Vergil's *Eclogues*

LANDSCAPES OF EXPERIENCE

Vergil's *Eclogues*

LANDSCAPES OF EXPERIENCE

Eleanor Winsor Leach

Cornell University Press

ITHACA AND LONDON

Cornell University Press gratefully acknowledges
a grant from the Andrew J. Mellon Foundation
that aided in bringing this book to publication.

First published 1974 by Cornell University Press.
Published in the United Kingdom by Cornell University Press Ltd.,
2–4 Brook Street, London W1Y 1AA.

International Standard Book Number 0–8014–0820–2
Library of Congress Catalog Card Number 73–17699

Printed in the United States of America by Kingsport Press, Inc.

MAGISTRAE SAPIENTI:
LOUISE ADAMS HOLLAND
FILIAEQUE CRESCENTI:
HARRIET OLNEY LEACH

❧ Acknowledgments

As Ovid expressed his satisfaction at belonging to an age that suited his personal disposition ("Haec aetas moribus apta meis," *AA* 3. 122), I consider myself fortunate to have taken up the study of Latin and English literature at the beginning of a *novus ordo*, a golden age of pastoral criticism. Although the marshes and meadows of Rhode Island, the green lawns of Bryn Mawr, and the dismal fogs of New Haven have all had their influence upon my evaluation of degrees of reality, reminiscence, artifice, and escapism in the pastoral landscape, still this is a field where "the art itself is nature," and I have had far more pleasure and profit than a handful of footnotes can show from the many critics and theorists whose insights have, for the past several years, challenged me to continual redevelopment and revaluation of my ideas. Likewise the list of those whose instruction and forbearance once sustained the early stages of my interest in pastoral would be long, but it is my pleasure here to mention the most outstanding obligations incurred in the writing of this book.

The poetry of the *Eclogues* and, almost equally important, a sense of their puzzles and problems, were first presented to me as a college freshman by Louise Adams Holland. It is with appreciation of her teaching, as well as with gratitude for her encouragement and assistance, but especially with admiration for her scholarly achievements in a field far different from this, that I mention her name in dedication. Professor Lawrence Richardson, Jr., has given me the benefit of his insight into the forms and problems of Republican poetry and of his expert

7

knowledge of Roman painting. His innumerable suggestions and canny questions have been a consistent source of new topics for investigation. My husband, Peter Leach, has read the manuscript in more versions than I like to count, and has shared in my speculations concerning pastoral fiction and contributed many thoughts on post-classical literature. Charles Segal produced a sympathetic and detailed commentary that not only saved me from many careless errors, but also prompted a rethinking of several points in the argument at the time of my final revision. I have had much assistance in my work on Roman painting from Kyle Phillips and information on historical questions from Robert J. Rowland, Jr. At all times I have profited from the learning, advice, and skepticism of Agnes Kirsopp Michels. Mary Ann Robbins, *socius* incomparable, has contributed liberally of her ideas and encouragement, as well as specific suggestions concerning Livy. I can hardly fail to mention my pleasant bucolic associates, those masters of the flock and flute, William Berg, Charles Fantazzi, Gilbert Lawall, Michael Putnam, and John Van Sickle, whose Arcadian discourse, not to mention occasional challenges to a contest, has made a sense of shared endeavor one of the greatest rewards of writing this book.

In the summer of 1966, Frank E. Brown, then Director of the American Academy in Rome, arranged permission for me to see several paintings not generally on exhibit in the Museo delle Terme. Ernest Nash and Karen Einaudi of the Fototeca Unione have filled my requests for photographs from Rome, and Karl Dimler, photographer for the Department of Classical and Near Eastern Archeology at Bryn Mawr College, provided the photographs taken from books. My debt to Yuldez Van Hulsteyn of the Bryn Mawr College Library is great. At the busy end of the semester, Susan Kane Trimble's help in correcting the galley proofs has made it possible to meet various deadlines without a total sacrifice of sleep.

Permission has been granted by the German Archeological Institute to reproduce the following photographs: a blue monochrome panel from Herculaneum, now in the National Archeological Museum in Naples; a fresco from the House of Obellius Firmus in Pompeii; three sacral-idyllic panels from the Red Room of the Villa of Agrippa Postumus at Boscotrecase, now in the Naples Museum; and the landscape showing Paris on Mt. Ida, from Pompeii, now in the Naples Museum. Permission has also been given by Fratelli Alinari for the landscape from the Villa Albani Collection, the frieze in stucco relief from the Villa Farnesina now in the Museo delle Terme, and the architectural landscape from the Villa of Fannius Synistor at Boscoreale, now in the Metropolitan Museum of Art in New York. Little Brown and Company and Jonathan Cape Ltd have given permission to quote from John Fowles' *The French Lieutenant's Woman.* The editors of the following journals gave me permission to reprint my own work: *American Journal of Philology* (87 [1966]:427–445; © by the Johns Hopkins University Press) for "Nature and Art in Vergil's Second *Eclogue,*" used in Chapter 5; *Latomus* (27 [1968]: 13–32) for "The Unity of *Eclogue* 6," portions of which are incorporated into Chapter 6; *Arethusa* (4[1971]:83–90) for "Eclogue 4: Sources and Symbolism," from which part of the argument is reproduced in Chapter 6.

E. W. L.

Austin, Texas

❧ Contents

❧ Illustrations

❧ Abbreviations

AJPhil	*American Journal of Philology*
Ann. Ist.	*Annali del Istituto di Corrispondenza Archeologica*
Bull. Com. Arch.	*Bullettino della Commissione archeologica comunale in Roma, 1872–*
CIL	*Corpus Inscriptionum Latinarum*
CQ	*Classical Quarterly*
CR	*Classical Review*
ELH	*English Literary History*
GRBS	*Greek, Roman and Byzantine Studies*
Harv. Stud.	*Harvard Studies in Classical Philology*
IL	*L'Information littéraire*
JDAI	*Jahrbuch des Deutschen Archäologischen Instituts*
JHS	*Journal of Hellenic Studies*
JRS	*Journal of Roman Studies*
MAAR	*Memoirs of the American Academy in Rome*
MDAI(R)	*Mitteilungen des Deutschen Archäologischen Instituts (Römische Abteilung)*
MLN	*Modern Language Notes*
MH	*Museum Helveticum*
PBSR	*Papers of the British School at Rome*
Rev. Et. Lat.	*Revue des Études Latines*
Rev. Phil.	*Revue de philologie*
Rh. Mus.	*Rheinisches Museum*
SEL	*Studies in English Literature*
SP	*Studies in Philology*
TAPA	*Transactions of the American Philological Association*
YClS	*Yale Classical Studies*

Vergil's *Eclogues*

LANDSCAPES OF EXPERIENCE

⚞ Introduction

Vergil's *Eclogues* do not easily yield a definition of pastoral; despite many centuries of study and imitation, they remain among the most haunting and elusive of all the poems we know. Even certain seventeenth-century critics who regarded them as the model of pastoral decorum found many of their elements difficult to reconcile. With their shifting, varied images of nature and their historical allusions, their herdsmen, farmers and soldiers, gods and Roman poets, they resist being classified as country poems, and they also elude those large-scale generic definitions so comforting to students of literary forms. Where the critic desires material for generalization, Vergil never generalizes. In no one passage or poem does he explain unambiguously what his ten poems are or should be. The few lines that in one poem appear as a definition will change to a hypothesis when we read the next. As one scholar said not long ago, "There is no such thing as a typical *Eclogue*."[1]

Looking back upon the history of pastoral criticism, we find the ambiguities of the *Eclogues* compounded by numerous definitions created to advance the theory of pastoral genre. To the poets and critics of the Renaissance, Vergil's rural subjects and characters seemed a mask for daring political allegories. The seventeenth-century critic Rapin was barely able to justify political allusion in poems whose purpose he wished to consider as the presentation of a rationalized image of the golden age. Rapin thought the *Eclogues* morally improving. Fontenelle, his

[1] G. Karl Galinsky, "Vergil's Second *Eclogue:* Its Theme and Relation to the *Eclogue* Book," *Classica et Mediaevalia* 26(1968):162.

contemporary, rejected both the politics and the morality, interpreting the poems as courtly fantasies of a rural life, like peasant costumes sewn of satin and silk.[2]

To Samuel Johnson the *Eclogues* presented a realistic image of the Italian countryside, and he directed English poets to copy Vergil's example, but not his words, substituting English landscapes for those of Italy.[3] In the reading of pastoral, Johnson found an experience akin to the recollection of childhood: by turning to the pleasant countryside, man might recapture his youthful, optimistic view of life. The great editor John Conington, whose literary judgments reveal Johnsonian standards, went further toward defining the *Eclogues* as a territory of imagination. A blending together of Sicilian and Mantuan scenery, of shepherds, nymphs, and Romans, gave Conington the impression of a fantastic, indefensible artificiality. Vergil had transformed the boorish Arcadia of other ancient writers into a "golden land where imagination found a refuge from the harsh, prosaic life of the present."[4] Despite his acute interpretations of specific phrases and metaphors, Conington believed that Vergil's language and imaginary descriptions lacked the vitality of Theocritean pastoral. The *Eclogues,* he said, were the product of literary, rather than actual, experience.

In our own century, the Arcadia that Conington described has been a major topic of discussion, but one that the critics themselves have idealized, regarding it as the symbol of a poet's freedom to create images superior to his experience of reality. Erwin Panofsky and Friedrich Klingner were among the first apologists for Arcadia. Like Conington, Panofsky found it

---

[2] George Puttenham, "The Arte of English Poesie," in *Elizabethan Critical Essays*, ed. G. G. Smith (Oxford, 1904), II, 39–40; Philip Sidney, "An Apology for Poetry," in *ibid.*, I, 175; *Rapin's "De Carmine Pastorali" prefixed to Thomas Creech's translation of the "Idylliums" of Theocritus* (1684), ed. with introduction and bibliographical note by J. E. Congleton, The Augustan Reprint Society, series 2, Essays on Poetry, no. 3 (Ann Arbor, 1947); Fontenelle, "A Treatise upon Pastorals," in *Monsieur Bossu's Treatise of the Epick Poem,* trans. Mr. Motteaux (London, 1695).

[3] "Pastoral Poetry I," in *Rambler* no. 36, July 21, 1750; here cited from *Eighteenth-Century Critical Essays*, ed. Scott Elledge (Ithaca, N.Y., 1961), 11, 579.

[4] *The Works of Vergil*, with a Commentary by John Conington and Henry Nettleship, vol. I, *Eclogues and Georgics*, rev. by F. Haverfield, 5th ed. (London, 1898; repr., Hildesheim, 1963), pp. 2–3.

compounded of unrealities, but saw in these the features of a better world: "a Utopia . . . where human suffering, the sadness of frustrated love and death, lose their factuality and are projected into the future or into the past."[5] In Klingner's writings, and also in a chapter of Bruno Snell's *Discovery of the Mind*, Arcadia becomes a refuge from the violence of history, a world of eternal innocence and imagination where history may be recast into the ideal patterns of myth.[6]

Although each of these interpretations is clearly influenced by aesthetic and literary assumptions of its time, there are convincing points in all. Each critic sees what he is prepared to notice, yet each seems to describe some genuine aspect of the poems. The fact that so many contradictory theories have been formed to explain the *Eclogues* — they have been called allegorical and plain, fantastic and naturalistic, mythical and real — is probably owing to the nature of the poems themselves. They are many-faceted works, susceptible of more than one kind of description, and they present a multiplicity of images and evaluations of the natural world.

In the face of so many varied and opposing opinions, one is tempted to recommend that the reader who wants a clear, unprejudiced impression of Vergil should forget his previous knowledge of pastoral criticism and the tradition. If so extreme

[5] "*Et in Arcadia Ego*': On the Conception of Transcendence in Poussin and Watteau," in *Philosophy and History: Essays Presented to Ernst Cassirer*, ed. R. Klibansky and H. J. Paton (Oxford, 1936), pp. 223–254, repr. in Panofsky's *Meaning and the Visual Arts* (New York: Anchor, 1955), pp. 295–320.

[6] In order of publication: Klingner, "Die Einheit des Vergilischen Lebenswerkes." *MDAI(R)* 45(1930):43ff., repr. in Klingner's *Römische Geisteswelt* 2d ed. (Munich, 1961), pp. 274–292; Klingner, "Virgil und die geschichtliche Welt," *Römische Geisteswelt* (Munich, 1943), pp. 91ff., repr. in *Römische Geisteswelt* 2d ed. (Munich, 1961), pp. 293–311; Snell, "Arkadien, die Entstehung einer geistigen Landschaft," *Antike und Abenland* 1(1944):26ff., repr. in Snell's *The Discovery of the Mind: The Greek Origins of European Thought*, trans. T. G. Rosenmeyer (New York: Harper Torchbooks, 1960), pp. 281–310. The discussions of Arcadia in these studies were preceded by that in Gunther Jachmann's "Die dichterische Technik in Vergils *Bucolica*," *Neue Jahrbuch* 49(1922):101–120. T. G. Rosenmeyer's *The Green Cabinet: Theocritus and the European Pastoral Lyric* (Berkeley, 1969), p. 18 and n. 51, traces the concept of the spiritual Arcadia to Herder, who associates it with the landscape of post-Vergilian pastoralists. In his most recent discussion of the subject, Klingner, in *Virgil: Bucolica, Georgica, Aeneis* (Zurich, 1967), pp. 12–14, suggests that Vergil found the model for his unreal world in the Alexandrian pastoralists who followed Theocritus.

a step is unnecessary, it is only because the intense critical interest in the pastoral that has sprung up during the past two decades is subjecting all our concepts of the pastoral tradition to re-evaluation and redefinition. Although Thomas Rosenmeyer has recently suggested, not without perspicuity, that Vergil often stands apart from the norms of this tradition,[7] a new reading of the *Eclogues* may contribute to the investigation and reconsideration of critical formulas, both old and new.

Accordingly, my purposes in this book are two. The study is, in large part, an exploration of the thematic patterns of individual poems in relationship to problems of unity and design posed by the *Eclogue* book as a whole. At the same time, I have attempted to broaden this investigation by consideration of some of the questions and theories that contemporary criticism has brought to the reading of pastoral literature. The discussion emphasizes three major topics that, although not entirely new in themselves, figure prominently in recent studies of pastoral: the literary issues of pastoral simplicity and complexity in association with the archetypal myth of the lost paradise, the interpretations of nature implied by Vergil's organization of his pastoral landscapes, and the symbolic value of the pastoral singers, especially their character patterns and their place in the pastoral world. In approaching these topics, I have attempted to modify the generic study of pastoral by giving particular attention to the importance of Roman ideas and habits of thought.

At the low point of Vergil's literary reputation, Conington thought the *Eclogues* wholly derived from Theocritus, yet inferior. Since twentieth-century criticism has defended the importance of literary allusion and adaptation and its contribution to poetic originality, there has been more talk of the *Eclogues* as original, Roman poems. Thus Brooks Otis writes of the first poem: "Pastoral, that most unhistorical of genres, has been Romanized and brought into history."[8] All the same, the question of Roman elements in the poems continues to pose some embarrassment to the critic whose thoughts turn to the chaotic civil wars, and to the violence of the political figures

[7] Rosenmeyer, p. 18.
[8] *Virgil: A Study in Civilized Poetry* (Oxford, 1963), p. 136.

who are named or suggested by the poet. Since it seems logical that this Roman atmosphere should be hostile to pastoral tranquillity, the poems have been read primarily as Vergil's effort to preserve the idyllic vision of Theocritus during the troubled years 42–37 B.C. In short, the concept of sentimental, Arcadian pastoral has influenced many readers and in its strongest form shows the poems as an escape from the historical world.

In my opinion, the *Eclogues* are not designed to show hostility between the pastoral and the Roman worlds. Here, as in other adaptations from Greek sources, the poet's creation of a distinctive Roman atmosphere and symbolism can safely be regarded as a major challenge to his originality. This study will show that Vergil does not restrict his Roman viewpoint to a scattering of contemporary allusions but manifests it in every aspect of his work: in his attitude toward the myth of pastoral innocence, in his definition of experience, in his representation of the natural world, and finally in his characterization of the poetic imagination as embodied in the figures of the pastoral singers and in the contents of their songs.

Such points can most easily be demonstrated by a consideration of hitherto neglected material that has bearing upon Vergil's portrayal of innocence, landscape, and poetic imagination. In the agricultural writings of Cato the Censor and Marcus Terentius Varro, as well as in certain philosophical works of Cicero, we find useful definitions, both practical and aesthetic, of natural order and of man's role in his environment that are of particular relevance to the Roman originality of the *Eclogues*. In addition, Vitruvius' brief outline of the history of Roman landscape painting may illuminate Vergil's interest in depicting a variety of natural settings, an interest that has its parallel in the considerable body of landscape paintings roughly contemporary with his work.

From the latter come the title and primary theme of this book. The landscapes of pastoral may be considered as symbolic patterns created by the poet's organization of images of the natural world. Landscapes, as the art historians tell us, are never entirely literal in their representation of nature and are always capable of revealing a philosophy and a point of view. The poet's depiction of landscapes is a reliable guide to his interpretation of man's place in his environment.

In discussing Vergil's images of nature, critics have often pondered the relative values of actuality and the unreal, but their definitions of reality and unreality have commonly followed their own contemporary aesthetic standards. No one has approached the matter speculatively, asking how a Roman poet or audience might distinguish between convincing and fantastic representations of nature. Roman painting is especially useful here. In his analysis of a group of landscape panels from the Villa of Agrippa Postumus at Boscotrecase, Peter von Blanckenhagen has given particular attention to the conventions of perspective and the question of verisimilitude in Roman landscape art.[9] He has shown that the representation of varying degrees of reality and unreality had its place in the development and refinement of this art. Comparisons between Vergil's landscapes and those of Roman wall painting may therefore present a new basis for distinctions between the real and the unreal aspects of nature in the *Eclogues*.

These distinctions will ultimately show that Vergil has created two different kinds of pastoral landscape, the natural and the fantastic, associating the latter with the most volatile of his pastoral characters. Not all shepherd singers rest contented in their natural environment. To some the woods and fields are a harsh, repressive home. The desire to escape from reality— even pastoral or agricultural reality—into an imaginary world of unspoiled innocence is a theme belonging to Vergil's Corydon and Damon, not to the Eclogue Poet or to Vergil himself. In this respect the symbolic values of landscapes are associated with conflicts of innocence and experience, simplicity and complexity, nature and civilization, and with the reflection of such conflicts in pastoral song.

[9] P. H. von Blanckenhagen and Christine Alexander, *The Paintings from Boscotrecase, MDAI(R) Sechstes Ergänzungsheft* (Heidelberg, 1962).

CHAPTER 1

⁂ Return from the Pastoral World

A passage from a somewhat theoretical contemporary novel goes beyond the scope of its immediate context to capture the essential conflict of emotions in the pastoral experience.[1]

It was this place, an English Garden of Eden on such a day as March 29th, 1867, that Charles had entered when he had climbed the path from the shore at Pinhay Bay. . . .

When Charles had quenched his thirst and cooled his brow with his wetted handkerchief he began to look seriously around him. Or at least he tried to look seriously around him; but the little slope on which he found himself, the prospect before him, the sounds, the scents, the unalloyed wildness of growth and burgeoning fertility, forced him into anti-science. The ground about him was studded gold and pale yellow with celandines and primroses and banked by the bridal white of

---

[1] The quotation from *The French Lieutenant's Woman* by John Fowles is reprinted by permission of Little Brown and Co. and Jonathan Cape Ltd; copyright © 1969 by John Fowles.

The study with which modern pastoral criticism begins is William Empson's *Some Versions of Pastoral* (London, 1935). My thinking owes much to this book and also to the following essays and books on English and American literature that deal with questions of pastoral complexity: Rosamund Tuve, "Theme, Pattern and Imagery in Lycidas," in *Images and Themes in Five Poems by Milton* (Cambridge, Mass., 1957), pp. 78–111; Northrop Frye, *The Anatomy of Criticism* (Princeton, 1957), *Fables of Identity: Studies in Poetic Mythology* (New York, 1963), *A Natural Perspective: The Development of Shakespearean Comedy and Romance* (New York, 1965), *The Critical Path* (Bloomington, Ind., 1971); Harry Berger, Jr., "The Prospect of Imagination: Spenser and the Limits of Poetry," *Studies in English Literature* 1(1962):193–220; Berger, "A Secret Discipline: *The Faerie Queene,* Book 6," in *Form and Convention in the Poetry of Edmund Spenser,* ed. William Nelson (New York, 1961), pp. 35–75; Berger, "The Renaissance Imagination: Second World and Green World," *Centennial Review* 9(1965):36–78; Angus Fletcher, *Allegory: The Theory of a Symbolic Mode* (Ithaca, N.Y., 1964); Leo Marx, *The Machine in the Garden: Technology and the Pastoral Ideal in America* (Oxford, 1964); John Armstrong, *The Paradise Myth* (Oxford, 1969).

densely blossoming sloe; where jubilantly green-tipped elders shaded the mossy banks of the little brook he had drunk from were clusters of moschatel and woodsorrel, most delicate of English spring flowers. Higher up the slope he saw the white heads of anemones, and beyond them deep green drifts of bluebell leaves. A distant woodpecker drummed in the branches of some high tree, and bullfinches whistled quietly over his head; newly arrived chiffchaffs and willow warblers sang in every bush and treetop. When he turned he saw the blue sea, now washing far below; and the whole extent of Lyme Bay reaching round, diminishing cliffs that dropped into the endless yellow saber of the Chesil Bank, whose remote tip touched that strange English Gibraltar, Portland Bill, a thin gray shadow wedged between azures.

Only one art has ever caught such scenes—that of the Renaissance, it is the ground that Botticelli's figures walk on, the air that includes Ronsard's songs. It does not matter what that cultural revolution's conscious aims and purposes, its cruelties and failures were; in essence the Renaissance was simply the green end of one of civilization's hardest winters. It was an end to chains, bounds, frontiers. Its device was the only device: What is, is good. It was all, in short, that Charles's age was not; but do not think that as he stood there he did not know this. It is true that to explain his obscure feeling of malaise, of inappropriateness, of limitation, he went back closer home—to Rousseau, and the childish myths of a Golden Age and the Noble Savage. That is, he tried to dismiss the inadequacies of his own time's approach to nature by supposing that one cannot reenter a legend. He told himself he was too pampered, too spoiled by civilization, ever to inhabit nature again; and that made him sad, in a not unpleasant bittersweet sort of way. After all, he was a Victorian. We could not expect him to see what we are only just beginning—and with so much more knowledge and the lessons of existentialist philosophy at our disposal—to realize ourselves: that the desire to hold and the desire to enjoy are mutually destructive. His statement to himself should have been, "I possess this now, therefore I am happy," instead of what it so Victorianly was: "I cannot possess this forever, and therefore am sad."

[John Fowles, *The French Lieutenant's Woman*, pp. 67–69]

A landscape, sensuous yet delicate, colored by the haunting atmosphere of early spring yet made particular by the names of plants, trees, and birds, presents itself to the protagonist of the novel as an unexpected and disturbing invitation. Tradition, both artistic and literary, has glorified such scenes as images of the archetypal paradise, the natural home of man. The novelist speaks of Botticelli's landscapes, thinking, doubtless, of the *Primavera,* an image of mythical transformation which for him represents the birth of an intellectual spring. The novel's Victorian protagonist is in need of such a spring, and the novelist has offered him this rich landscape to encourage the discovery of a freer, less conventional self. Yet the protagonist hesitates. His own awareness of the traditional symbolism of such landscapes stands in his way, for to him it represents a discomforting primitivism: a "childish myth." Cut off by his knowledge and his rationality, he is incapable of accepting the invitation and of altering his accustomed relationship with nature. The suspicion that nature has here, in some mysterious manner, transcended her normal limitations and created a new season before its time gives rise to a protective assertion of human limitations. Even in its promise of release, the new landscape has threatened the beholder's identity and self-assurance. Thus his response is a gentle melancholy that is in itself a pleasing substitute for the stronger, more joyous emotion the landscape demands. Such a response is not so specifically Victorian as the novelist appears to indicate, but common to the characters or readers of pastoral. As a "flower passage," a *topos* well known in the pastoral tradition, this description may be compared with two others: one from Milton's *Lycidas;* one from Vergil's second *Eclogue.*

> Return Alpheus, the dread voice is past,
> That shrunk thy streams; Return Sicilian Muse,
> And call the Vales, and bid them hither cast
> Their Bels, and Flourets of a thousand hues.
> Ye valleys low where the milde whispers use,
> Of shades and wanton winds, and gushing brooks,
> On whose fresh lap the swart Star sparely looks,
> Throw hither all your quaint enameld eyes,
> That on the green terf suck the honied showres,
> And purple all the ground with vernal flowres.
> Bring the rathe primrose that forsaken dies,
> The tufted Crow-toe and pale Gessamine,
> The white Pink, and the Pansie freakt with jeat,
> The glowing Violet.
> The Musk-rose, and the well attir'd Woodbine,
> With Cowslips wan that hang the pensive hed,

And every flower that sad embroidery wears:
Bid Amaranthus all his beauty shed,
And Daffadillies fill their cups with tears,
To strew the Laureat Herse where Lycid lies.
For so to interpose a little ease,
Let our frail thoughts dally with false surmise.
Ay me! Whilst thee the shores and sounding Seas
Wash far away, where ere thy bones are hurld,
Whether beyond the stormy Hebrides,
Where thou perhaps under the whelming tide
Visit'st the bottom of the monstrous world;
Or whether thou to our moist vows deny'd,
Sleep'st by the fable of Bellurus old,
Where the great vision of the guarded Mount
Looks toward Namancos and Bayona's hold;
Look homeward Angel now, and melt with ruth,
And O ye Dolphins waft the haples youth.   [*Lycidas* 132–164]

huc ades, o formose puer: tibi lilia plenis
ecce ferunt Nymphae calathis; tibi candida Nais,
pallentis violas et summa papavera carpens,
narcissum et florem iungit bene olentis anethi;
tum casia atque aliis intexens suavibus herbis
mollia luteola pingit vaccinia calta.
ipse ego cana legam tenera lanugine mala
castaneasque nuces, mea quas Amaryllis amabat;
addam cerea pruna (honos erit huic quoque pomo),
et vos, o lauri, carpam et te, proxima myrte,
sic positae quoniam suavis miscetis odores.
rusticus es, Corydon; nec munera curat Alexis,
nec, si muneribus certes, concedat Iollas.
heu heu, quid volui misero mihi? floribus Austrum
perditus et liquidis immisi fontibus apros.   [*Ecl.* 2. 45–59]

(Come here, o beautiful boy: behold, for you in full baskets the
Nymphs bear lilies; for you a shining Naiad, plucking pale
violets and the heads of poppies, joins the narcissus and the
blossom of the sweet-scented dill, then intertwining cassia with
other sweet herbs, she colors the soft hyacinth with saffron
marigold. I myself shall choose fruits, whitened with soft
down, and chestnuts that my Amaryllis loved. I will add waxy
plums [honor shall be given this fruit also]. And you, oh

laurels, I shall pluck and you nearby myrtle, so joined that you mingle sweet odors. You are countrified, Corydon: Alexis does not cherish your gifts; nor will Iollas give in to you if you wage a contest of gifts. Alas, alas! What have I wished upon my poor self. Senseless, I have let the south wind loose upon my flowers, and the wild boars into my clear-running streams.)[2]

In the *Lycidas* passage, after St. Peter's awesome accusation of the irresponsible clergy—bad shepherds of the modern world—comes an image of spring returning to English valleys, a luxuriant flower passage in the tradition of Sicilian pastoral. Homely English nicknames give these flowers reality, while their colors, both dark and pale, make them an appropriate and fragile tribute to the young, dead poet. Spring's profusion, the renewal of the creative powers of earth, is a reminder of the continuity of a universal nature whose cyclical processes are untouched by individual death. Yet the poet lacks confidence in his own image.[3] The flowers are gathered together in imagination only for the momentary comfort of Lycidas' mourners. Although poetry creates the tranquil image of the laureate hearse, the ordered ceremony to dispel grief, the body of Edward King finds no certain repose, but driven by endless tides is cast about the undersea rocks of the British coast. These seas belong to the world of experience where the reality of sudden death destroys illusions and threatens aspirations—indeed the poetic aspirations of the speaker who mourns for Lycidas here. As his thoughts turn from "false surmise" to follow the real body of Lycidas, the poet acknowledges that the harsh world of turbulent seas, not the gentle and unreal pastoral, is his challenge, the world with which his ambitions, fears, and talents must come to terms. The springtime flowers of English vales are no more than a poetic convention, emblem

[2] The text of Vergil is *P. Vergili Maronis, Opera*, ed. R. A. B. Mynors (Oxford, 1969). All translations, save for those from Greek authors, are my own.

[3] With an echo of Ovid's lament for the death of Tibullus (*Am.* 9. 21–22), he invokes the myth of Orpheus, the futility of the poet's kinship with nature:

What could the Muse herself that Orpheus bore
The Muse herself for her enchanting son,
Whom universal nature did lament,
When by the rout that made the hideous roar,
His gory visage down the stream was sent.   [59–62]

of a nature offering no security to man. They belong to an illusion of innocence the poet has already outgrown.

In the second *Eclogue*, Corydon has created a dream world, immensely pleasing to himself, at whose center he presides as a munificent bestower of pastoral wealth. Yet such dreams cannot prevail against the material sophistication of the city. Fearing exposure to an unsympathetic eye that will strip his whole existence of meaning, he anticipates failure by destroying his vision himself. Corydon knows that his imaginings have not even the permanence of nature; thus he pictures nature as a force too crude and violent to sustain a refined sensibility. His paradise of crystal fountains and delicate flowers is blighted by the scorn of an insensitive world. Yet the poem closes with a more equitable vision of nature, a corrective to the singer's self-indulgence, that anticipates Milton's realistic acknowledgment of the actual world. Corydon's imaginative freedom is compromised. He has stolen it by neglecting the tasks that define his real place in nature, yet inevitably he will take up these tasks and forget his disappointment, dreaming again in the future another version of the same dream:

> a, Corydon, Corydon, quae te dementia cepit!
> semiputata tibi frondosa vitis in ulmo est:
> quin tu aliquid saltem potius, quorum indiget usus,
> viminibus mollique paras detexere iunco?
> invenies alium, si te hic fastidit, Alexin.   [2. 69–73]

> (Ah, Corydon, Corydon, what madness has captured you? Your vine is half-pruned on the leafy elm. Why don't you, at least, set about weaving, with twigs and pliant reed, something which practical use demands? If this one scorns you, you will find another Alexis.)

The symbolic values of these passages from Fowles, Milton, and Vergil are similar, although the landscape of one professes to copy nature while two are consciously drawn in imagination. Such flower passages sum up the ideal fertility and spontaneity at the heart of the pastoral vision. References to Eden, to Arethusa, to the magical realm of the nymphs, warn us that the landscapes are unreal. But the unreality is not in any poetic misrepresentation of nature, which often shows itself profuse and seductive to human eyes. Neither the wild seacoast garden, nor the flowers of the English countryside, nor even Corydon's garland of fruits and flowers exceed the limitations of natural possibility. The mind of the beholder has created the unreality. While he remains in restless exclusion from his vision, he confesses his bondage to another, harsher environment whose actualities are less satisfying than the seductive images before him. At the very point of losing himself amidst nature's spontaneous profusion, he hesitates, doubtful that her influence can effect a desirable transformation of self. His longing for freedom is doomed to gentle, melancholy frustration.[4] The pastoral impulse has virtually intensified his alienation from nature, for it has existed only to illuminate an unattainable and even discomforting ideal.

Behind the pastoral vision lies the archetype of the primeval paradise, commonly called the golden age or the garden of Eden, and from these associations the pastoral draws its ideal coloring.[5] The desire to enter the pastoral world — to recreate in imagination the infancy of mankind — is the expression of a longing for rebirth,[6] for the awakening of some freer, hitherto

[4] The undertone of melancholy in pastoral is discussed by Erwin Panofsky, "*Et in Arcadia Ego:* Poussin and the Elegiac Tradition," in *Meaning in the Visual Arts* (New York: Anchor, 1955), pp. 295–320, as a result of the poet's translation of real human sorrows into a utopian setting. Thomas Rosenmeyer, *The Green Cabinet: Theocritus and the European Pastoral Lyric* (Berkeley, 1969), pp. 224–229, attributes melancholy to a self-conscious recognition of pastoral illusion: "an awareness that the bower does not really exist."

[5] The particular consistency in the recurrences of this myth is aptly described by Armstrong: "Some constituents of the human mind persist which can only be sufficiently expressed in symbolic form and . . . the most subtle poetic structures which the mind creates at different times for this purpose tend not to become outdated. It follows that comparable new poetic forms are likely to bear important resemblences to old ones" (pp. 5–6).

[6] For imagery associated with the archetype of rebirth see C. G. Jung, *The Archetypes and the Collective Unconscious,* trans. R. F. C. Hull (New York, 1949), pp. 80–81, 130; Maud Bodkin, *Archetypal Patterns in Poetry* (New York: Vintage, 1958), pp. 106–110. Empson sees the reconstitution of the self in relationship to the social norms which he considers the major point of pastoral: "Normally the idea of including all sorts of men in yourself brings in an idea of reconciling yourself with nature and therefore gaining power over it," (p. 262). Renato Poggioli's influential essay, "The Oaten Flute," *Harvard Library Bulletin* 11(1957): 147, speaks of pastoral rebirth as a rather simplistic, artificial, and easily attaina-

unrealized self whose potential has been repressed by the limitations of mortal nature or everyday life. The landscape of an ideal world with its abundant fertility, eternal greenness or unusual tranquillity contains intimations of a new beginning and promises to elicit hidden resources of self. Yet paradoxically, the myth that embodies these promises would never exist if its garden of innocence were not irrevocably lost to mankind. Pastoral fantasies lure us with the impossibility of their fulfillment. We may wonder if the fault lies entirely with man and his society, or whether, as Milton suggests in *Lycidas*, the very concept of the garden does not conceal some fatal inherent deficiency.[7] This failure to satisfy the same longings that give it birth is, in fact, the major source of complexity in pastoral.

Unlike many of his predecessors who expected little more than a pleasing simplicity in pastoral, the contemporary reader expects complexity.[8] The past two decades have brought forth a revolution in pastoral criticism, an ever-increasing series of symbolic and thematic investigations spurred by William Empson's proposal that pastoral literature is written chiefly to clarify

---

ble goal: "The psychological root of the pastoral is a double longing after innocence and happiness to be recovered not through conversion and regeneration, but merely through a retreat." More recently Northrop Frye has explained the new perspectives – the ideal or microcosmic experiences of pastoral, comedy, and romance in accordance with a traditional, intellectualized interpretation of the Fall: "Adam was capable of a preternatural power of experience before the fall and we have lost this capacity. Our structures of reason and imagination are therefore analogical constructs designed to re-capture, within the mental processes that belong to our present state, something of a lost directness of apprehension" (*The Critical Path*, pp. 31–32). This ideal experience, Frye explains, cannot be achieved in life without a total relinquishment of identity, and therefore is sought vicariously in literature.

[7] The insufficiency of the garden as "ideal enclave" – a fantasy world oriented toward pleasure and therefore static – is considered in Armstrong, pp. 3–7 *et passim*.

[8] For the tradition of pastoral simplicity in the seventeenth and eighteenth centuries see J. E. Congleton, *Theories of Pastoral Poetry in England, 1684–1798* (Gainesville, Florida, 1952). Concepts of pastoral simplicity are expanded and re-evaluated in Thomas Rosenmeyer's recent comparative study, *The Green Cabinet*. But, although Rosenmeyer consistently emphasizes simplicity as the substance of the ideology and literary texture of pastoral, many of the themes and situations he discusses go beyond the narrow boundaries of his theory and must be treated, somewhat unconvincingly, as aberrations from the pastoral norm.

experience by translating its complexities into simple and unaccustomed forms. Empson has shown that pastoral can be comprehensive ("You can say everything about complex people by a complete consideration of simple people"), that it can serve for social or philosophical anatomy ("You can take a simple thing and imply a hierarchy in it"), that it can create universals ("The clash and identification of the refined, the universal and the low is the point of pastoral").[9] These suggestions have been of major importance to scholars who now define pastoral as a method or perspective rather than as a rigid and formalized genre, and they have enriched the possibilities of literary comparison by showing the ability of all forms—comedy, epic, satire, devotion, the novel—to make use of pastoral themes and points of view.[10] Under the influence of Empson we have come to understand the convention of pastoral simplicity as a vehicle for the exploration of ideas, and to describe the thematic organization of pastoral poems with such terms as "dialectic" or "balancing of opposites."[11] Thus while the older theories maintained that the entire substance of pastoral literature might be seen as a gratification of man's longing for nature, newer theories subordinate this impulse to other ends: to some experience of knowledge or discovery. We have moved from a theory that was almost entirely emotional, or affective, to one that is highly cognitive.

All the same, with his strong prejudice toward ideology and social criticism, his preference for the analytical uses of the green world or garden over its physical or visionary attractions, Empson often leaves the modern reader uncertain how to

[9] Empson, pp. 137, 143, 249.
[10] Thus Poggioli, p. 184: "There is a pastoral cluster in any form of poetry and we find 'pastoral oases' even in non-pastoral writing."
[11] In writing of Theocritus, Gilbert Lawall, *Theocritus' Coan Pastorals: A Poetry Book* (Cambridge, Mass., 1967), pp. 4–5, 11, speaks of a tension of ideal and real worlds that he regards as a projection of the poet's own emotional conflicts. Rosenmeyer speaks of defining "a unique pastoral mood which prevails when tempers clash, or when sadness jostles joy" (p. 15). Expanding upon Lawall, Patrick Cullen, in *Spenser, Marvell and Renaissance Pastoral* (Cambridge, Mass., 1971), pp. 1–2, observes: "But while pastoral can portray an escape from reality or a desire to escape reality, the pastoral *mode* itself from Theocritus onward involved, implicitly or explicitly, a critical exploration or counter-balancing of attitudes, perspectives and experiences."

reconcile the literary complexity of pastoral with the simplicity of its myth.[12] This problem is particularly acute for students of the ancient pastoral lyric, which, falling outside the boundaries of his critical speculation, remained for Empson no more than a simplistic embodiment of a naïve paradise of innocence. Consequently the lyric often appears at the center of a multiplicity of forms that easily surpass it in complexity and range of subject. Some of the most distinguished and profitable books on later pastoral have concerned themselves primarily with the larger and less traditional forms, while those devoted exclusively to the ancient lyric tend to seek a specialized theme or function proper to this form by which we may acknowledge its seminal position and, at the same time, its obvious limitations. Often the pastoral lyric is understood as an essentially private exercise in self-examination, providing freedom for the projection of the individual mind or sensibility.[13] Among the more current of such subjectively oriented interpretations is the notion—based on the preeminence of bucolic songmaking in Theocritus and Vergil—that the primary concern of such poetry is the formulation of a poetics; i.e., that the complexity and dialectic of pastoral are oriented toward the illumination of conflicts in its own creative process or toward the discovery and refinement of an aesthetic ideal.[14] There is, of course, nothing greatly objection-

[12] Thus Rosenmeyer, pp. 5–7, 16–17, finds it necessary to narrow Empson's broad definition in preparation for his discussion of simplicity in the pastoral lyric.

[13] Poggioli fosters the idea of a subjective point of view in pastoral with his identification of one mode of pastoral discourse as "pastoral of the self," and with his statement, in contradiction of Empson, that "bucolic poetry is largely indifferent to the lot of men in collective terms" (p. 170). He suggests an interrelationship of subjectivity and poetics in observing that the pastoral poet often enters his poems in disguise, masking his public face for the sake of personal expression.

[14] Thus John Van Sickle, "Studies of Dialectical Methodology in the Vergilian Tradition," MLN 85(1970):884–928, reads the *Eclogues* as an illumination of their own mythopoesis, analogous to the Orphic balancing of poetic triumph against "the poetic myth of failure through passion and fatal discontinuity—negation and contradictory elements." Michael Putnam, *Virgil's Pastoral Art: Studies in the "Eclogues"* (Princeton, 1970), pp. 8–9, understands pastoral as an expression of "the poet's life of the imagination and his concerned search for freedom to order experience." Rosenmeyer, pp. 267–281, whose concept of the pastoral ideal is associated with an objectified Epicurean simplicity, believes that emphasis on the topic of writing poetry has been exaggerated as a pastoral theme.

able in this theory, for the outlines of a poetics may be traced in any poem whose creator reveals the interaction of his imagination and his subject. One should, perhaps, not even object that such thinking is apt to transfer ideal simplicity from its place in the psychological background of pastoral to the position of an ultimate literary goal. Yet before we make this concept a common denominator of the pastoral lyric, we must question whether it is not too narrow to encompass the range of experience in such poems as Vergil's *Eclogues*. It does not fully provide for Corydon's loss of faith in his dream world, for the conflicts between his private vision of nature and the real natural world.

It is a rather different matter to propose that the intellectual explorations or dialectical processes of pastoral must be understood in their relationship to the archetype of rebirth not only as it affects the poet's hopes of self-realization through creativity, but also in its larger relevance to all human aspirations toward imaginative fulfillment of which creativity is only the most articulate and sophisticated form. This process, as I hope to show, is as fundamental to the lyric as to any of pastoral's more inclusive forms. It is here that we must reinvoke the essential elusiveness of the lost garden, which colors not only the myth but also the specific literary shapes the myth assumes. These forms are articulations of the paradoxical situation proposed earlier: the ambivalence of man's attitude toward a return to nature.

The garden of Eden and the golden age—the legendary ideals of the pastoral—are primitivistic, fertile, indeed maternal, intrinsically threatening to the security and identity of civilized man. Although man may long for the freedom of a pastoral world, he does not wish to remain there. Thus by accepting and dramatizing the elusiveness of the garden, he renders it subject to control; it need not endanger his established selfhood or his allegiance to the imperfect world that he knows, a world to which he is bound not only by practical necessity but also by strong ties of humanity, and one that he would not easily relinquish. The continual tension between the pastoral impulse and the need to preserve a known identity in the face of the overwhelming power of nature gives rise to conflict and complexity in pastoral.

Thus the more complex forms of pastoral do not embody a glorification but rather a critical evaluation of the pastoral dream. What we study in this literature may be called a displacement of simple gratification, a turning aside of the original pastoral impulse into some more demanding form of intellectual or emotional activity, inspired by proximity to nature, yet based upon recognition of the futility of the pastoral ideal.[15] In this manner specific poems both incorporate and exceed the paradox of their archetypal myth. As Empson realized, the garden is not an end in itself but an opportunity. Its function is not to satisfy but to breed a restlessness that impels man toward some higher end. For the undisturbed garden, which in its essence contains both birth and growth without challenge or decay, is a static and enclosed world. In the four quoted passages it is easy to see how the desirability of the garden can be established by intensive rhetorical elaboration; yet active significance begins, not in the physical charm of the place, nor even in its symbolic possibilities, but rather in man's gestures of hesitation, drawing back, and reflection. The insights into self and nature that may be gained from the garden are ultimately of little use within its confines. New knowledge must be tested in the world of ordinary experience, even at the price of destroying the dream that is its source. Thus we cannot seriously complain of the interruption of pastoral tranquillity, for disturbance is the ultimate justification of its existence. The goal is subordinated to the search, and the search itself to the real world where it began. The paradox of man's ambivalence toward nature can only be resolved in one way: when the desire for escape or recreation gives way to a reconciliation of the two conflicting worlds.

The familiar term "pastoral limitation," in its trivial sense, justifies the exclusion of all but simplicity from the garden, but it can also encompass the deficiencies of the pastoral world. As a mode that invites speculation, pastoral often takes on problems larger than it can solve, problems sometimes generated by the atmosphere of the garden, but just as often imported from the great world. Consequently, pastoral situations often end in

[15] Marx, pp. 5–11, explores the distinction between sentimental pastoralism — the idea of a return to nature in everyday thought — and complex, literary pastoral.

balance or impasse: pastoral loves go unrewarded; pastoral philosophers fall short of satisfactory solutions; pastoral singing is only a preliminary step in the mastery of poetic power. The limitation of pastoral stems both from man's helplessness in the face of nature and from the lack of sophisticated resources in nature itself, but ultimately it serves to keep alive a necessary communication with the great world. Like the original garden, the pastoral world is a place of beginnings whose culmination and maturity lies elsewhere.

Rightly enough, the pastoral is often compared with the heroic, for both kinds of literature have human aspiration as their theme.[16] They are alike in offering to their readers the potentially gratifying fantasy of a nobler self. But although the heroic mode, by its characterization of the fallibility of the epic hero and its dramatization of the limitations imposed upon his ambitions, embodies its own self-criticism, the pastoral is the only mode that contains the image of its own dissolution.

Almost no pastoral grants its characters a continuous or untroubled sojourn within the natural world. Rather, an ultimate turning back to the great world is the common denominator of pastoral literature: the point at which the individual work yields to the archetypal pattern, expelling man from his dream of innocence into the experienced world.[17] But the potential sense of loss or desolation is tempered by the fact that the return from the pastoral is the gesture by which man may assert his indi-

---

[16] Empson, pp. 140–141, 196, and elsewhere; and, for a concise discussion of the Renaissance linking of pastoral with the "desire for greater things," Cullen, pp. 6–10.

[17] A return from the pastoral necessitated by the fragility of ideal experience is proposed by Poggioli, p. 154, but in a limited manner. Observing that "man may linger in the pastoral dream world a short while or a whole lifetime," he goes on to say that the ideal appears more poignant when the sojourn is short. A stronger and broader interpretation is suggested in Harry Berger's general discussion of the pattern of withdrawal and return: "This withdrawal from life to fiction is seen as fulfilled in a return to life which has two aspects: a return to the image of life within the play-world of art and a return to life itself at the end of the fictional experience" ("The Renaissance Imagination," p. 42). Berger is speaking not merely of pastoral, but of all fictions, and from this perspective the return from the pastoral may be seen as the prototype of all fictional returns. The pastoral experience is accordingly a paradigm of all fictional experiences; its drive toward the recognition of an ideal, toward rebirth and self-discovery, is an intensification of these drives in general literary experience.

viduality against the influence of nature. Here, especially, the ambiguity of the natural ideal shows clearly, for the return to the great world takes many forms: sometimes a fortuitous conclusion to discovery, sometimes an escape from rustic isolation, sometimes a sad awakening to an imperfect and oppressive reality. Thus the pastoral may lead toward vision, or, contrariwise, demonstrate that man's capacity for vision is lost. Although the mode is unique in its derivation from a single mythic ideal, it is also unique in its capability for innumerable modifications of that ideal and for variations in literary pattern, verging sometimes on comedy and romance, sometimes on tragedy or satire.[18] By tracing some of these patterns in larger forms of pastoral, I shall prepare for a later, minute examination of their significance in Vergil's lyric. The manner in which the pastoral world must be abandoned is the final evaluation of the quality of pastoral experience.

The simplest return from the pastoral occurs when the garden has in some way answered to expectation or desire, when nature performs a restorative function or possesses magical powers. Under such conditions, problems may be solved in the pastoral that human obstinacy or shortsightedness make insoluble within the great world. An early version of pastoral reconciliation occurs in Menander's *Dyskolos* where the courteous, city-bred Sostratus, son of a wealthy Athenian landowner, must take up field labor to win a virtuous country bride. Although his wealth arouses the resistant pride of an impoverished rustic family, his perseverance and humor demonstrate sincerity, showing that sophisticated ease has not tainted his own rural heritage. As the farmers acknowledge that poverty is not essential to nobility, the marriage of Sostratus and Cnemon's daughter and a rustic feast in honor of Pan celebrate the be-

---

[18] These categories obviously coincide with Northrop Frye's classification of the *mythoi* of comedy, romance, tragedy, and irony in *The Anatomy of Criticism*. Poggioli's often cited classifications of pastoral ("pastoral of the self," "pastoral of friendship," "pastoral of happiness," "pastoral of melancholy") are based upon the particular aspects of personal experience that the critic finds in each poem, but they tend to negate the larger relationship to mode or genre. It is, in fact his opinion (p. 183) that "all the subgenres of pastoral must be reduced to the common denominator of the lyrical mode."

ginning of a new society founded upon the alliance of city and country virtues.[19]

Joyous return from the pastoral is the familiar conclusion of Shakespeare's green-world comedies.[20] In *A Midsummer Night's Dream*, the confused young lovers are trapped by their capricious emotions and by a harsh Athenian marriage law until chance brings them into the power of Oberon in the midnight forest. Here the follies of infatuation assume their proper perspective as accidents of nature's drive toward fertility when Oberon insists that each lover must have a mate. The couples wake to find a society grown favorable to their loves, and, looking backward, see their forest night already fading into the ambiguity of a dream. As Duke Theseus remarks, lovers and poets are similar in their capacity to transform their world through vision and fantasy.

In *As You Like It*, the courteous, civilized court of the elder Duke takes refuge from a harsh usurper in Arden Forest, a free, green kingdom like Robin Hood's, yet empty of citizens to govern. Love is the pastime best suited to Arden.[21] In the freedom of her boy's disguise, Rosalind explores the idiosyncrasies of love, teasing country couples for their shyness and ill humor, while she urges Orlando to learn to love her realistically, unblinded by sentiment and illusion. Yet Arden remains an isolated play world until the repentance of Duke Frederick opens the way for its inhabitants to put off their forest disguises and return to the real world. The island of *The Tempest* is a setting for more difficult social readjustment since the injustices of the great world have been more complex. Under the influence of Prospero's magic, the spirits of the island show nature's extremes of savagery and refinement; their world is both a snare to apprehend and baffle evil and a charm to encourage self-knowledge and rebirth. Such magic is too intense for man's ordinary life. As Prospero explains when he dissolves his wed-

[19] See the excellent interpretation by Kenneth Reckford, "The *Dyskolos* of Menander," *SP* 58(1961):1–24, who speaks of Menander's countryside as "a testing place for sincerity of character."

[20] See esp. C. L. Barber, *Shakespeare's Festive Comedy: A Study in Dramatic Form and Its Relation to Social Custom* (Princeton, 1959), pp. 119–162, 222–239.

[21] *Ibid.*, p. 223. The tension between ideal freedom and natural realities in the play is also discussed by Poggioli, pp. 180–182.

ding pageant of beneficent spirits, commanding Prince Ferdi-
nand to "look cheerful," man cannot hope to remain within the
tenuous ideal constructs shaped by imagination. Prospero himself must relinquish his powers and entrust himself to the
benevolence of that society he has labored to re-create.[22]

In these plays the transition from pastoral to reality is both
desirable and painless, for the semblance of man's better self,
discovered within the pastoral world, stands ready to be trans-
planted into the real. Such discoveries are most closely associated
with comedy, where they answer to the generic demand for the
reformation or renewal of a faulty society, but they also figure
in two other forms of pastoral: the prose romance and the
visionary lyric. In such a tale as Longus' *Daphnis and Chloe*, the
pastoral world offers glamorously fearful adventures to test
the courage of its heroes, but the assured termination of these
adventures is a part of their charm. Unlike the epic hero whose
existence is synonymous with his exploits, the hero of romance
experiences adventure only as an interlude in life, and is ready
to sacrifice pastoral freedom for the security of the civilized
world. The possibilities of such temporary freedom are exploited in Walter Scott's highland novels, where the forbidding
moors and mountains, so barbarous to a tame lowland eye, offer
a new version of the return to nature. In a country whose
shepherds and herdsmen are poor clansmen and villagers, the
wars of Britain are played out upon a reduced scale in intrigues
and skirmishes of soldiers and chieftains. Sudden and unexpected involvement in these actions gives scope for the restless-

---

[22] The dual temptations to intellectual withdrawal or tyrannical self-assertion
that Prospero faces in consequence of his magic are discussed by Berger in
"Miraculous Harp: A Reading of Shakespeare's *Tempest*," *Shakespeare Studies*
5(1969):253–283, and the exploration of man's imaginative powers is also the
keynote of Armstrong's analysis of the play, pp. 77–96. Prospero's intuition of
the need to relinquish his magic in favor of the actual world is well explained by
Berger's comments on the analogous vision of Colin Clout in *Faerie Queene* 6:
"The triumph of imagination is partly measured by the extent to which it has
converted frustration, brute fact, the world of first sight and first nature into a
symbolic intuition of the real. . . . But the triumph is also measured by the acceptance of what the mind cannot transform, by the awareness of limit. . . . The
complete self-sufficiency of the second nature, the total inward mastery of experience—this is no triumph at all, only delusion, if it takes itself seriously. For
then it would have nothing to do with the poet *now*, a man still faced by life,
fortune, malice, Providence" ("A Secret Discipline," p. 74).

ness of Scott's youthful protagonists, many of them lowlanders in quiet or unconscious rebellion against the dull lives urged upon them by their conventional fathers. Thus Edward Waverly, a phlegmatic young aristocrat with a habit of changing his mind, finds his first real commitment as an unintending participant in the Rebellion of the Young Pretender. Amidst the emotional conflicts of warring against his homeland, Waverly discovers his potential for loyal friendship in his adherence to a quarrelsome, ambitious highland chief, and his shifting fancies give place to love for a Jacobite's daughter. With the self-assurance that comes from tested identity, he welcomes the royal pardon that admits him to his obligations as his family's heir.

Among the most intensive of experiences in nature are the visions of the Romantic poets, such as Wordsworth's "Resolution and Independence" and "Immortality Ode" or Keats's "Ode to A Nightingale." Here, in fleeting moments of insight, the poet looks beyond the outward forms of reality to the source of creative power, the interaction of imagination with a universal spirit of life. Here, especially, the recognition of a natural ideal is transient. Wordsworth's concept of "emotion recollected in tranquillity," the reinterpretation of visionary experience amidst the calm of ordinary life, embodies the principle of pastoral return. In *The Prelude*, a nocturnal ascent of Mt. Snowdon brings the poet before an awesome scene — mist-enshrouded promontories and hills, a clear moonlit sky, and the sound of many waters rising toward the moon — that for him becomes a unifying vision of a dynamic nature and a majestic intellect: "a mind that feeds upon infinity, that broods/over the dark abyss, intent to hear/its voices issuing forth to silent light/ in one continuous stream" (14. 70–74). This experience is the culmination of a series of visionary moments uniting pastoralism and the search for poetic understanding that have haunted and shaped the young poet's growth. Yet only while the vision is dissolving does the poet begin to translate it into the vocabulary of his poetics, perceiving the resemblance between the Eternal Mind whose power creates unity in nature and the shaping mind of a poet: "They build up greatest things/from least suggestions, ever on the watch,/willing to work and to be wrought upon" (14. 101–103). When pastoral nature opens to man a genuine new world, yet a world oriented toward the reinterpretation or re-creation of reality, its literary pattern is close to those of comedy and romance.

In other cases, the pastoral world, although not openly in conflict with reality, yet appears too naïve or too uncouth to stand against the sophistication of the great world. Hence pastoral characters may turn against or flee from their rustic surroundings in search of worldly experience or freedom from limitations. A rather crass version of such pastoral inadequacy appears in Calpurnius Siculus' seventh *Eclogue,* when the rustic Corydon, dazzled by the sights of Rome, and especially by the exotic, artificial imitations of nature in the Neronian amphitheatre, returns home with rude condemnations of his lowly rustic surroundings. Here we may doubt the rustic's judgment, suspecting that the humble world he now scorns is worthier than the glamorous spectacles that have distorted his vision.[23] A more philosophical loss of faith in nature forms an underlying theme of Spenser's *Shepheardes Calendar,* and is equally pertinent to its Christian philosophy, its theoretical consideration of poetry, and its image of the human condition. In the January Eglogue, Colin Clout's love for Rosalind, the scornful maiden of the town who "laughs the songs that Colin Clout doth make," has disturbed his pastoral tranquillity. Finding no comfort from his rural muse, the despondent swain breaks his oaten pipe. In the December Eglogue, Colin's pastoral existence seems insufficient in a deeper way. As the year's dismal progress toward winter coincides with human despair and frustration, Colin sees the pastoral as a wasteland, himself as a natural creature bound to the cycle of the seasons. He laments a withered spring and a decayed harvest, looking forward only to the symbolic end of his pastoral youth:

> Winter is come that blows the bitter blast
> And after winter, dreary death must haste.

[23] Calp. *Ecl.* 7. 4–6, 12–18, 79–84. Such phrases as "resupinis arboris," "inter continuous montes," "silvestria monstra," referring respectively to the timbers, the *cavea,* and the animals of the theatre, betray the perversion of nature. The poem is not, as Rosenmeyer suggests (pp. 123; 208), a judicious balancing of city and country, but rather a demonstration of their incompatibility as is argued in Eleanor Winsor Leach, "Corydon Revisited: An Interpretation of the Political *Eclogues* of Calpurnius Siculus," *Ramus* 2(1973):53–97.

In living with complete dependence upon nature, man finds himself devoid of resources of spirit.[24]

In Shakespeare's *Cymbeline*, a play steeped in pastoral themes and allusions, the contrast of rustic isolation and cosmopolitan sophistication is translated into legendary history. Under the influence of his chauvinistic, scheming queen, Cymbeline maintains a proud, provincial defiance of Rome. His Britain, "ribbed and paled in with rocks unscalable and roaring waters," provides an illusory freedom from the great world. But the sterility of such isolation is manifested in the naïveté of the British character. Honesty is paired with gullibility; both the king and his daughter's husband Posthumus are victims of deception. Cymbeline's innate nobility cannot be fully realized until he rises above insular pride and makes a gesture of reconciliation as a victorious leader, freely granting tribute to Rome. The Roman eagle soars toward the sun, signifying a majestic alliance between Caesar and Cymbeline, and men rejoice in a new world harmony.[25]

The incompatibility of rustic isolation and the noble mind is reflected in one of the subplots of the play: the discovery of the king's stolen sons. Educated in the security of a forest cave, amidst untainted nature, the boys learn gentle manners and manly skills; yet they chafe at their ignorance of the world and their obscurity, longing for honor: "an invisible instinct frames them to royalty unlearned." Here the pastoral life is to be valued only as a preparation for heroic experience. The tale of these princes is a variation upon the legend of Rome's founders, Romulus and Remus, and this pattern, in which a limited rustic environment serves both to disguise and to mold a heroic character, is particularly Roman.

Although nature may foster the development of a hero, the limitations of rustic perspective sometimes obscure his true worth. Such is the case in *Tom Jones*. The foundling's native

[24] E.g., Isabel MacCaffrey, "Allegory and Pastoral in the *Shepheardes Calendar*," *ELH* 36(1969):95: "Those aspects of his life which indicate its congruence with nature are unsatisfactory or inadequate to the demands made upon them."

[25] *Cymbeline* V. v. 465–474. This prophecy is of a new pastoral golden age; the eagle is the emblem of Christ and Cymbeline the British king at the time of Christ's birth, as Spenser notes in *Faerie Queene* 2. 10. 50 and Frye explains in *Anatomy of Criticism*, p. 219.

honesty and generosity, clouded by the mystery of his parentage and misguided in his well-meaning friendship with the family of Black George the gamekeeper, incur only misunderstanding and disgrace in his country home. The conventional rural piety of Squire Allworthy makes him an easy victim for the deceptions of Tom's enemies, and he is unable to interpret the young man's true merits until he sees them set off by contrast with the corrupt manners of the city. When the pastoral world is dominated by awkwardness and inexperience, man's life there is often no more than a prelude to self-discovery. Departure from the pastoral may appear as the beginning of wisdom. But since the pastoral hero, despite such early isolation, is often in progress toward a fuller society or a heroic destiny, this kind of pastoral also verges upon comedy and romance.

A more painful transition from the pastoral to the real world, the opposite of the comic pattern, appears when the pastoral world is suddenly destroyed, when the loss of an idyllic environment leaves its naïve or unwary dependents at the mercy of the great world. Such a startling catastrophe is witnessed by Sir Calidore in *Faerie Queene* 6. His pursuit of scandal—the Blatant Beast—ceases temporarily as the knight finds unexpected haven in the shepherd community presided over by Meliboee and his gentle daughter Pastorella, a world that to him seems far removed from "storms of fortune and tempestuous fate." Although the philosophical old shepherd, himself a fugitive from the great world, explains that true contentment adheres to no given place or condition of life, but is established only in the mind (6. 9. 18–33), Calidore insists upon undertaking the pastoral life as an experiment. Only when Meliboee's sheepfolds are invaded by brigands, the old man brutally murdered, and Pastorella imprisoned and threatened by a robber chief does Calidore understand that his tranquil refuge was but a secluded corner of that real world wherein courtesy must struggle constantly to maintain order and keep violence at bay.

The pastoral in which the golden world is destroyed follows most closely the archetypal myth of lost innocence. Accordingly, this pattern is often united with themes of education, initiation, and the awareness of maturity. In *Lycidas*, the security and ambitions of the young poet, confident in his promise, have been shaken by the death of his coeval, and human achievement must be re-evaluated in terms of man's inevitable end. The themes of education and initiation are especially strong in American literature where the atmosphere of the new world, the dream of innocence rediscovered, is constantly in the background.[26] Ishmael's journey in the *Pequod* is a journey of initiation. The green world of the sea, a second pastoral refuge for the man who already fears to see "the green fields gone," becomes the context for discovery of the restless, self-destroying violence of the human heart. Here nature does not perish, but man who in projecting his own fears and obsessions upon nature transforms his paradise into hell. In a not uncomparable voyage, Huck Finn discovers the universal nature of man's duplicity in his glimpses of life near the great river. The river is his way to freedom, and under its influence he has, with agony of con-science, committed himself to procuring freedom for black Jim. But the journey ends abruptly, and Huck's commitment is debased by the conventional make-believe of Tom Sawyer's romantic imagination. Concealing his knowledge of Jim's manumission, the carefree Tom becomes a deceiver, forcing the old slave to undergo an incomprehensible ritual of escape from bondage.[27] For Tom, freedom is no more than a toy; his youthful passion for adventure is in bondage to generations of civilized imaginers. In American literature, pastoral inexperi-ence—or an ignorance of social bondage—is often thus em-bodied in a youthful protagonist. Faulkner's *The Bear* centers about the cutting of the wilderness where Isaac McCaslin has been initiated into the romantic rituals of the gentleman's hunt. The hero's early ideal of maturity, the meeting with the bear whom he does not wish to kill—a meeting that symbolizes his kinship with nature—must be revised when the bear dies with violence, the lumber company possesses the land, and Isaac confronts the unromantic face of the South: a land that God has blessed with forests and game and man has cursed with injustice. Attempting to maintain his old ideals of woodland

[26] Marx, pp. 73ff.
[27] Marx sees the ascendancy of Tom as a symbolic death of Huck as hero (*ibid.*, p. 339).

purity, Isaac repudiates his background, rejecting his inheritance of land in inconclusive withdrawal from the guilt of his ancestors, unable to leave a pastoral world that has already been taken from him.

In plots such as these that follow a tragic model, the pastoral world remains a physical reality, a nature with an integrity of its own that man is unable to share. But sometimes the pastoral world must be rejected, and often again with sorrow, because it becomes known for a wishful fiction, an illusion of something unattainable and unreal. A simple form of this rejection is in Raleigh's poem "The Nymph's Reply to the Shepherd." The lady who knows the world is no paradise is sophisticated, almost too sophisticated in her suspicions of the shepherd's invitation:

> The flowers do fade and wanton fields
> To wayward winter reckoning yield.
> A honey tongue, a heart of gall
> Is fancy's spring, but sorrow's fall.

The knowledge that innocence is already gone from the world turns pastoral delights to seductions and false promises.

A more complicated awareness of the emptiness of a pastoral paradise is the disillusionment in Fitzgerald's *The Great Gatsby.* Gatsby's American dream of prosperity, success, and love finds its emblem in the green light that shines across the harbor from Daisy's dock. To his still naïve faith, her material world of green lawns and white dresses remains an innocent world where romantic trust is possible. But his illusion blinds him to the callousness of Daisy's society, the cause of his own destruction, and finally appears to the narrator as only one of the haunting, sad dreams that have endlessly been nourished at "the green breast of the new world."[28] Such sad dreams are not infrequent in novels of this century where American literature has preserved the pastoral bias of earlier times but with new notes of irony.[29] The Los Angeles of Nathanael West's *Day of the Locust*

[28] See Marx, pp. 359–364. Like Isaac McCaslin, the narrator, Nick Carroway, rejects the flawed world in favor of another pastoral withdrawal, a return to the Middle West. To Marx this is a somewhat futile and melancholy gesture; a token move in the direction of nature and the vanishing American pastoral myth.

[29] *Ibid.*, pp. 354–369. Poggioli, p. 176, speaks of random survivals of the pastoral perspective in post-eighteenth-century literature, the majority mock-pastoral and ironic in point of view.

is a fallacious green world where mediocre men, hoping to escape their drab lives, "come to die." In its midst is Hollywood, a mock-microcosm where the movie cameras record history re-enacted in costumes and flimsy trappings; a painted field of Waterloo collapses under an untimely charge. To the protagonist, this paradise is Hades. His apocalyptic panorama, the burning of Los Angeles, anticipates the chaos of hysterical, stampeding moviegoers that concludes the novel.

A skillful adaptation of mock-pastoral characterizes J. L. Herlihy's recent novel *Midnight Cowboy,* a work whose ironic elevation of the rogue to sympathetic protagonist recalls the inversions in the *Beggar's Opera.* Here the fabled green plains of the west are sordid and dry, and the naïve wanderer, taking on the guise of a cowboy—the embodiment of the American legend of masculinity—travels east seeking a new pastoral dream of leisure and abundant fertility by fulfilling the mythical sexual desires of the nymphs of the big city, a world whose greenness is that of cash alone. As the cowboy's dream fails, he contrives a new escape, traveling to Florida, another seductive, legendary paradise. But the death of his sole companion leaves him amidst a reality that is to be confronted, not with expectation, but with fear. The pastoral illusion whose disappearance may bring mingled sadness and relief is a more abstract form of the destruction of the pastoral world and is well adapted to satirical contexts. Here the innocent paradise bears little physical resemblance to the traditional ideals of nature. Its beauty is projected upon it by a dreamer who, laboring under some misconception or blindness, makes his ideal world the mirror of his own naïve folly.

Whether it involves a genuine sojourn in nature or a mere cohabitation with illusions, the pastoral experience is always temporary. Return from the pastoral world is inevitable, either to save man from sterile isolation or to rescue him from himself. As a world created in imagination for the gratification of human longings, the pastoral demands a relationship with reality, either the reader's world of reality or some image contained within the poem itself.[30] In the final meeting of the pastoral

[30] Berger regards the transition from the fictional world to the real as the critical point in the cognitive process: "Profit is immanent in the very nature of

world and the great world, a meeting that may be either a clash or a reconciliation, we come to understand the distance between the two regions, the ways in which each may reflect the other, and the possible interrelationships between the pastoral characters' experience and our own. As fully as natural simplicity, innocence, or ideological conflict, the abandonment of the pastoral world has become an aspect of the pastoral tradition.

In Vergil's *Eclogues* we find the roots of this tradition. From beginning to end the poems are characterized by disappointment, frustration, and lost illusion. Already in the first poem, one farmer warns another that the tranquil fields of their fatherland have become turbulent. Land is torn from its rightful owners in the aftermath of civil war. In *Eclogue* 2, Corydon's dreamworld vanishes before the city-bred scorn of his beloved. In *Eclogue* 3, a pair of quarreling herdsmen accuse each other of offenses against nature: profaning a shrine, cutting a vineyard, stealing a prize. Even their pastoral singing match is no more than a protraction of animosities. The poet of *Eclogue* 4 rejects the humble tamarisks and the orchards, emblems of pastoral rusticity, and calls upon the Muses for a higher strain of song, one worthy of a consul's name. The lament for Daphnis in *Eclogue* 5 portrays the cessation of nature's activities: the breaking of rural order after the death of an ideal leader. In *Eclogue* 6, the poet again desires to free himself from the pastoral and embark upon celebrations of *reges et proelia*, but Apollo holds him back, insisting that he maintain the decorum of the shepherd's art. Thyrsis of the seventh poem looks cynically upon pastoral idealism, depicting nature as a country of dry hills and rejected loves. Again in the eighth, the Eclogue Poet reveals his impatience with the pastoral and the song he relates is that of a disappointed lover who turns his back on nature in death, escaping from a world that had deluded him with dreams of a prosperous love. The ninth poem shows the farm possessed

---

artifice and fiction; yet . . . fiction can fulfill itself only by going beyond itself and invading life. It does this through open gestures of self-limitation, as when, by revealing itself as mere make-believe, it seals off its image, breaks the transference, releases the audience and consigns the fate of its rounded image to their wills" ("The Renaissance Imagination," p. 75).

by a soldier, and displaced herdsmen on a journey to the city, recalling snatches of song from better days. In *Eclogue* 10, the pastoral dreaming of the elegiac poet Gallus is incapable of changing the course of his unrewarded love. Bidding farewell to visions of a new life amidst nature, he turns back to a harsh world of reality governed by cruel love.

In these negative illuminations of the pastoral are the prototypes for the varied patterns of pastoral return in later literature. The tragic is present in the violent destruction of natural tranquillity, while vanishing illusions of an unattainable beauty create an ironic relationship between man and the world of his desires. The limitations of rustic simplicity are in the foreground when the Eclogue Poet compares pastoral and heroic, seeking for a poetry that can incorporate the deeds of the real world. Yet Gallus, a poet from the real world, can in turn seek a new identity in the pastoral, discovering only that the complexities of human emotion are easier to discover than to transform. Each of the poems contains some reminder of frailty or inadequacy in nature or of the human weakness that makes man incapable of adopting the natural world as his home. The reader is constantly aware of man's ambivalent attitudes toward nature.

For Vergil this ambivalence is bound up with a persistent creative problem: the adaptation of pastoral poetry to his own world. From Theocritus he had inherited pastoral as the expression and exploration of a human impulse, an impulse whose universal validity was apparent, yet one whose specific goals were, in many respects, incomprehensible to a Roman point of view. Thus it is impossible to read Vergil save as the second major pastoral poet, a reinterpreter and re-evaluator, for his reactions to his predecessor play an integral part in the cognitive experience of his poems. In his hands the pastoral changes from a mode emphasizing self-expression and felicitous withdrawal to one that makes nature a vehicle for the contemplative study of man. The personal turns to the universal, innocence yields to experience, and the pastoral paradise gives way to a microcosmic nature wherein poetry, at its best, may undertake to shape new patterns for the world of reality. If, as a critic has recently proposed, the dialectic of Theocritean poetry stems from conflicts of the ideal and the real,[31] Vergil places ideals in conflict. His new design incorporates a double perspective whereby man's search for ideals is constantly balanced against overlying standards by which the validity of the ideal must be judged. Within the book of poems, the ultimate judge is the Eclogue Poet, whose own ideal is the search for a viable form of poetic expression, a self-critical search that gives ultimate unity to the collection by its relinquishment of pastoral poetry.

The poet of the *Eclogues* does not leave the pastoral reluctantly with expressions of sorrow and loss, but deliberately, as if a period of controlled poetic experimentation had reached its limits and timely conclusion. Man's ambivalence toward nature is not merely a function of the psychological substratum of the poems, but rather a conscious element in their literary design. Another means of understanding this ambivalence may be derived from an examination of the specific directions taken by the pastoral impulse in Roman thought.

[31] See Lawall, pp. 4–5, 11, and John Van Sickle's interpretation, "Is Theocritus A Version of Pastoral?" *MLN* 84(1969):942–946.

CHAPTER 2

The Pastoral Impulse in Rome

In Christian literature, one principle of ideology gives particular impetus for the rejection of the pastoral world. Man's uneasiness in nature is a condition imposed upon him by the Fall.[1]
Theoretically, as well as practically, he is unable to recapture his
innocence by living as a natural creature amidst the natural
world. In his error of disobedience, Adam not only lost paradise
for himself but also bequeathed his guilt and ruined condition
equally to all members of his race. His descendants are constantly liable to repetitions of the Fall. Properly speaking,
the Christian must define innocence as a condition of the spirit
and understand Eden, the lost physical paradise, as a symbolic
manifestation of spiritual wholeness.[2] It was in token of Adam's

---

[1] Renato Poggioli, "The Oaten Flute," *Harvard Library Bulletin* 11(1957):147–
149, proposes a rather moralistic distinction: that the bucolic ideal stands at the
opposite pole from the Christian, since it sanctions a retreat from responsibility
not permitted to Christianity; he adds (p. 161) that the writing of Christian
pastoral is an effort to make Christianity idyllic. Both statements depend upon
his notion that the classical pastoral does indeed provide an illusion of "happiness" as well as an image of simplicity. Recently, several critics have taken up
this generalization: Patrick Cullen, *Spenser, Marvell and Renaissance Pastoral*
(Cambridge, Mass., 1971), finds an irreconcilable conflict of Arcadian leisure
and Christian responsibility to be the basis of the ideological debate in the
Shepherd's Calendar; John Knott, Jr., *Milton's Pastoral Vision: An Approach to
"Paradise Lost"* (Chicago, 1971), finds a successful fusion of classical and Christian
ideals in Milton's mythical Eden; Thomas Rosenmeyer, *The Green Cabinet:
Theocritus and the European Pastoral Lyric* (Berkeley, 1969), challenges Poggioli's
moralizing on the grounds that the ideal of simplicity transcends ideology in all
pastorals.

[2] August. *De civ. D.* 13. 21. The argument of this chapter is that Paradise is an
allegory of the spirit: its four rivers are the four virtues—prudence, fortitude,
temperence, and justice; its trees are useful knowledge; its fruits the customs of
the godly; its tree of life is wisdom herself; and the tree of the knowledge of

51

departure from spiritual integrity that God turned him from the garden, and thus the loss of Eden's physical beauty is only secondary to the decline of human nature under its legacy of ancestral sin.

The Christian myth of the Fall requires that man be dissatisfied with all earthly environments. With the disappearance of Eden, earthly nature comes to symbolize the limitations of the human condition and is deeply attached to mortal weakness. Eden can never again return on earth and all semblances of Eden are mere shadows of the past or foreshadowings of the higher paradise to be attained beyond nature.[3]

In his turning from the pastoral world, Christian man does not merely acknowledge a dependence upon civilization, for his sights must be fixed upon spiritual goals transcending his mutable and untrustworthy environment. Whatever images of innocence the physical world may seem to offer are potentially dangerous, for they represent an untutored and aspiritual innocence powerless for salvation.[4] Milton's fallen Adam learns that he must strive for paradise, but it is "a Paradise within thee, happier far." Man's quest for a renewal of innocence is unending but can never be fulfilled on earth, where his best occupation is to live so as to prepare himself for a rebirth in spirit.

This doctrine has given the Christian pastoral a peculiar poignancy in its expression of the tension between the love of earthly nature and the fear of its influence. In the November Eglogue of Spenser's *Calendar*, the singer reminds the shepherds that it is folly to weep for Dido, that they must celebrate her translation to a world above the imperfections of pastoral nature:

> Unwise and wretched men, to weet what's good or ill,
> We deem of death as doom of ill desert;

---

good and evil is the experience of a broken commandment. The garden is at once a definite terrestrial place, an allegory of the church, and a prophecy of heaven.

[3] For Milton's interpretation of this principle in a catalogue of lost mythical gardens inferior to Eden see *Paradise Lost* 4. 268–285.

[4] See the discussion of the fallability and deceptiveness of earthly paradises in A. Bartlett Giamatti, *The Earthly Paradise and the Renaissance Epic* (Princeton, 1966), p. 85 and elsewhere.

But knew we, fools, what it us brings until,
Die would we daily, once it to expert!
No danger there the shepherd can astert;
  Fair fields and pleasant lays there bene;
  The fields aye fresh, the grass aye green.
O happy herse!

Likewise Milton's Lycidas need not care for spring's tribute of
flowers or the mourning tears of nymphs and shepherds when
he is received into "blest kingdoms meek of joy and love." The
death of Shelley's Adonais leads to an acknowledgment that
"the One remains, the many change and pass . . . The world is
a dome of many colored glass, shattering the white ray of eter-
nity, till death tramples it to fragments on the floor." It is hardly
surprising that the Christian pastoral has reached one of its
peaks of articulation in elegy where the loss of earthly beauty
may be interpreted as a triumphant step in achieving release
from mortality.[5]

Turning backward from Christian to classical thought, we
find that the ideological background for the rejection of the
pastoral world must, at first, seem less clear, since neither doctrine nor philosophy places ultimate barriers between man and
his enjoyment of the natural world. Although the myth of the
lost golden age is archetypally similar to that of the loss of Eden
and can similarly be used to explain man's restlessness or sense
of alienation from his environment and his longing to return to
a better self, its hold upon the individual is less binding.

Classical thought has no concept quite equal to the spiritual
innocence of Christianity. The myth of the golden age implies
a physical abundance in nature sufficient for man's needs and
a consequent absence of the baser emotions that attend upon
want or the increase of possessions.[6] Although man is un-

---

[5] In Poggioli's opinion (p. 165), the Christian pastoral of death conflicts most
strongly with the pagan ideal by substituting a new image of happiness in the
afterlife of the soul. Rosenmeyer, pp. 117–125, treats elegy as a subspecies of
the genre, which, in the Western tradition, ultimately degenerated into en-
comiastic dirge. But he argues against Poggioli's view that the heavenly paradise
makes the beauty of pastoral nature seem insufficient, suggesting rather that it
enforces the pleasures of the *locus amoenus*.

[6] For the golden age and its varied relationships with the civilized world in
classical authors, see the material collected and analyzed by A. O. Lovejoy and

troubled by feelings of limitation and his life passes harmoni-
ously, and sometimes piously, there is more passive primitivism
than active purity in this life. Then, too, the disappearance of
the golden age is a myth far more flexible than the Christian Fall,
capable of interpretation according to the poet's wish. Hesiod
attributes man's misfortune to the gods, who inexplicably replaced the first sublime human generation with members of a
lesser race. Aratus, whose *Phaenomena* is a standard locus for
the myth, does not attempt to fathom the change from golden
age to silver but speaks of the departure of justice from the
earth as a consequence of the decline of man. In some authors,
the golden reign of Saturn is overturned by a violent, ambitious
Jove; in others, the ancient concord falls victim to human greed
and the desire for power.

All these legends have one element in common that we may
cite as typical of classical thought. Their interpretations of man's
fall explain the imperfections of history and society. As a social
and historical being, man feels the effects of the Fall. Human
corruption does not rest upon the shoulders of one special
person but is the product of a general failure in the quality of
mortal existence.[7] The individual may regret his alienation from
felicity while feeling no responsibility for the loss. Should he
choose to withdraw himself from the corruptions of a degener-
ate society and seek an individual return to nature, he is not
troubled by warnings of spiritual insufficiency. Instead, he may
take nature for his model in formulating patterns for an ideal
environment or a better self.

Unlike the Garden of Eden that can be recaptured only in
spirit, the golden age can theoretically be restored on earth. In
the *Works and Days,* Hesiod preaches that the just and righteous
man can regain a semblance of primal felicity:

George Boas, *Primitivism and Related Ideas in Antiquity*, vol. I of *A Documentary History of Primitivism and Related Ideas,* ed. A. O. Lovejoy (Baltimore, 1935), reprinted as vol. I of the series Contributions to the History of Primitivism (New York, 1965).

[7] "While for the pagan poet the salvation of mankind meant conjuring away the curse of war, for his Christian readers it meant instead the redemption of the human race from original sin" (Poggioli, p. 163).

the earth gives them great livelihood,
   on their mountains the oaks
bear acorns for them in their crowns,
   and bees in their middles.
Their wool-bearing sheep are weighted down
   with fleecy burdens.   [232–234] [8]

Even Plato sometimes maintains the outlines of this mythology. In the *Laws*, he likens the nature of the ideal ruler to that of the benevolent Daimons whom Saturn had established as men's governors in the golden age. By imitating the justice of the age of Saturn, a modern state can become ideal. To Plato the conventional trappings of the golden age, its spontaneous crops and natural abundance, are useful metaphors for the prosperity of well-governed states.[9]

This revivified golden age, less mystical and less spontaneous than the first but infinitely more practical, has wide-spread echoes in classical literature. In the *Georgics*, Vergil adopts the Hesiodic pattern for his idealization of Italy, the land whose richness offers always the potential for a recaptured Saturnian age, and where the atmosphere of the world's first spring returns each year to the vineyards and orchards (2.323–345), where a disciplined life in nature once shaped men to a virtue whose traces are still inherent in the agricultural life (2.532–540). The more political Platonic ideal figures in the *Aeneid*, summed up by King Evander when he speaks of the reign of his ancient predecessor Saturn as a time when unruly and ignorant men learned to live peacefully under good laws and a just rule: "He brought together a race unteachable and scattered throughout the high mountains and he gave them laws, and preferred to call the land Latium, since he had found safe refuge hiding on these shores. Some maintain that the ages under that king were golden: thus he ruled over the peoples in quiet peace" (8.321–325). When the golden age is thus transposed from lost ideal to a model for human endeavor,

---

[8] The translation is by Richmond Lattimore, *Hesiod* (Ann Arbor, 1959).
[9] Plato *Laws* 4.713B–714A. For discussion of Plato's reinterpretation of Hesiodic myth see Friedrich Solmsen, "Hesiodic Motifs in Plato," in *Hésiode et son influence*, Entretiens sur l'antiquité classique, 7 (Geneva: Fondation Hardt, 1960), pp. 171–212.

from a counsel of despair to a canon of perfection, little senti-
mentality colors the image of man's life in nature. His role is
an active one; his duty to create order in the universe in cooperation with nature's own activity. Consequently, we find little
practical difference between such allegorical adaptations of
mythology and the principles of rationalist thinkers who espouse
the antiprimitivist concept that nature is unfallen, that her true
perfection still remains to be discovered by man. This tendency
is apparent in the philosophical writings of Cicero, whose
general convictions are opposed to an idealization of primitivism.[10] In the *De Legibus* he argues that man should seek understanding of the law of nature as the surest guide to reason and
virtue:

But certainly this principle holds true, that a life in accordance with
nature is the highest good: that is, a life that is temperate and fitted
both to enjoy virtue and to follow nature and live as if by her law. A
man who lives thus omits in no manner, so far as is humanly possible,
to answer to the demands of nature, among which is her wish that man
should take virtue for his law.   [1. 21. 56]

Cicero does not believe that man has lost his ability to live in
accordance with nature. The rational order of nature is unchanging; it is man's task to discover this order and translate
it into concepts that will give a corresponding order to human
life. Since the human and the natural worlds are similar in their
capacity for order, the harmony of man and nature is neither
unstable nor imaginary but real and ever present. In a passage
describing man's place in the universe, Cicero shows how the
discovery and understanding of this harmony provide a basis
for self-knowledge:

When the mind has looked with understanding upon the sky, the earth,
the sea and the nature of all things, realizing where they had their
beginnings and to what they will return and in what manner they will
perish; when it understands what part of things is mortal and prone to
destruction, and what part of things is eternal and divine, when it

---

[10] Lovejoy and Boas analyze Cicero's attitude toward primitivism on pp.
243–259. Cicero tends toward the anthropological view that man, at the outset
of his history, was not superior to the animals. Human goods are the product
of civilization and dependent upon the development of man's reason.

comes near to comprehending the force that governs and tempers all things and recognizes that it is not hemmed in by walls like the people of some fixed place, but lives as a citizen of the whole world, as if the whole world were one city, then amid this magnificence of creation and before the spectacle and knowledge of nature, how well it will know itself, immortal gods, in keeping with the teaching of Pythian Apollo.

[1. 23. 61]

Cicero's counsels on the observance of natural law are no less exacting a discipline than Milton's search for a spiritual paradise, but the writers differ in their opinion of nature as a source of ultimate truth. Here the classical thinker depends on nature as the Christian depends on scripture and revelation. The physical universe is his book of revelation. In *Paradise Lost*, Milton showed an awareness of this difference between the two modes of thought when he made the world that Adam learns of in innocence a rational universe with classical overtones. Only after the darkness of sin has clouded his reason and his dependence on God has changed from adult understanding to childlike faith does Adam see nature as mysterious.

With their emphasis on disciplined human activity, both the concept of the restored golden age and the investigation of universal order are in keeping with Roman attitudes toward nature in that period of the late Republic that preceded the composition of the *Eclogues*. As we go on to examine some of these attitudes more fully we should realize that they are less often embodied in philosophical statements concerning man's existence in nature than in images of nature as a background for the development of the Roman character.

On the simplest ideological plane, Roman legends and Roman institutions show a disposition toward a pastoral longing for nature in their idealization or preservation of associations with nature in the past. The founders of Rome were inhabitants of a pastoral world. Evander, the Arcadian exile, lived as a shepherd king in Italy, the first settler on the Palatine Hill.[11] Descendants of his community educated Romulus and Remus as

---

[11] For references see G. Lugli, *Regio Urbis Decima Mons Palatinus, Testi et Documenti*, vol. VIII, part 1, Fontes ad Topographia Veteris Urbis Romae Pertinentes, Universita di Roma, Instituto di Topographica Antica, no. 19 (Rome, 1960), pp. 51–53.

shepherds. The pastoral life concealed the identity of the royal boys in childhood while preparing them for a career in the historical world. Roman interest in the primitive life of Romulus is attested by careful preservation of the iron-age hut on the Palatine known as the hut of Romulus. In addition to her legend of the shepherd founders, Rome had gained the makings of her own golden-age legend when Ennius, in the second century, promulgated the story of King Saturn's second reign in Italy following his expulsion from the old world by Jove.[12]

The traditions and religion of the city tend to preserve associations with an ancient bucolic or agricultural life. Many festivals of the state religion trace their supposed origins to pastoral times, among them the Parilia, birthday of the city, celebrated with quaint bucolic rituals honoring Pales, the protector of shepherds. The Lupercalia, whose exact significance no historical Roman seems to have understood, was generally interpreted as a feast of Lycean Pan, brought from Arcadia by Evander. There was a rustic cast to the *Suovetaurilia*, the sacrificial procession of sheep, sow, and bull that marked the completion of the census or the purification of armies after war but was originally a ceremony for the purification of the fields. As he comments on such rituals in the *De Re Rustica*, Varro emphasizes their linking of the Roman past and present. The unquestioning re-enactment of traditional ceremonies, many whose meaning was already lost, shows a desire to preserve the continuity of ideology against the changes brought by progress and time.[13]

In the middle years of the Augustan era these ancient survivals took an inevitable turn toward the glorification of a primitive past. Especially in the elegiac poets Propertius and

[12] *Euhemeris sive sacra historia*, frg. V. 87–97, (Vahlens, pp. 224–225), and see Lovejoy and Boas, pp. 55–65. The kingdom is merely a political one, not conceived on the ideal model of the Hesiodic golden age.

[13] For sources see Lugli, pp. 37–40, 45–49. The urban and rustic aspects of the Parilia are described by Warde Fowler, *The Roman Festivals of the Period of the Republic* (London, 1899), pp. 79–85. The Lupercalia is discussed in Lugli, pp. 45–49 and R. Ogilvie, *A Commentary on Livy Books 1–5* (Oxford, 1965), pp. 51–53. The formula for the *Suovetaurilia* is given by Cato *Agr.* 141; Varro *Rust.* 2. 1. 10 mentions its connections with the Lustrum. In sections 9–10, Varro speaks of the Parilia and the *Suovetaurilia* as evidence of the honored position of husbandry in Roman tradition.

Tibullus is a longing for escape from the complexities of the present, a note of regret for Italy's loss of the second golden age.[14] But during the late years of the Republic such sentimental attitudes toward nature and primitivism are more notable by their absence than by their presence.

The last years of the Republic are sometimes characterized as a time of intellectual turning toward nature,[15] a time when Romans sought relief from the struggle of contemporary politics in thoughts of the country or the early days of their city. In some respects this is true. The years from 55 to 36 saw the composition of Cicero's dialogues with settings often far removed in time or place from contemporary Rome: the *De Legibus*, a conversation conducted on the banks of the River Liris in the author's native Arpinum; the *De Re Publica*, set in the villa of Scipio Aemilianus a hundred years before; the *Cato Maior*, with its eloquent glorification of retirement to an agricultural life. In similar fashion, Varro's three books on agriculture use rural settings to emphasize their themes, and both the first and second books have fictional dates somewhat earlier than the actual years of composition. As the speakers in this treatise reveal their knowledge and experience of its three subjects (cultivation, husbandry, and the farmstead), it becomes clear that Varro has coupled his practical information with the affectionate delineation of an idealized image of the complete villa farm, a beautiful and self-sufficient world.[16] Not unrelated to literary interest in nature is the movement in the graphic arts toward the use of landscapes in wall decoration.[17] Natural motifs occur in vignettes and friezes as well as in large mural prospects that seem to dissolve the confined space of a room into illusions of spatial expansion and prospects of a world outside.

[14] The theme is ironic in Propertius 2. 25; 2. 32. 47–57, more straightforward in 4. 1. 1–70. In Tibullus 1. 3. 35–50 and related poems with agricultural imagery there appears a more sentimental view of the country.

[15] Pierre Grimal, *Les Jardins Romains*, 2d ed. (Paris, 1969), pp. 358–398.

[16] For the symbolic value of this work see *ibid.*, pp. 366–367, and Phyllis Williams Lehmann, *Roman Wall Paintings from Boscoreale in the Metropolitan Museum of Art* (Cambridge, Mass. 1953), p. 94; she speaks of the villa as "that ideal microcosm cherished by the men of the late Republic and early Empire."

[17] For the association of landscape painting with "escapism" see Karl Schefold, "The Origins of Roman Landscape Painting," *Art Bulletin* 42 (1960):92.

And from this same period come expressions of lament for a decline of the Roman character, a sense that its essential virtues have been lost. The picture of ancient Rome in Sallust's *Catilinae Coniuratio* portrays a community of vigorous citizens actively competing for honor in the military and civic life. Almost twenty years later, Livy's preface to the *Ab Urbe Condita* glorifies the lost virtues of economy, moderation, and civic devotion, virtues that had remained stable at Rome longer than in any other city, only recently yielding to corruption and greed.

Yet in none of these works is an antidote for contemporary problems posed by a return to pure natural simplicity or by dreams of isolation in nature. Even the scenes of Roman landscape painting blend together elements of nature and civilization—shrines and shepherds, buildings and trees—as if images of the rural world would be incomplete without some reminder of the occupations and institutions of man.[18] Likewise, the discussions of the Roman past and Roman agriculture have an ethical orientation that emphasizes the relationship between the rural and the civic life. Although lacking the Christian doctrinal basis for avoidance of natural simplicity, Roman writers tend toward a similar point of view.

Insofar as we may identify a Roman approximation of the concept of natural innocence, we find it colored by realism and practicality. Roman attitudes toward nature are ambivalent. While Livy may speak with admiration of the self-discipline and modesty of Cincinnatus plowing his four *iugera* (3. 26. 7–10), the blighted prospects of the young T. Manlius, confined by his proud father to a life of agricultural servility on account of his sluggish talents, is a subject for indignation (7. 4. 6–7).[19] On the one hand, the Roman shows a desire to link present and past by demonstrations of a continuous strain of virtue in the national character, a virtue whose source may be seen in the activity of cultivating and controlling the rural world. On the other, he

---

[18] Rosenmeyer, pp. 127, 183, mentions this well-known point to demonstrate that Campanian painting is not pastoral.

[19] "But, by Hercules, Lucius Manilius augmented his son's inherent badness by ill-use and repressed his sluggish nature by his authority, and, if there was any small element of natural energy in him, he crushed it out by confining him to a country life and a rustic upbringing amid the herds."

suspects that a life of pure natural simplicity is neither an end in itself nor a suitable condition for man. From this perspective, innocence tends to assume the shape of ignorance — hardly a subject for idealization since it cannot provide sufficient basis for action or even for integrity in a complicated world.

Republican writers show little inclination to interpret the pastoral days of their city as a vanished golden age. In invoking the bucolic milieu, they are less apt to idealize than to demonstrate how far the city has risen from its humble origins. When Cicero and Livy mention Romulus in their histories they are concerned primarily with rationalizing his story, making it probable that a young man bred in pastoral obscurity could stand ready for a position of leadership in the historical world. In the *De Re Publica*, Cicero stresses the hardiness and vigor of personality that Romulus developed during his rustic life:

Tradition maintains that the shepherds reared him in country discipline and labor so that he reached maturity so surpassing all others in strength of body and fierceness of spirit that all men living in the fields where this city stands today were glad to grant him their obedience with the feeling that it was just. [2. 2. 5]

Livy's image of the shepherd Romulus is even less idealized. His community lives by plunder taken from robbers, the citizens of King Amulius. This aggressive life makes Romulus and Remus ready for necessary deeds of agression in the future:

As they gained in hardiness of body and spirit, they lived not only by hunting wild animals, but also by making attacks on robbers laden with booty, dividing their spoils among the shepherds. With these men, a band of youths daily growing larger, they engaged in serious matters and in sport. [1. 4. 9]

Although Romulus and Remus are not gentle shepherds, the arts they learn in the country are rough foreshadowings of civic virtue. In Cicero, Romulus displays almost miraculous historical acumen as he chooses the most advantageous territory in Latium for the site of Rome. In Livy's account, the young founders of the city are stirred by emotions both noble and competitive: "There also joined them shepherds, all of whom easily conceived the hope that Alba and Lavinium would be small cities in comparison with that city they were about to establish" (1. 6. 3). The pastoral origins of the city form a background for ambition and energy. Romulus does not remain long in his simple hut but soon occupies the curule chair, attended by lictors. In Livy, the city develops so rapidly that the scoffing Sabines who have refused to marry their daughters to the Romans are taken aback when they see its size. "The age of Romulus," says Cicero in the *De Re Publica*, "was a civilized age" (2. 10. 8).[20]

In the second and fifth books of his history Livy again refers to the shepherds who founded the city, observing in the first chapter of Book 2 that the early association of shepherds and fugitive plebeians was a community hardly capable of rational, independent government. In Book 5, the great speech of Camillus appeals to Roman patriotism by reminding the discontented citizens how quickly their fathers had left behind the shepherd life, founding a city with institutions and traditions:

> If in all the city no structure could be found better or larger than that hut of our founding father, would it not be preferable to live in huts in the manner of shepherds and country-folk surrounded by our sacred objects and our Penates, than to go publically into exile? Our forefathers, strangers and shepherds, when there was nothing in these regions save forests and marshes, built a new city in so short a time: should we, with our Capitolium, our citadel unharmed, the temples of the gods still standing, be ashamed to build up what has been burned?
> [5. 53. 8–9]

The moral that the Romans read into the lives of their shepherd ancestors has nothing to do with pristine innocence but rather is derived from the energy and industry by which these men transformed their slender holdings into the foundations of a state. In attempting to make inspirational history from legend, Republican writers ignore the picturesque or idyllic possibilities of their material in favor of a celebration of progress.

The pattern followed by these treatments of pastoral Rome is echoed in Roman discussions of agriculture, an occupation that

---

[20] The statement is in support of the authenticity of the story of Romulus' apotheosis, which did not take place in primitive times but after the establishment of historical and literary documentation and must therefore be considered credible.

Varro places in history as the successor to herding: a second and more sophisticated stage in man's development of the civilized arts (2. 1. 4–5). At Rome the beginnings of agriculture were sometimes attributed to Numa, the most virtuous and religious of the kings. It was he, says Cicero in the *De Re Publica* (2. 14. 26), who distributed the lands conquered by Romulus as farmlands, teaching the warlike citizens how to live without taking plunder by cultivating the arts of peace. Although the agricultural writings of the late Republic are not without their aesthetic dimension in their praise of the beauty and order of the countryside, again the chief emphasis is on industry and contributions to the state. The active and disciplined spirit that characterized the early years of Rome lived on in the cultivation of her fields.

The great age of Roman agriculture is closely linked with the great age of Roman civic virtue. Its setting is not the legendary pasture, but the real Italian countryside. In almost all Roman writers the mention of agriculture carries an aura of sanctity that preserves the flavor of earlier times. To the farmer goes the honor of maintaining the image and spirit of old Rome, for more than half its years an agrarian community. In the *De Re Rustica*, Varro gives a mythical coloring to the qualities of piety and industry traditionally attributed to farmers: "Not without reason are they used to calling the earth 'mother' and 'Ceres,' and to believing that those who cultivate her are engaged in a dutiful and useful life, that they alone are the survivors from the stock of King Saturn" (3. 1. 5). In Cicero's *Cato Maior*, a laudation by old Cato elevates the life of the farmer to the height of the philosophical *vita beata*:

It is my opinion that I do not know of any life that can be happier, not only because of its service, for the cultivation of the fields benefits the whole race of man, but also because of that pleasure I have mentioned and that overpowering abundance of all things that pertain to the nourishment of man and even to the worship of the gods. [16. 56]

Not only for its contribution to human welfare does the agricultural world demand honor, but also because of its long-standing association with political service. For many years the country has been the breeding ground for the discipline, endurance, and devotion to duty that are fundamental to the

Roman state. A classic expression of this sentiment occurs in a fragment of a speech in which the elder Cato holds up the example of his own youth: "I, even from my origin in a life of economy, hardship, and industry, kept my whole youth continent by cultivating the fields, breaking down Sabine rocks and flints, and seeding the land" (Malc. 32. 128). In the preface of the *De Agricultura*, Cato praises the civic virtues of ordinary citizens reared on the farm: "From the ranks of the farmers come the bravest men and most energetic soldiers; their profession is considered most dutiful, most stable, and least subject to envy, while the men busy about this calling are almost never prone to rebellious thoughts" (1. 4). His statement is echoed by Varro, who observes that men from the country have always been considered more industrious than city men (*Rust.* 2. 1). Even Cicero can take this line of argument when it suits his purpose, as in defending the country man, Roscius Amerinus, against members of the Sullan faction: "Among our ancestors those very noble and famous men who in every age ought to sit at the helm of the state nonetheless spent a portion of their time and labor in the cultivation of their fields" (51). Since Roscius is no Cincinnatus but only the undistinguished manager of his father's farm, we may suspect that Cicero has designed this reference to defame the members of the accusing party, creatures of Sulla who compared poorly with the great statesmen of the past.

Even in their aesthetic appreciations of the farm world, Republican writers invoke the ideals of discipline and practicality. Thus Cicero's Cato professes enjoyment of the order of the farm, speaking both of that which comes from nature and of that imposed by the hand of man.[21] He marvels at the generative force of the seeds and the orderly maturing of the plants (51–52). The earth, he observes, never rejects man's authority and always repays what is lent her with interest. He

[21] As Cicero well knows, there is no such aesthetic appreciation in Cato's own agricultural handbook. Obviously there is some deliberate humor in his attribution of such sensations as *delectatio* and *voluptas* to the old moralist whose own perspectives are consistently utilitarian. Thus he comments: (1. 3). "[Cato] will thus seem to argue with greater erudition than he usually does in the books he wrote himself. You may put this down to the Greek literature that he is known to have studied very zealously in his old age."

notices the farmer's skill in directing and controlling the vine (53), and delights in the orderly spectacle of fields and crops: "What more shall I say about the green of the fields or the orderly ranks of trees or the spectacle of vineyards and olive groves? I shall be brief. Nothing surpasses a well-tilled field; nothing is richer in fruition or more elegant in appearance" (57).

In Varro, discussion of the beauty of the farm world is turned to a moralizing purpose to emphasize the contrast between industry and luxury. To all right-thinking men, a well-managed farm is a more pleasing sight than an elegant country mansion (1. 2. 10). Beauty and economy are one. The orderly appearance that bears witness to the proper management of a farm and increases its monetary value is also the condition most pleasing to the eye: "Many of the practices that make a farm appear more honorable when cultivated not only render it more productive — as when the orchards and olives are set out in rows—but also make it more salable and add to the worth of the farm" (1. 4. 2)

Although both Varro and Cicero wrote in times when the sturdy citizen farmer was slowly disappearing and the great landowners seldom visited the *latifundia* they cultivated with slaves and hired labor,[22] both writers aim to convey a sense of immediacy in their praises of agriculture. Varro's *De Re Rustica* urges the purchase and personal management of farmland. One of its strategies is to attribute to owners of *latifundia* those same virtues celebrated in the honest country men of the past. The speakers in the dialogues are such men. All are renowned for their scientific command of farming, but none hesitates to labor with his own hands. Furthermore, these are men whose careers or family backgrounds embody the noble association of agriculture and public service. Among the speakers in Book 1 is Gaius Licinius Stolo, descended from that Licinius who had proposed

[22] W. E. Heitland, *Agricola: A Study of Agriculture and Rustic Life in the Greco-Roman World from Point of View of Labor* (Cambridge, 1921), pp. 151–212, argues that few wealthy landowners shared the high-minded attitudes of the speakers in these books, and few had personal experience in farm management. As to the balance of large and small landholdings, Kevin D. White, *Roman Farming* (Ithaca, N. Y., 1970), pp. 47–67, 384–412, tempers the conventional picture of the prevalence of *latifundia*, using evidence from recent excavations and aerial surveys to indicate the continuity of smaller farms in many regions of Italy.

the first law restricting landholdings to 500 *iugera*.[23] In the Book 2, Varro portrays himself, during an interlude of his successful naval campaign in Epirus, discussing husbandry with old farmers of that country. Clearly he places himself among the noble descendants of King Saturn and among those whom Cicero terms worthy to sit at the helm of the state.

In the days of the late Republic these praises of Roman agriculture betray a pastoral impulse, a desire for return to nature; yet this impulse is tempered and given its moral justification by an emphasis on order and industry in the country life. In speaking of the agricultural world, the Roman seeks regeneration through communication with an ancient source of virtue. Discipline and reason give their support to an experience of self-gratification that could never be so acceptable if labeled as escape. Participation in the agricultural life implies no withdrawal from the political world. The traditional ancestral rustic virtues create no divorce between city and country, but a strong bond. A life amidst rural simplicity involves confrontation with the realities of nature and is thus a commendable preparation for life in the great world.

Among Republican writers only Sallust refuses to join in the general tribute to agriculture. *Serviles officii* ("slavish duties") is the name he gives to the arts of farming and hunting. The reasons behind his scorn are worth consideration, for they add a second dimension to our understanding of practical Roman attitudes toward rustic simplicity and innocence. When confronted with the insidious perils of a corrupt society, pure innocence may cease to be a gleaming example and become a negative good. It is so in Cicero's defense of Roscius Amerinus. His client is a country person of the old tradition who has passed his mature years in the isolation of the farm. Although his honor is above question, he is also a helpless rustic, scarcely

---

[23] 1. 2. 9: Gaius Licinius Stolo, "who by the diligence of his agricultural activity confirmed the appropriateness of his family name, since you could not find a single useless sucker (*stolo*) on his farm [so effectively] did he dig around his trees." Also 2. 1. 11: "Our Scrofa, to whom this generation awards the palm in all matters pertaining to the country." Other examples are given in the discussion of villas in 3. 2. 5.

aware of the evils his enemies have gathered against him. His innocence is pure ignorance and no preparation for the dangers of experience.

Such a disposition is particularly clear in Sallust's introduction to the *Catilinae Coniuratio*. The work begins with a sketch of Roman history that embodies the traditional pattern of the disappearance of the golden age through human greed. The early days of the city were remarkable for their tranquillity. When the Trojans came to Italy, they found the *Aborigines,* an agricultural people, living freely without need for rulers and laws. Sallust remarks on the ease with which the wanderers and natives united, peoples of different ancestry, languages, and customs joining together in a harmonious state (6. 6. 8).

In the early years of the Republic, honor was the basis of Roman life, sustaining a healthy competition for distinction in service to the state. So long as Rome campaigned against external enemies, honor flourished, but the unaccustomed peace that followed the conquest of Carthage destroyed opportunity for glory. The particular virtues of Roman soldiers — their craving for distinction and their habituation to rigorous military circumstances — made them easy victims of leisure, wealth, and the desire for novelties. The process that began at Carthage was repeated under Sulla. Bound in loyalty to their commander, Romans followed his evil example, helpless before the temptations of an unindustrious life.

The story of Catiline is that of a man belonging wholly to the age of corruption. Catiline never knew innocence. His bold spirit was guided by an evil nature that exercised it only in pursuit of vice (5. 2). But the story of Rome's fall from virtue has significant bearing on a different aspect of this history. It is repeated in the story of the author's own life.

Sallust presents himself as a man whose simplicity and enthusiasm made him the victim of evil times. Full of noble intentions, he entered upon his political career and found himself in a world of recklessness, bribery, and greed:

Although my mind, inexperienced in evil practices, disdained these vices, all the same, in a world so vicious, my unprotected youth, broken

in upon, was held fast by ambition. Even though I withheld my consent
from the evil customs of the rest, no less did that same lust for distinction that vexed others with gossip and envy become a trouble
to me.   [3. 4][24]

Sallust's tone in these autobiographical reflections is bitter.
He resents both the corruption that thwarted his career and the
inexperience that left him open to wrong influences. But the
bitterness is not without pride and a certain self-righteousness,
an assertion of innate superiority to the world. Although he is
aware that most men who fail in politics may as well withdraw
themselves from public attention, his own choice is not escape.
Instead he seeks to capture the honor that had previously
eluded him by the writing of history. As compensation for the
loss of innocence, he resolves to make use of experience.

Sallust feels strongly a Roman horror of obscurity, of a life
passed without recognition. Although he accepts retirement, he
must continue, even vicariously, his involvement in Roman
affairs. The writing of history is the one political exercise now
open to his frustrated ambition:

Therefore, as soon as my mind was at rest from many troubles and
dangers, and I decided that the remainder of my life must be spent
far from the state, my plan was not to wear away good leisure in self-
indulgent laziness, nor again to carry on a life obsessed by farming
and hunting, tasks that belong to slaves. Instead I returned to a pursuit
I had begun once before, from which my unfortunate ambition had
distracted me, and I determined to write some portion of the deeds of
the Roman people, whatsoever seemed worthy of preservation. This
task was the more suitable to me because my mind was now released
from expectation or fear concerning the factions in the state.   [4. 1. 2]

In his scorn for the traditional country life of retirement,
Sallust is, as I have observed, unique among writers of his time.
Yet his remarks are in keeping with the circumstances of a
career that had placed the nobler symbolic value of agriculture
beyond reach. He could not pose as a Cincinnatus or a Cato,
looking upon the farm life as an interlude in public service or

[24] For discussion of this passage see G. M. Paul, "Sallust," in *Latin Historians*,
T. A. Dorey and D. R. Dudley, *Studies in Latin Literature and Its Influence* (London,
1966), p. 86. Paul doubts the accuracy of Sallust's portrayal of his own naïveté,
thus suggesting that his comments have some literary purpose.

as the final regimen of a well-ordered career. For him this life could only betoken genuine seclusion, a permanent separation from the Roman world.

The realistic disillusionment of Sallust is a useful counter to the idealism of his contemporaries. His monograph makes use of a concept of lost innocence to rationalize his errors and those of his times. Corruption in human society is not only hostile to innocence but has proven it a precarious defense against unforeseen dangers of experience.

Amidst these opinions of agriculture and the duties or virtues of the Roman citizen, we may begin to find a background for the *Eclogues.* Vergil's involvement with the world of nature, his delineation of rustic simplicity and its confrontation with the world of experience, are not apart from the interests of his time. These interests are directly related to the Roman's definition of his own and of his nation's identity, and of the character that both should present to the contemporary world. To Roman writers of the Republic, the images of nature, and of that world of agriculture where men and nature most frequently meet, have a clear symbolic value. In its original form this symbolism may seem very distant from what we conventionally call pastoral, and for this reason it is useful to consider.[25]

[25] I cannot agree with Rosenmeyer, pp. 20–27 and elsewhere, that pastoral must exclude all references to Hesiodic elements — i.e., to the practical aspects of human life in nature. Although the simple pastoral impulse may remain as unchanging as the human heart, pastoral poems tend to modify this impulse by absorbing aspects of the culture and ideology of their times.

CHAPTER 3

A Roman Design
for Nature

Students of the pastoral have developed a custom of speaking, sometimes too glibly, of "the pastoral world." The phrase encompasses both autonomy and coherence but blurs a necessary distinction between the two. When we think of autonomy—of the pastoral world as an independent place—we are accepting a convention by which a limited segment of nature is temporarily allowed to stand as a whole, and to be set, if need be, over and against its implied external context: the great world. In this respect, the pastoral world is a continuous fiction that one poet inherits from another.

Coherence cannot be inherited, but with each new venture into pastoral fiction it must be created anew. The concept of a pastoral world must, therefore, encompass that texturing of specific details and images that gives unity and character to a bucolic environment and, by a combination of imitation and originality, distinguishes one poet's creation from that of another. Thus we may think of a pastoral world as an interpretation of nature with all its components—the concrete particulars of a physical setting—and the intangible indications of passing time. It implies a poet's manner of relating characters to their environment, and the manner in which each poet has structured his individual landscape as an extrapolation from the larger world of nature.

Automatically we look for the ideal qualities of a pastoral world, but specific poems demand that this expectation be modified. Inevitably, the return from the pastoral world forces recognition of certain imperfections in its image of nature. In fact, the imaginary worlds of pastoral exist at a midpoint between the ideals of myth and the realities of physical nature; yet the relative distance from each extreme is not the same in every

70

poem. In varying degrees, pastoral nature contains the semblance of those forces that govern the real world. At times it
offers no more than a secure and static background for human
action, while at others it is dynamic and exercises an influence
upon man. The stronger the force or influence of nature, and
the more pre-eminent its role in the dramatization of pastoral
experience, the greater we may find the complexity, or cognitive
content, of pastoral. Thus the relationship of man to his environment is a major element in the development of pastoral
themes.

Questions of a relative degree of idealism and realism have
always entered into comparisons of Vergil and Theocritus. The
older canon of pastoral simplicity used to designate the world of
Theocritus as a real one, vivid and specific, while that of Vergil,
having less apparent unity, was either artificial, or fantastic, or
Utopian—that is to say, wholly unreal. This tidy distinction does
justice to neither poet, assigning to Theocritus the role of
primitive beginner and to Vergil that of idealizer or refiner:
both essentially simplistic roles. Two recent books have altered
our thinking on Theocritus. Despite their differences on many
issues, Gilbert Lawall and Thomas Rosenmeyer are in agreement on the characteristics of Theocritean nature, whose
precise, economical descriptions they see as an idealization, a
refinement of the natural world. In making nature a background for human freedom, Theocritus ignores traditional
Greek suspicion of the country life as rigorous or debased but
emphasizes its narrow perspectives and distance from the complexities of civilization. Although the great world is not blotted
out of existence in the *Idylls,* the reader is not invited to compare
it with the country.[1]

Such is not, as I have demonstrated, a Roman habit of think-

---

[1] An example of the older view is Bruno Snell, *The Discovery of the Mind: The
Greek Origins of European Thought,* trans. Thomas Rosenmeyer, (New York:
Harper Torchbooks, 1960), pp. 282–287. Thomas Rosenmeyer, *The Green
Cabinet: Theocritus and the European Pastoral Lyric* (Berkeley, 1969), pp. 29–30,
urges that Theocritus' work be read "as if it were that of a fellow writer, a com-
petitor, of the later pastoralists, rather than the source that it is." Gilbert Lawall's
book is entitled *Theocritus' Coan Pastorals: A Poetry Book* (Cambridge, Mass.,
1965). Rosenmeyer, pp. 20–24, sees the pastoral poet's exclusion of the rigors
of country life as a rejection of Hesiodic *ponos* in favor of Epicurean *hasychia.*

ing about city and country. To the Roman these worlds are vitally interrelated; the country becomes narrow only when the link of communication is broken, and agrarian virtue, left in solitude, degenerates into naïve rusticity.

In the *Eclogues,* Vergil has exploited this pattern of thought, creating an interdependence of city and country, of nature and civilization, entirely new to the pastoral. In its first appearance this interdependence is politically oriented and reveals a paradox: while pastoral freedom cannot exist in isolation from the great world, still the great world threatens the well-being of the country. But, as the poems progress, this literal and ominous beginning gives way to more abstract and symbolic considerations, with the world of nature encompassing a range of human activities. Thus the Roman moral justification of the pastoral impulse—the view of the country as the source of civic virtue —is extended to make the pastoral life into a model for the exploration of human conduct. For the sake of this new program, a new texturing of the pastoral world is necessary. The microcosm must incorporate elements of reality. Symbolic distinctions require distinctions among the images of nature.

Thus in its entirety the Vergilian landscape is less easy to describe than that of Theocritus, for superficially it is not all of one piece, but, rather, is composed of contrasting locations and topographies. Although order is its ideal, it is not always orderly. Its coherence does not appear as the artful coherence of simplicity and refinement, but rather as a unity amidst contrasts that approaches the coherence of real nature. The landscapes of the *Eclogues,* imaginary though they may be, give a far stronger approximation of nature's realities than those of Theocritus. Their order and disorder are analogous to the conditions of the natural world. The point is not that the Roman poet is more observant or more appreciative of his physical environment than the Greek, but rather that he has given greater attention to the interaction of human and natural forces, and that he is more willing to assign symbolic complexity to nature. In discussing Vergil's image of nature, I shall take up three topics: the sense of time that governs his world; the variety that distinguishes the individual landscapes of each poem; and the poet's techniques of organizing the landscapes to provide for his reader a vantage point, a position from which to interpret man's relationship to his world.

Both Vergil and Theocritus have incorporated a temporal dimension within their ideals of order. The contrast between them may be introduced by a comparison of two passages showing well-defined relationships between man and nature: the descriptions of two carved bowls offered as prizes for the singers of *Idyll* 1 and *Eclogue* 3. These descriptions are based on the pictorial convention of Homer's Shield of Achilles. They are symbolic microcosms reflecting their larger poetic context. Such objects are always the creation of artists, never of the persons to whom they belong.[2] Their images differ from those of the poems where they appear, but are thematically related.

The bowl in the first *Idyll* has a decoration of three scenes that Lawall terms representations of childhood, youth, and age.[3]

And I will give thee a deep cup, washed over with sweet wax, two-handled and newly fashioned still fragrant from the knife. Along the lips above trails ivy, ivy dotted with its golden clusters, and along it winds the tendril glorying in its golden fruit. And within is wrought a woman, such a thing as the gods might fashion, bedecked with cloak and circlet. And by her two men with long fair locks contend from either side in alternate speech. Yet these things touch not her heart, but now she looks on one and smiles, and now to the other she shifts her thought, while they, long hollow-eyed from love, labor to no pur-

[2] In the *Idyll*, the maker is unknown, but the goatherd has purchased the cup from the ferryman of Caladria for a goat and a cheese (1. 57–58). In *Ecl.* 3. 37, the maker is *divinus Alcimedon*. Lawall comments: "The cup is an alien intrusion into their simple world. It reaches outside the chaste rustic world to embrace conditions of men which have no place in the lives of Thyrsis and the goatherd" (p. 27). C. P. Segal comments: "Vergil treats the cups with a seriousness which derives from the fact that they are not just rustic gifts, just as his pastorals are not just rustic songs or realistic genre scenes. . . . He is self-consciously aware that his cups are an *opus*, a work of art" ("Vergil's *caelatum opus:* An Interpretation of the Third *Eclogue*," *AJPhil.* 88 [1967]:289).

[3] Segal, p. 283, takes Theocritus' bowl as a panoramic view of the poet's pastoral world. But Lawall, pp. 27–31, interprets their symbolism differently, seeing the figures as representations of the commonplace world of everyday experience. Three aspects of this world are represented: the folly of wasted passion, the innocence of childhood, and practical labors with rewards. Thus the figures outline a pattern for the life of ordinary man. The translations of Theocritus, here and elsewhere are taken from A. S. F. Gow, *Theocritus*, edited with a translation and a commentary (Cambridge, 1952).

pose. By these is carved an old fisherman, and a rugged rock, whereon the old man eagerly gathers up a great net for a cast as one that labors mightily. You would say that he was fishing with all the strength of his limbs, so do the sinews stand out all about his neck, grey-haired though he is; yet his strength is as a youth's. And a little way from the sea-worn old man there is a vineyard with a fair load of reddening clusters, guarded by a little boy who sits upon its dry-stone wall. About him hang two foxes, and one goes to and fro among the vine-rows plundering the ripe grapes, while the other brings all her wit to bear upon his wallet, and vows that she will not let the boy be until [she has raided his breakfast bread]. But the boy is plaiting a pretty cricket-cage of bonded rush and asphodel, and he has more joy in his plaiting than care for wallet or for vines.   [1. 27–56]

The decorated bowl resembles a Theocritean pastoral, a pictorial arrangement of human attitudes against a natural background, composed with careful art. We recognize a lifelike quality in the figures, but we are even more aware of the self-conscious perfection of their detail. Each scene comprises an action both limited in scope and continuous in time. The poet describes the carved figures as if they were living persons, moving and thinking within the small compass of the design. Their attitudes and states of mind are convincing; yet the actions have neither beginning nor end. Although they maintain the semblance of motion, these figures are truly static.

Under such conditions work and play are scarcely distinguishable. Even the straining old fisherman with the vigor of eternal youth can indulge in his labor as a sport. The lady who smiles on both lovers and the boy who neglects both food and duty are embodiments of an unawareness of reality and time. The position of the lady is secure in the endless rivalry of her lovers, and the boy need never turn from his art to satisfy hunger or account for the stolen grapes. They are inhabitants of a world where no decisions are made, no questions asked; where the beginnings and ends and causes of action count for less than its continuity. Such relaxation and security cannot even pretend to exist amid real nature, but are nourished only by a nature that is the creation of art. The art of the Theocritean pastoral supports an illusion of emotional freedom, by raising human action above the ravages of temporal process. Thus it creates a world free from the influence of time.

In the third *Eclogue,* Vergil has followed Theocritus so far as to make his singers offer decorated cups as their prizes. The second of these cups, which I will discuss in another place, shows Orpheus leading the forests after him by his music, the creation of an ideal and dynamic order in nature through art. The first, like that of the *Idyll,* embodies a relationship between time and the order of human life, but its manner of suggesting this relationship is entirely new. Instead of a group of scenes, the decoration consists of two portrait figures. The first is Conon, the mathematician; the second a scientist whose name the herdsman has forgotten:

> in medio duo signa, Conon et — quis fuit alter,
> descripsit radio totum qui gentibus orbem,
> tempora quae messor, quae curvus arator haberet?
>
> [3.40–42]

(In the center are two figures, Conon and — who was he, the other who described to men the whole circle of the heavens measured with his rod, and showed the seasons belonging to the harvester and those for the stooping plowman?)

Unlike the finely carved bowl in the *Idyll,* this one is scarcely distinguished for picturesque value. It has no vivid images of man in action and no representations of the natural world. The meaning is not in the pictures, but in what they imply. It is too far-reaching to be conveyed in a single scene. In place of limited, self-contained actions in their settings, are figures symbolizing a knowledge of nature that reaches to all the peoples of the world. Instead of timelessness and continuity, we are reminded of time as a measure of natural order, determining the proper beginnings and ends of human labor.

The unknown scientist is one whose thinking encompasses the relationship of parts to a whole.[4] His description of the course of the year with its proper times for planting and for harvest, gives a practical knowledge necessary to human life. Measurement is important. Man needs rules and systems of

[4] The second, unnamed figure has often been taken for Aratus. As Segal observes: "The figures make large suggestions of benefactions to all mankind, and the rhythms of the natural world which astronomy helps indicate. . . . The contrast of the cups is that between creative activity for purely utilitarian purposes and the 'pure' creativity of poetry" (pp. 288–289).

measure to help him respond to nature's demands and anticipate the dictates of time. The man who explains the heavens is
an intermediary between nature and humanity. The absence
of his name is appropriate, for such a person has his real identity
as a part of the great working order of nature.

While Theocritus' scenes are careful descriptions of a static
nature, Vergil's symbolic figures imply a dynamic natural order.
The difference is a result of three new elements: Vergil's emphasis on time, his use of agricultural images as an ideal of
nature, and his awareness of the cosmos as a whole.

A sense of changelessness is essential to Theocritus' hedonistic naturalism. He procures this effect not only by excluding
influences exterior to the pastoral world, but also by restricting
the influence of time and natural alteration within its confines.
Neither morning nor evening enters the poems. The shepherds
sing at endless high noon, the moment of leisure. Their day's
activities have no beginning or end.

Five *Eclogues* close with the coming of evening. The hour
when daylight and song cease together has seemed to many
critics a time of ideal harmony between nature and man.[5] But
in the first *Eclogue*, night is a reminder of loneliness and exile,
while in three other poems that end in this manner the approach
of evening interrupts unfinished song. In the second, the close
of day finds Corydon, the unhappy lover, still restless and
troubled by passion, out of harmony with the natural world. At
the end of *Eclogue* 6, we hear that the gods themselves want the
song of Silenus to continue, but the relentless evening star
moves up the sky, and the cattle turn homeward from pasture;
nature has overcome divine art. Finally, in the ninth poem, a
threat of rain and the nearness of the evening keep the travelers
from resting on their unwelcome journey to the city and cut off
their exchange of remembered fragments of song. Thus night
interrupts human action. Nature's firm order contrasts with the
emotional, less ordered life of men who are unable to resolve
their passions or alter their fortunes to enjoy the tranquillity

---

[5] "With only slight exaggeration, we might say that he [Vergil] discovered the
evening" (Erwin Panofsky, *Meaning in the Visual Arts* [New York: Anchor Books,
1955], p. 300).

of the pastoral world. The passage of diurnal time is a reminder of human weakness and instability.

Although Theocritus excludes changes in time of day, he does not exclude the names of the seasons. Still, when he mentions these, it is almost to deny their effects on the pastoral world. In the Cyclop's song of *Idyll* 11, both summer and winter have their offerings of flowers: the one the red poppy and the other the snowdrop. The wealth of the Cyclops does not vary with the seasons: "Cheese I lack not in the summer, nor in the autumn, nor in the depth of winter" (11. 36–37).

Spring is the season most often mentioned; its sweetness is like the sweetness of love. At times we may suspect that Theocritus' seasons do not literally refer to stages in the cycle of nature but are simply metaphorical expressions of states of mind. Thus, in the eighth poem, the lover praises his beloved as the bearer of a prosperous spring: "There does the sheep, there do the goats bear twins, and there do the bees fill their hives with honey where fair Milon steps" (8. 44–47). The fullest and most elegant of such metaphorical descriptions is that of the harvest festival in *Idyll* 7, which Gilbert Lawall interprets as an allegory of poetic creation, taking its wine and water as symbols of the poet's sources of inspiration and its abundant fruits as a harvest of verse.[6] This harvest does not fade away into winter, but merges into the timeless realm of myth:

And the four-year seal was loosened from the wine jars. Nymphs of Castalia that haunt the steep of Parnassus, was it such a bowl as this that old Chiron served to Herakles in Pholus' rocky cave? Was it such nectar that set the shepherd by the Anapus dancing among his sheep-folds, even the mighty Polyphemus that pelted ships with mountains? Such nectar as ye nymphs mingled for us to drink that day by the altar of Demeter of the Threshing floor?   [7. 147–155]

The wine carries man into a world of poetic legend, linking him with divine figures existing beyond time and change. Such harvests and vintages are recurrent, uniting the worlds of poetry and myth. The abundance of nature signifies a constant fertility of the creative mind that is timeless and reassuringly stable. The

---

[6] Lawall, pp. 102–108.

poetic beauty and symbolic resources of seasonal description are what is most valuable to Theocritus.

In the *Eclogues*, the seasons also suggest nature's permanence, but it is a permanence of a different kind. The seasons are the measure of the orderly progress of the year. In the fifth poem, the shepherds promise their patron, Daphnis, a series of seasonal festivals: before the hearth in winter, in the autumn in the shade with new wine, in spring when vows are paid to the nymphs, and in summer at the lustration of the fields (5. 65–75). This cycle of festivals embodies the order of the changing year. With its repetition, Daphnis assumes a permanent role in the agricultural life, whose stability man's devotion binds him to preserving:

> ut Baccho Cererique, tibi sic vota quotannis
> agricolae facient: damnabis tu quoque votis.   [5. 79–80]

> (Just as to Bacchus and to Ceres, the farmers will make vows to you each year; by giving fulfillment, you will hold them to their vows.)

A similar bond between the divine protector and the order of the agricultural life is suggested by the twelve monthly sacrifices that Tityrus, of the first *Eclogue*, vows to the benevolent Roman deity who has sent him home to live in freedom on his farm. In the fourth poem, a progress not unlike that of the seasons marks the growth of a new benefactor of mankind. The infancy of the divine child brings forth a springlike profusion of flowers, his adolescence witnesses flourishing summer crops, and his maturity is sponsor to the perpetual harvest of the golden age.

Several poems have definite seasonal settings. In the third, it is spring; likewise in the seventh, where the farmer has set out his young trees and the baby lambs in his farmyard are already of an age to be weaned. In the second poem, the harvesting, plowing, and pruning indicate late summer, the season of the Dog Star.[7] The hopeless love of Corydon must burn itself out like the seasonal heat; but Corydon, whose fantasies are images of springtime, feels helpless to dispel his fiery passion.

---

[7] Varro *Rust.* 1. 32. 1: "In the fourth period between the solstice and the dog star most [farmers] make harvest. Plowing is to be completed."

In *Eclogue* 1, it is autumn. Tityrus had been in Rome during late-summer harvest when his apples hung ungathered on the trees. Now he can hear the song of the leaf-cutter (*frondator*), cutting foliage to store for winter fodder. He speaks of his stored-up apples, chestnuts, and cheese. Meliboeus has been driven from his farm after the fall sowing and anticipates the spring harvest when the soldier will reap the grain he planted.[8] The setting is consistent with the themes of the poem: Tityrus' harvest with his long-awaited freedom, and the coming winter with the bleak future of Meliboeus, whose country summers are over. In Vergil, the progress of the changing seasons is associated with the mutability of human life.

In contrast to the cycles of nature that are identical from year to year, is the time that measures human life, drawing it toward age. There are old men in Theocritus, but none like Tityrus whom *libertas* has favored only after many years of servitude. Moeris, of the ninth poem, is an old man looking backward who has lost his power of singing and his memory for songs. In the first, the dispossessed Meliboeus muses upon the many years of his coming exile, hoping to return to his home after much time has passed. The poet in the fourth *Eclogue* prays for a long life to witness and celebrate the deeds of the divine ruler. Unlike the seasons of sowing and harvest, whose consistent alterations follow a predictable pattern, the lives of men suffer permanent change. The passage of time brings thoughts of lost opportunity and vanished potential. Awareness of time is disturbing as man acknowledges that nature is always superior in vitality and constancy to himself.

The *Eclogues* incorporate the effects of time, not only within the pastoral, but also within the historical world. History accelerates the process of change in human life, imposing its sudden alterations upon the more gradual pattern of nature. Under the influence of its changes, pastoral characters are forced to understand that their countryside belongs within the

---

[8] *Rust.* 1. 34. 1: "In the sixth period after the autumnal equinox the writers say that [the farmer] should sow up until the ninety-first day. . . . He should harvest the grapes and make the vintage between the autumnal equinox and the setting of the Pleiades and then begin to prune the vines, set out new vine slips and plant fruit trees."

framework of the great world. The pressure of historical change weighs heavily upon the first and ninth poems with their alternating visions of a prosperous and a declining world. Here individual persons interpret history in accordance with its effects on their own lives; its order and chaos correspond to the expectations and disappointments of personal experience. In the fourth and sixth poems, the scope of history is broadened, and the experience of society supersedes that of the individual. The Parcae of the fourth *Eclogue* echo the hopes of mankind as they promise stability and continuity for a better Rome in accordance with the design of fate. The Silenus song combines science and mythology, looking backward to the origins of a world man already knows. Accounts of man's troubled confrontations with nature extend the uncertainties of the present world far back into the past. Thus Vergil's poetry of time draws the pastoral into the Roman world, and the Roman, in turn, into a context of universal history. Both individual lives and human society are unstable, although they pursue their courses amid an orderly nature.

An equivalent sense of the limited or expansive perspectives that foster security or uncertainty, is inherent in the poet's creation of pastoral landscapes. In comparing Vergil and Theocritus, we may again see that the *Idylls* present a context of reassuring stability, while the *Eclogues* contrast order and disorder.

The complexity of Theocritus' poems derives from expressions and conflicts of human emotion, especially those of love.[9] Although nature offers freedom to emotion, it has little influence over human actions. Rosenmeyer has rightly observed that the poems do not attempt to establish a complex intellectual relationship between nature and man: "The Greek pastoral does not attempt to solemnize man's power over nature, or his

---

[9] "These country people are not distracted by business, extensive responsibilities, intellectual ideas or artificial moralities. They are bound in no way by convention; their own intense emotions are their only preoccupation, their only justification for existing. Pastoral leisure and freedom permit undistracted concentration on the emotional core of man's being. Viewed in this setting men are close to the beasts" (Lawall, pp. 6–7).

response to nature's guidance, nor does it, overtly, assert any kind of bond between man and nature."[10]

Accordingly, Theocritean herdsmen look at nature with easy familiarity. The landscapes take shape incidentally, as the characters speak casually of the trees, grass, and streams that surround them, assessing their promise of comfort and their appropriateness as backgrounds for song. Man is always in the foreground; his activity is more intense than that of nature, and he is too absorbed in his own emotions and pastimes to appreciate nature solely for itself. To the reader, the Theocritean landscape appears as a series of elegant, artfully stylized designs; yet he can also understand that this art is a striving for artlessness, an invitation to take nature for granted as the perpetual, unchanging home of man.

In this carefree image of nature Rosenmeyer sees the outlines of the *locus amoenus*, the idealized scene that is never a microcosm of reality, but only an aesthetic background:

The *locus amoenus* is a highly selective arrangement of stage properties. The character of the properties is decided, not by the ideals or the needs of man, but by the pastoral demand for freedom and pleasure. The stage is set in such a way that the herdsmen may pursue their objectives, their affections and their dreams, as easily as possible, against the smallest number of obstacles. The ease of the rural scene, with its tree, its greensward and its brook is a dramatic convenience, not a philosophical necessity. It is because the herdsman has no obligations whatever toward the trees or the brook, except for a laisser-faire attitude of respect and enjoyment, that he is placed among them. Neither the city, nor the fields and the pastures which call for work and hardship, would do.[11]

Within these limitations, Theocritean stage settings are used to highlight poetic themes or dramatic interchanges between characters. The Nymphs' spring in *Idyll* 1 is a fitting place for

[10] P. 186; discussion on pp. 186–196.

[11] Pp. 186–187. Rosenmeyer's discussion of pastoral landscape follows in the tradition of Ernst Curtius, *European Literature and the Latin Middle Ages*, trans. Willard Trask (New York, 1953), pp. 185–195, who sees in these descriptions the basis for the elaborate, rhetorical landscape *topoi* of the Middle Ages and Renaissance. In his opinion there is little essential difference between the landscapes of various *Idylls* and *Eclogues*.

Thyrsis' song of Daphnis, the beloved of a nymph, who died by
water (1. 140–141). In *Idyll* 5 the cocky young Lacon sits by the
wild olive (5. 31–32) whose fruitfulness without cultivation
reflects his self-confidence and refusal to submit either to the
erotic or to the artistic domination of his elder rival Comatas,
while Comatas boasts of the superiority of his station by an oak
tree surrounded by bees (5. 45–46, 59) in which we may understand an allusion to the "honey" of skillful song. The hill that
the herdsmen climb in *Idyll* 4 appears to John Van Sickle as a
symbol for pastoral poetry, and the harvest world of *Idyll* 7, the
one landscape away from the pasture, is, as we have already
seen, rich in symbols for poetic inspiration. Lawall speaks of
subtle differences in the tone of several descriptions: a Utopian
background for the Daphnis song; an air of comic rusticity in
the landscape of the snub-nosed goatherd's wooing song in
Idyll 3.[12] These subtleties are a part of Theocritus' poetic stylization and reflect the idiosyncrasies of his characters, but they do
not increase the visual complexity of his landscapes or disturb
their consistency and uniformity. Although each poem contributes new images, all are the features of one endless pasture.
The entire, unchanging landscape is a *locus amoenus*.

In Rosenmeyer's opinion, the Vergilian grove is also a *locus
amoenus*, a pleasant, inconsequential background for pastoral
song,[13] but many elements in Vergil's descriptions belie this
point of view. It is true that several *Eclogues* offer glimpses of a
timeless, dreamlike pastoral scene. The vision of Corydon in
Eclogue 2 is among these, and another is evoked by Gallus in
10: a paradise of cool springs, soft meadows, and groves where a
man might waste away his life in happy ease. But unlike the
pleasant descriptions in Theocritus, these do not pretend to

[12] Lawall, p. 63, sees erotic connotations here, associating the olive with
pederasty and the oak with heterosexuality, while Rosenmeyer, p. 188, finds
a note of pastoral failure in the singers' inability to accept each other's versions
of the pleasaunce. On the landscape of *Idyll* 3, the two are essentially in agreement (Lawall, pp. 35–36, Rosenmeyer, pp. 173, 202), but Rosenmeyer differs
greatly in seeing in that of *Idyll* 7 a near surfeit of natural fertility (p. 191).
Van Sickle's discussion of symbolic landscape is in "The Fourth Pastoral Poems
of Virgil and Theocritus," *Atti e Memorie dell'Arcadia*, series 3a, 5(1969):10–20.

[13] "Neither author seeks to distinguish between the natural and the contrived, except as utopia excludes the hard work that the Hesiodic landscape
carries with it" (p. 196).

recreate the immediate surroundings of the speakers. Corydon sings his love song on the farm, Gallus amidst the Arcadian wilderness. The contrast between each speaker's actual environment and the paradisical *locus amoenus* shows that the latter is a purely imaginary creation, a subjective design for nature. The presence of a precise and varied landscape topography has forced the ideal simplicity of the *locus amoenus* into a tenuous position where it can no longer represent the actual face of the world. Vergil asks his reader to follow him through the complexities of a more intricate visual pattern that is based upon contrasts rather than uniformity.[14]

The variety of Vergil's landscapes equals the variety of nature. The *Eclogues* have not one landscape, nor even ten, but countless glimpses of the natural world. The most ordered is that of Tityrus' farm in *Eclogue* 1, the wildest that of Mt. Maenalus in Arcadia where shepherds complain to Pan and Gallus laments his lost love. Between these extremes is a range of scenes: pastures, caverns, roads, vineyards, grainfields, groves. Although these scenes are obviously not intended for representations of real geographical places, they are vividly imagined landscapes, frequently quite precise in their topographical detail. Such diversity is essential to Vergil's new interpretation of the pastoral, but it is also in keeping with other Roman methods of visualizing and describing nature. The orderly farm scene we have already encountered in the agricultural writers. Analogies for other scenes are to be found in the visual arts. It is only natural that the poet should form his images in keeping with contemporary conventions of representing nature; that he should not only create his own symbolic dispositions but should also exploit whatever symbolism might already be inherent in these conventions.

An interest in the variety of natural scenery equivalent to that revealed by the *Eclogues* is apparent in the landscape paint-

---

[14] The explicit distinction between the actual and the imaginary within a fictional structure might be seen in relationship to those changes in thought process—the increased amount of visualization—that are part of the change from an aural-oral to a written culture that Walter J. Ong, S.J., describes in *The Presence of the Word: Some Prolegomena for Cultural and Religious History* (New York: Clarion Books, 1970), pp. 17–35.

ing of the late Roman Republic. The development of this new phenomenon, its place in the history of wall decoration, and its orientation toward realism are recorded by Vitruvius in the seventh book of his treatise *De Architectura*. After a glance at the early imitation masonry or "incrustation" style — a Hellenistic method that we traditionally call the Pompeian first style — he describes the painters' progress toward the illusionistic representation of the forms of buildings, columns and overhanging pediments that mark the beginnings of the second style and then to its scenic compositions. His catalogue of subjects includes tragic, comic and satiric stage settings; scenes with landscape backgrounds depicting the wanderings of Ulysses, and especially diverse representations of objects in nature:

Ambulationibus vero propter spatia longitudinis varietatibus topiorum ornarent ab certis locorum proprietatibus imagines exprimentes; pinguntur enim portus, promontoria, litora, flumina, fontes, euripi, fana, luci, montes, pecora, pastores.

Their corridors, indeed, on account of their long expanses of space they decorated with varied representations of places, images that imitated the particular characteristics appropriate to the places. They painted harbors, headlands, coastlines, rivers, springs, canals, shrines, groves, mountains, flocks and shepherds.[15]   [7. 5. 2]

Like the ten *Eclogues* this catalogue includes both wild and civilized aspects of nature. Paintings of this kind, Vitruvius maintains, take their models from the actual world ("quae sunt . . . ab rerum natura procreata" [7. 5. 2]; "haec quae ex veris rebus exempla sumebant" [7. 5. 3]). What the Roman audience demanded from its landscape painters would seem to have been eclectic variety within a convention of generically accurate topographical representation.

Although Vitruvius mentions pastoral elements as only two of the many topics for landscape, a large number of the surviving paintings are pastoral. Even within this specialized category,

---

[15] My interpretation of this passage is based on that by Peter H. von Blanckenhagen and Christine Alexander, *The Paintings from Boscotrecase*, MDAI(R) Supplement 6 (Heidelberg, 1962), 54–55. The text of Vitruvius is F. Krohn, ed., *De Architectura Libri Decem* (Leipzig, 1912).

there is great variety in the tone and organization of the pictures.

At times, the animals appear merely as random, decorative forms that add interest to a scene. In the painting of a sacred grove from the House of Livia on the Palatine (Figure 1), a few sheep wander near a stream which flows by a shrine.[16] No shepherd is present, although herdsmen's implements have been placed as offerings at the base of the shrine. In a monochrome panel from Herculaneum (Figure 2), straying animals are used in place of more extensive rustic details to indicate a country setting.[17]

In other instances, the flocks are under the care of their shepherds. A yellow monochrome panel in the House of Obellius Firmus at Pompeii (Figure 3) seems to depict the shepherd on his farm.[18] Surrounded by his grazing flock he stands at ease on a hillside shaded by a spreading tree whose vertical line is balanced at the right of the picture by that of a structure in three tiers, too badly faded to identify, but probably a shrine. On the crest of the hill, close to the top of the picture, a group of buildings indicates the farmstead. Thus the shepherd is enclosed within the boundaries of his world. We think of the pattern of his life with its morning walk to pasture, noonday rest and evening return. Although he is a solitary figure in his posture of duty, he belongs to the life of the farm. In a more severe style, the farm landscape is also suggested in one of a series of panel sketches from the Colombarium of the Villa Pamphili.[19] It is, in fact, the only extant painting that shows laborers working in the fields with plow and hoe (Figure 4). A second panel in this series depicts rough country huts, perhaps of the kind used as field shelters for shepherds.

More highly developed rural settings appear in two groups of

[16] Guilio Emmanuele Rizzo, *Monumenti della pittura antica scoperti in Italia*, section 3, vol. 3: *Le pitture della Casa di Livia* (Rome, 1936), pp. 52–59.

[17] Naples Nat. Mus. 8593. Another such panel is 9413. See von Blanckenhagen, p. 28.

[18] V. Spinazzola, *Pompei alla luce degli scavi nuovi di via dell'abbondanza* 3 vols. (Rome, 1953), II, 360–361 and III, Plate 81, and von Blanckenhagen, p. 24.

[19] Goffredo Bendinelli, *Monumenti della pittura antica scoperti in Italia*, section 3, vol. 5: *Le pitture del Colombario di Villa Pamphili* (Rome, 1941), Plates 6 & 8.

1. Landscape depicting a sacred grove. Fresco in the Hall of Landscape Paintings in the House of Livia on the Palatine in Rome. Photograph from G. E. Rizzo, *Monumenti della pittura antica scoperti in Italia*, sec. 3, vol. 3: *Le pitture della Casa di Livia* (Rome, 1936), fig. 42.

2. Blue monochrome panel depicting rural buildings. Fresco from Herculaneum, now in the National Archeological Museum in Naples. Photograph by courtesy of the German Archeological Institute, neg. 61.1270.

3. Yellow monochrome landscape representing a herdsman with his flock on a hillside. Fre
no longer visible, in the House of Obellius Firmus at Pompeii. Photograph by courtesy o
German Archeological Institute, neg. 56.1299.

4. Landscape with figures of two country men at work. Fresco from Wall C, the Colomba
of the Villa Pamphili, now in the National Museum of the Baths of Diocletian in Rome. Pl
graph from *Monumenti della pittura antica scoperti in Italia*, sec. 3, vol. 5: Goffredo Bendi
Le pitture del Colombario di Villa Pamphili (Rome, 1941), plate 6, fig. 1.

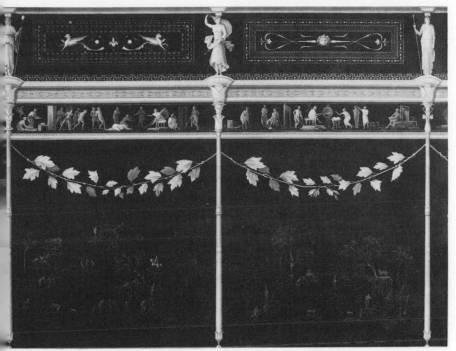

Pastel sketches of landscapes on a black background. Fresco from the Villa Farnesina, now ⟨th⟩e National Museum of the Baths of Diocletian in Rome. Drawing in Auguste Mau, *Monu-⟨ment⟩i Inediti Pubblicati dall'Instituto di Corrispondenza Archeologica* 11(1882), plate 44.

paintings found in the Villa Farnesina in Rome.[20] In a series of delicate pastel sketches on a black ground (Figure 5), animals and their keepers wander at random amid scattered houses and shrines. The second landscape, a frieze in blue, green and white, gives a more organized and formal character to the herdsman's life (Figure 6). A shrine with a gracefully curved schola dominates the foreground, and cowherds, shepherds and goatherds appear to have driven their flocks together while they sacrifice and rest beneath the trees. The bucolic life appears pious and tranquil. A similar tone of rural piety characterizes the herdsmen in an elegant panel from the Villa Albani collection (Figure

[20] Auguste Mau, in *Ann. Ist.* 11(1882):12(1884):307ff.; 12(1885):302ff.

6. Sacral-idyllic landscape in blue and green on a white background. Fresco from the W Ambulatorium G of the Villa Farnesina, now in the National Museum of the Baths of Diocle in Rome. Drawing in Auguste Mau, *Monumenti Inediti Pubblicati dall'Instituto di Corrisponde Archeologica* 12(1884), plate 5.

7).[21] Here, on an islet, beneath a tree garlanded with fillets, men are resting and sacrificing. A herd, returning homeward from pasture, crosses an arched bridge near a shrine and moves toward a harbor and a hillside town. Thus the herds-man's activities are no longer enclosed within the countryside. The pasture has become the threshold of the town. Finally, the most complex and intriguing of all such juxtapositions of pastoral and civilized elements in landscape appears in a series of three panels from the red room of the Villa of Agrippa Postumus at Boscotrecase (Figures 8–10). In each of these, a quiet rural foreground of herdsmen and wayfarers resting and worshiping is placed against an obliquely seen background of

[21] M. I. Rostovtzeff, "Die hellenistich-römische Architektur Landschaft," *MDAI(R)* 26(1911):24 and fig. 5. See discussion in von Blanckenhagen, p. 37.

Sacral-idyllic landscape with herdsmen, shrines, and a harbor. Fresco from the Villa Su-ana dei Quintilli, now in the collection of the Villa Albani. Photograph, Alinari 27630A.

porticoes and elegant buildings. Here especially the painter has captured the refined, idyllic spirit of the *locus amoenus*.

When pastoral figures appear in mythological landscape paintings they are often transported into wilder environments in keeping with the requirements of the stories represented. The sheep of Polyphemus cling to their seacoast crags, while the giant pipes to Galatea and the flock of Paris browses in the forests of rocky Mt. Ida (Figure 11).[22]

Each of these scenes creates a different impression of the pastoral life: some rigorous and austere, others tranquil and leisurely. In the mythological paintings, the pastoral no longer appears for its own sake but is absorbed into the symbolism of the fictional representation. In all the paintings, the presence of architectural monuments (shrines, houses, temples) estab-lishes a link between bucolic leisure and the civilized world.

[22] For general discussion see Christopher Dawson, "Romano-Campanian Mythological Landscape Painting." *YClS* 9(1944): repr. *L'Erma di Bretschneider* (Rome, 1965).

8. Sacral-idyllic panel. Fresco from the north wall of the Red Room of the Villa of Agrippa Postumus at Boscotrecase, now in the National Archeological Museum in Naples. Photograph by courtesy of the German Archeological Institute, neg. 59.1973.

9. Sacral-idyllic panel. Fresco from the east wall of the Red Room of the Villa of Agrippa Postumus at Boscotrecase, now in the National Archeological Museum in Naples. Photograph by courtesy of the German Archeological Institute, neg. 59.1989.

10. Sacral-idyllic panel. Fresco from the west wall of the Red Room of the Villa of Agrippa Postumus at Boscotrecase, now in the National Archeological Museum in Naples. Photograph by courtesy of the German Archeological Institute, neg. 59.1983.

Mythological landscape representing Paris as a shepherd on Mt. Ida. Fresco from Pompeii, in the National Archeological Museum in Naples. Photograph by courtesy of the German ...ological Institute, neg. 56.1460.

The varied landscapes of the *Eclogues* similarly create various interpretations of the pastoral life and its relationship with the civilized world. Although each poem has a setting unique in its details, we may distinguish four general types: the farm scene, the rustic countryside, the wilderness, and, finally, the *locus amoenus*, which contrasts with the former three. Each has its particular characteristics of order and disorder and each its symbolic associations.

The farm landscape places the bucolic life within a pattern of agricultural organization.[23] If they are not roughly realistic, still Vergil's images of the farm world contain many elements that identify them as typically Italian. The majority of the persons in the *Eclogues* are not merely herdsmen, but cultivators as well. This innovation should not surprise us if we take Varro for our authority, for he explains that the best and most efficient kind of farm is one that combines the benefits of agriculture and husbandry.[24] The juxtaposition of these interdependent activities makes the farm self-sufficient, contributing to the aesthetic completeness of the whole. The small farm of Tityrus in *Eclogue* 1 is a miniature of the well-balanced *latifundium*, where the farmer cultivates apple trees, nut trees, sheep, cattle, bees, turtledoves, and pigeons. To the dispossessed Meliboeus this farm is a symbol of human security and felicity. Sadly he

[23] Agricultural elements in the *Eclogues* have caught the attention of readers since the seventeenth century but have often been regarded as a violation of pastoral decorum. Thus Rapin in *"De Carmine Pastorali" prefixed to Thomas Creech's translation of the "Idylliums" of Theocritus*, ed., with an introduction and bibliographical note by J. E. Congleton, The Augustan Reprint Society, series 2, Essays on Poetry, no. 3 (Ann Arbor, 1947), p. 27, observes that country occupations that allow man no leisure are incompatible with pastoral's golden-age ideal. In more recent years, Jean Hubaux, *Le réalisme dans les "Bucoliques" de Virgile* (Paris, 1927), pp. 72–89, has treated the agricultural descriptions as an aspect of the poet's Roman originality: "What attracts Vergil is the image of nature made productive by the labors of man." Michael Putnam, *Virgil's Pastoral Art: Studies in the Eclogues* (Princeton, 1970), likewise gives attention to the farm scenes, although he distinguishes this "georgic" touch from a purely pastoral landscape, a world of undisturbed leisure that to his mind represents an intellectual ideal.

[24] *Rust.* 1. 2. 11–1. 3; 2. 1. 1–10. On the two kinds of life in the *Eclogues*, see Hubaux, p. 97. Observing that the herdsmen in the *Georgics* are addressed as farmers, he suggests that Vergil makes no strong distinction between a pastoral and an agricultural life: "There are in the *Bucolics* as many agricultural realities as pastoral realities."

remembers the similar scenes he has just been forced to abandon: the seeded fields, the pruned vines and grafted pear trees, and the high rocky pastures where he once tended his goats. The disruption of such farms as this, places of ideal cooperation between man and nature, brings home with particular forcefulness the waste of civil war.

The landscape of *Eclogue* 2 is also that of a farm. At first we see a dense beech grove where Corydon sings his love complaint. Nearby is a vine-draped orchard where the lover wanders in the sunshine, and also a harvest field where the workers rest, awaiting a noonday meal. In the shade of the trees, the flocks rest also; all beings are in harmony with nature save for the restless lover whose passion gives him no repose. At the close of the poem, the farm world is again before us in the images of a tired plowman returning homeward and a vineyard with its unpruned vines. This setting tells us much about the singer. Corydon is not the owner of this villa farm but a hired laborer or slave. His rightful tasks and proper place in nature are determined by the activities of the farm. For love, he has neglected his duties, leaving vines untrimmed on the elm; he might at least have been weaving a basket while he sang.[25]

In *Eclogue* 7, Meliboeus, a farmer much poorer than Corydon's master, seems hard put to manage his varied tasks. While he tends his sapling myrtles away from the farmstead, his cattle wander without a guide. He cannot even afford a servant at home to pen up his lambs.[26] In taking time to hear the song contest, he feels some pangs of neglected duty. In him we may see some reminiscence of that ideal Roman farmer who does not shrink from accomplishing his tasks with his own hands.

In creating such farm scenes, Vergil shares in that idealized vision of cultivated nature so prominent in contemporary Republican writers.[27] Meliboeus' praise of Tityrus' farm is

[25] Both Cato *Agr.* 31. 1 and Varro *Rust.* 1. 22. 1 mention basket-making as an important part of farm work, since harvesting and storage require numberless baskets, and both advise planting trees and shrubs suitable for this purpose.
[26] For advice on penning the lambs away from their dams at night see Varro *Rust.* 2. 2. 16–18; for the suitability of girls for tending animals around the farmstead see 2. 10. 2.
[27] Although many scholars have thought of the details of rustic life in the *Eclogues* as completely picturesque and unreal (e.g., Bruno Snell, p. 288), many

slightly reminiscent of a Ciceronian passage in which old Cato describes his pleasure in contemplating the whole panorama of his farm, where every feature has its place in one great pleasing design: "Not only on account of its seeded fields, its meadows and vines and orchards is the agricultural life delightful, but also because of its gardens and fruit orchards; its pasture for the flock; its swarms of bees and its profusion of all kinds of flowers" (54). With such appreciations of the intellectual rewards of farming, Cicero and Varro show a Roman's native reverence for order and practicality while adding a new aesthetic sophistication to the rugged old ethic of the country life. The countryside is most beautiful when tamed and enriched by cultivation. To the Roman eye the farm is the best design for nature, the best opportunity for the organization of man's skills in governing his environment.

Thus the orderly landscape of the farm bears witness to a cooperative relationship between man and his environment wherein the farmer's authority as cultivator and controller is adapted to nature's instinctive order of growth and fruition. In the agricultural writings this relationship often fosters the pragmatic parallel between agricultural and civic discipline, but in the *Eclogues* it emerges metaphorically in a series of correspondences between human and natural life.

---

do have a place in the regular life of the farm. Even the flowers that lend charm to Vergil's landscapes can be reckoned among the products of commercial farming, as Varro (1. 16. 3) and Cato (8. 1) indicate. If the farmer keeps bees, his flower plantings are of the greatest importance. Those Varro recommends for honey are among the most common in the *Eclogues:* roses, poppies, clover, and especially the wild and domesticated thyme (3. 16. 26).

As Snell has observed, Vergil does not stress hard labor or the harshness of the elements, but the normal program of the shepherd's life in Varro shows a round of activities quite similar to those in the *Eclogues.* The greater part of the day is spent in grazing the animals. In summer they must be driven twice to water (*Ecl.* 9. 23–24; 7. 45–46; *Rust.* 2. 5. 15), and they must go out to graze before dawn when the grass is wettest and sweetest (*Ecl.* 8. 14–15; *Rust.* 2. 2. 10). Providing a shady resting place for the flock is among the keeper's major duties (*Rust.* 2. 2. 11). In summer the herdsmen stay in rough huts in the pastures or mountains far from the farmstead (*Ecl.* 2. 29; *Rust.* 2. 2. 9; 2. 10. 6). The farm owner is advised to provide female companions for his herdsmen to keep their huts and hold them near their flocks (*Rust.* 2. 1. 6). These women, Varro suggests, should be strong, but not unattractive (*Rust.* 2. 10. 7).

In *Eclogue* 5, the death of Daphnis brings a hiatus in the order of the agricultural life. Animals forget their food (24–26) and weeds spring up where crops have been sown:

> grandia saepe quibus mandavimus hordea sulcis,
> infelix lolium et steriles nascuntur avenae.
>
> (From the furrows to which we have often entrusted the swelling grain, unlucky cockle weeds and barren oats are born.)
> [5. 36–37]

The reader may recall the first *Idyll* where nature's mourning for Daphnis evinces a magical sympathy between man and his world. But here, the disturbance of nature is more acute. The processes of growth are perverted; the farmer's hopes are deceived. The death of Daphnis has shaken the security of human expectations. We are aware that some event of large compass has here been translated into agricultural terms.

In such a passage the order of nature is no longer a literal order but has become a metaphorical expression of an ideal relationship between man and his world. In the same poem, terms of natural harmony and interdependency express the importance of Daphnis to the shepherds' world. He is as the vine to the tree; the grapes to the vine; the bull to the herd; the crops to the rich fields (32–34). In the ninth *Eclogue*, the optimistic Lycidas sings in a similar manner of the rising of Caesar's star:

> astrum quo segetes gauderent frugibus et quo
> duceret apricis in collibus uva colorem.   [9. 48–49]
>
> (The star by whose influence the seeded fields might rejoice in fruits; by whose power the grape might lead its color over the sunny hillsides.)

The divine leader has become the intermediary between man and nature, the power that guarantees the fulfillment of nature's promise. Yet his role is only that of the order-giving farmer, translated to a supernatural plane.

The center for such idealization of agriculture is in the fourth *Eclogue* where the poet envisions a new Roman age of gold in images related to the whole context of the *Eclogue* book. The infancy of a divine child is surrounded by bucolic abundance. Flowers pour forth about his cradle; deadly plants lose their poison, and flocks come home unguided. As the child grows older, the wild world turns into farmland; the corn ripens in untilled fields and the grapes on the uncultivated vine. With his maturity, a spontaneously creative nature obviates all need for cultivation:

> non rastros patietur humus, non vinea falcem;
> robustus quoque iam tauris iuga solvet arator.   [4.40–41]

> (The earth will feel no rakes; the vine no pruning hook; the sturdy plowman will lift the yoke from his bulls.)

Within the agricultural context of the *Eclogues*, this description has specialized implications. The complementary processes of natural fertility and human cultivation are at last united. The golden age brings to the landscape a permanent and civilized order that is in perfect harmony with the life of man. Here, again, as we shall see, Vergil does not intend this formula literally, nor as an expression of wishful magic, but rather as a metaphor for the prosperity of the harmonious, well-governed state.

The agricultural design of nature has given the poet not only a pattern for depicting immediate landscapes, but also a means of associating his landscapes with the greater world. The ideal organization of nature, rooted in images of the farm, in the simple occupations and responsibilities of farmers, becomes a microcosm of ideal world order. The defeat or fulfillment of man's hopes of nature, the harvest or loss of his rewards, can become a symbolic statement of his fate as a historical being. It is not exactly as Samuel Johnson said, that the grandiose subject of the fourth *Eclogue* is presented in terms of its effects upon the country life.[28] Rather, the country life is a paradigm of man's thinking about the organization of the world.

In the farm world, the crops and vines bear witness to man's control over nature, but in a purely rustic world his ability to order his surroundings is less secure. The rustic landscapes of

[28] "Pastoral Poetry II," *Rambler* No. 37, July 24, 1750, in *Eighteenth-Century Critical Essays*, ed. Scott Elledge, (Ithaca, N.Y., 1961), II, 582–583.

the *Eclogues* have their closest analogy in landscape paintings of the sacral-idyllic type.[29] The works that are commonly thus classified present a general impression of the country, neither cultivated nor wholly wild, combining groves or roadways with graceful buildings or shrines. Man's occupations in such settings are generally quiet ones, herding and worship, although he may occasionally appear as a traveler moving through the countryside or as the inhabitant of a country house. In the blue and white frieze of the Farnesina Villa (Figure 6), the emphasis is on herding and worship, while in a stucco frieze from the same house (Figure 12), scenes of worship are combined with indications of domestic life. The well-known yellow frieze from the Palatine House of Livia (Figure 13) incorporates a number of secular and commercial activities against a continuous panorama of scenes ranging from the urban to the rural.[30]

Rustic landscapes provide settings for *Eclogues* 3, 5, and 9; they also figure in the songs of these poems as well as in those of 7. Occasionally these scenes portray a quiet harmony comparable to that of the more idealized sacral-idyllic paintings. In the third poem, the judge, Palaemon, describes the season. It is spring; the trees have begun to put forth leaves and the grass to grow green. The setting of the fifth poem includes a quiet grove and a cavern overhung with vines. In the second song of that poem, the description of the rustic festivals for Daphnis and of the peaceful prosperity promised to the country by his apotheosis suggest such an atmosphere of quiet piety in a rural community as that depicted by the Farnesina landscapes. In the seventh poem, Corydon describes a sacrifice: small Micon humbly presents a stag's and a boar's head to Diana.[31]

But in other places, Vergil's rustic descriptions show the quiet countryside as a background for disorder in human activity. The opening dialogue of the third poem would appear

[29] For definition of the type see Rostovtzeff, pp. 1–185; H. G. Beyen, *Die pompeianische Wanddekoration von zweiten bis zum vierten Stil*, vol. I (The Hague, 1938), vol. II (The Hague, 1960).

[30] Emily L. Wadsworth, *MAAR* 4(1924):23–4, pls. 1–9; Rizzo, *Tavole* 5–8.

[31] Rizzo, p. 57 and figs. 35, 37–38; W. J. T. Peters, *Landscape in Romano-Campanian Painting* (Assen, 1963), p. 43.

12. Sacral-idyllic frieze in stucco relief from the Villa Farnesina, now in the National Mus
of the Baths of Diocletian in Rome. Photograph, Alinari 2508.

to take place in the fields, near a small village. The landmarks of
the sacral-idyllic world are present: a shrine, a crossroads, a
vineyard, rustic homes. But the two quarreling herdsmen,
Damoetas and Meliboeus, have little reverence for their environment. One accuses the other of desecrating the shrine,
and his companion, in turn, accuses him of destroying the
vineyard. Only Palaemon, who enters later, seems capable of
appreciating the beauty of the natural world.

In the ninth poem, the rustic landscape assumes a melancholy tone. The travelers pause to rest on their journey to the
city. Before them the countryside lies quiet; a tomb stands in
the distance and nearby is a grove where farmers cut leaves for
their cattle and spread them to dry. A threat of rain is in the air.
The tomb, the drying foliage, the coming rain, are emblems of
finality and sadness.

Unlike the farm landscapes, the rustic scenes do not show
man as the organizer of his environment but merely as a small,

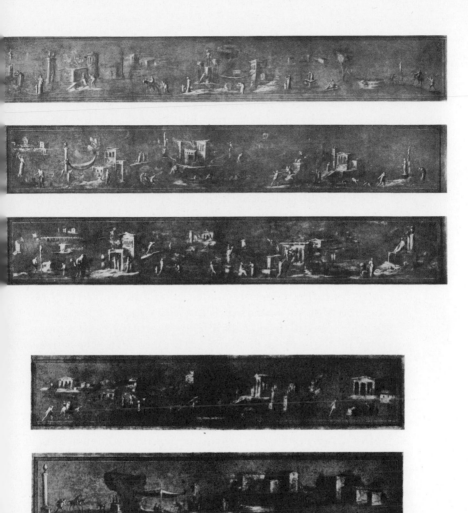
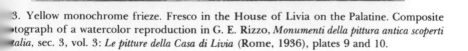

3. Yellow monochrome frieze. Fresco in the House of Livia on the Palatine. Composite photograph of a watercolor reproduction in G. E. Rizzo, *Monumenti della pittura antica scoperti ...alia*, sec. 3, vol. 3: *Le pitture della Casa di Livia* (Rome, 1936), plates 9 and 10.

sometimes helpless inhabitant of an impersonal world. Nature herself is less orderly, and man more sensitive to her disorder, or more liable to create disorder himself. Lacking the farmer's ability to utilize his own resources, the herdsman fears the external forces that govern his world. Thus, in the first *Eclogue,* a sinister omen has preceded Meliboeus' alteration from farmer to wanderer, and Moeris, in the ninth, has come to believe that the world is directed by an indeterminable and unlucky chance.

A third type of setting with analogies in Roman landscape painting is the wilderness of *Eclogues* 6, 8, and 10. In 6, a wild cavern is the place of an encounter between two shepherd boys and the sleeping Silenus. In the songs of 8 and 10, the Arcadian forest hears the complaints of rejected lovers. Wilderness is an aspect of nature seldom pleasing to the Roman eye, for it offers no contact with the reassuring order of civilization. We may remember the bristling forests of the African shore in the *Aeneid,* or the dark, fearful woods of Tacitus' Germany.[32] In Roman paintings of the late second and early third style, the forests and mountains become a background for such events as the punishment of Acteon, the rape of Hylas, the meeting of Endymion and Selene: awesome encounters between man and divinity that end in loss of identity, transformation, or death for man. In the wilderness he meets with forces beyond his control or experiences the release of fearful unknown forces within himself.[33] Thus the wilderness setting is appropriate to the song of Silenus, a song of man in the natural world. Although the god's singing gives order to nature, making the trees bend their heads and the wild fauns dance in rhythm, the tales he tells are of human disorder: the passion of Pasiphaë, the rape of Hylas, the metamorphosis of Phaeton's sisters, and the transformation of Philomela. All show the dire fate of man, alone in nature, alienated from the civilized world.

In a milder form, the chaos of human emotion is the subject of *Eclogues* 8 and 10. The introductory stanza of the unhappy

[32] Tacitus *Ann.* 1. 65–67; *Germ.* 5. 1.
[33] C. P. Segal discusses the aesthetic and psychological significance of forest scenes in mythological narrative in *Landscape in Ovid's Metamorphoses: A Study in the Transformation of a Literary Symbol,* Hermes Einzelschriften 23 (Wiesbaden, 1969), pp. 12–19.

lover's complaint is an evocation of the Arcadian wilderness, a land of groves and shrill-sounding pine trees, where shepherds sing their love songs to Pan — whose shepherd's pipe is itself an emblem of frustrated love. As an uncouth rustic with shaggy eyebrows and untrimmed beard, despised by his beloved Nysa, the goatherd-lover is well suited to such a setting. He recalls the often cited Roman image of Arcadia, a boorish wilderness, the home of men who lived before the moon.[34]

In the tenth *Eclogue*, the Arcadian wilderness is more fully described. We see its cold rivers, high crags, and mountains: harsh, disorderly objects that mirror the lover's own state of confusion.[35] As Gallus lies prostrate and self-pitying beneath the cliffs of Maenalus, he is visited by the inhabitants of Arcadia, who themselves are rough-appearing creatures: Menalcas the swineherd, dripping with acorns, Silvanus crowned with rustic garlands, and Pan with his face stained red with *minium*. All are amazed by the lover's grief, which to them denotes a failure to comprehend the implacable nature of love. With cold honesty, Apollo reminds the lover that his faithless mistress has gone beyond reach, following her new lover through an even wilder landscape of Alpine crags and snow. This image recalls the unhappy lover's description of the birthplace of love (8. 43–44):

[34] Panofsky, pp. 297–299, suggests that Vergil's utopian idealization of Arcadia departs from this tradition as shown in Ovid *Fast.* 2. 289–292 and Juvenal 7. 160. But, although Vergil seems to have made use of Polybius' remarks on the excellence of Arcadian singing (*Histories* 4. 21. 1), his Arcadian forest is not out of keeping with the concept of Arcadian hard primitivism.

[35] The interesting, although somewhat fulsome description of Mt. Parthenius in Aelian (*VH* 13. 1) might be an elaboration of Vergil's suggestions, but might also bear witness to a lost tradition of Arcadian *ecphrasis* associated, like this passage (and also Prop. 1. 11–15 and Ovid *AA*. 185–196), with the myth of Atalanta and Milanion: "There was a canal bringing water, and gigantic oaks and pines above that offered dense shade. In the hollow curve of the valley was a cave, very deep and fortified by a steep ascent. Ivy crept over it and embraced the sapling trees as it climbed over their tops. Here were crocuses, springing up in the soft, thick grass and one single hyacinth blossom, as well as other flowers of many diverse hues that not only afforded a pleasant prospect for the eye, but also filled the air all around with the sweetest odors. Laurels, whose thick leaves are always a pleasant sight, grew upright and crowded together, and the vines flourishing with their abundant fruit before the cave gave testimony of Atalanta's industrious nature. Moreover, there were eternally flowing fountains, both clear and cool that were delightful to the touch and the taste; and since they bubbled up unceasingly, were also very useful for watering the trees."

among the flinty rocks of Tmaros or Rhodope or the far-off
Garamantes. Such frozen, sterile regions are the natural homes
of the faithless, where the absence of any trace of nature's
greenness or fertility signifies a lack of emotion or kindness.
Unhappy lovers imagine such regions but never visit them,
remaining instead in Arcadia where nature can still be human-
ized, where the cold rivers are emblems of tears and the hard
rocks that suggest suffering are still covered with vegetation,
the life needed to support self-pity.

Within this imagistic scheme, we may understand Gallus'
restlessness in Arcadia, a restlessness that leads the poet's
imagination to wander as he attempts to transform the uncom-
fortable land of self-pity into a paradise of love. Although his
grief has led him to Arcadia, Gallus desires still further escape.
Begging the Arcadians to remember and sing of his passion,
he begins his own song. He wishes that he, too, were an Arcadian
and not a soldier in love. He dreams of a rural landscape, pleasing and soft, with willows, flowers, meadows, and streams. He
sees himself amidst pastoral lovers who sing and weave garlands
for him, or even with Lycoris among the groves and streams.
This visionary landscape, composed of intermingled images
from the *locus amoenus,* the farm world and the rustic scene,
has no relationship to the crags and forests of Arcadia. It is a
projection of the lover's desire, created in hopes of reordering
the wilderness of the mind. Once Gallus remembers reality — the
infidelity of Lycoris and her distance from him — he abandons
his vision and turns back to wild Arcadia. He vows that its forests
will be his new home, where he will dispel his passion in hunting
the boar over the rocks and marshes. Thus there are two landscapes in Gallus' song: Arcadia and the *locus amoenus.*

Throughout the *Eclogues,* glimpses of the *locus amoenus* appear
in the songs of the pastoral singers, always in contrast with the
real world. The singers in the third, seventh, and ninth poems
include such images in their songs, picturing briefly the shade
beside the brook, the tree that bears golden apples, the meadow
dotted with flowers. In the third poem, these pictures figure in
the singers' competitive boasting of their prowess in love and
song. In the seventh, they are the substance of Corydon's
idealized pastoral art. In the ninth, they are visions of a better

world, now lost, remembered from past time. In the second and eighth poems, the *locus amoenus* appears as a more sustained creation in Corydon's invitation to the pastoral and the unhappy lover's memories of the orchard where he first became acquainted with innocent love. No single descriptive formula governs the composition of the *locus amoenus;* at times it appears as an idealization of Vergil's agricultural or sacral-idyllic countryside, at times it looks backward to the genial pastures of Theocritus, and at others it drifts toward a world of pure myth. Unlike the Theocritean *loci,* descriptions of the real surroundings of the herdsmen, the Vergilian *locus* is always an imagined ideal, never present to the eye but actively sought by the mind. Even so, the emotional associations of these pictures and their frequent assimilation to the quest for love are not sufficient to explain their dreamlike quality. They are designed in a manner entirely different from other landscapes. To consider their style of composition, we may turn to another principle illustrated by Roman painting: the use of perspective arrangements to create realistic or unrealistic representations of the natural world.

Roman landscape painting is often characterized by its ability to render an illusion of space, to establish a sense of the topographical interrelationship of objects in a scene. For this purpose, the painters use two simple techniques of perspective: the diminution of size in background objects and, more notably, the placing of background objects above foreground objects to produce the illusion of receding planes.[36] This latter technique, commonly known as "bird's-eye perspective," is a cartographical method for presenting a record of actuality, the impression of appearances that meet the eye. Peter von Blanckenhagen sees a relationship between this practice and Vitruvius' mention of landscapes that depict the "actual characteristics of places." He speaks of the development of bird's-eye perspective in landscape painting as a consequence of the Roman desire for factual reporting, suggesting that the cartographical method may well have characterized the earliest of Roman

[36] The discussion here is greatly indebted to Peter von Blanckenhagen, pp. 54–58.

paintings, those carried in triumphal processions to present a journalistic record of battles and events. In landscape painting, the use of bird's-eye perspective makes it possible for natural objects to be more than a decorative background, assuming their relative positions as the features of a self-contained place.

Many Roman paintings use this technique effectively. The Villa Albani panel (Figure 7) is composed on three planes: the spreading tree in the foreground where the herdsmen rest and the cattle crossing the bridge stand out against the distant background of harbor and town. In the Farnesina landscape (Figure 6), the background subjects are of the same kind as those in the foreground, but a series of lightly sketched hills and depressions provides for consistent recession from foreground to background. The Villa Pamphili landscapes (Figure 4) are almost uniformly composed on two planes, foreground and background, with little clear designation of the distance between, but the sketchy, two-dimensional quality of the background objects indicates their removal in space. In the mythological paintings, the natural elevation of the mountains creates a horizon, providing not only a sense of distance but also an impression of enclosure and isolation in the foreground space.

In creating the landscapes of his poems, Vergil is aware of the sense of coherence and self-containment to be obtained through the clear designation of foreground and background objects. By distributing his descriptive passages throughout each poem, beginning always with the immediate foreground, he places his speakers in a definite spatial relationship to their surroundings and at the same time creates for the reader impressions of a landscape unfolding on successive planes as it meets the eye. In *Eclogue* 1 the farm appears through the eyes of Meliboeus. In the foreground is a spreading beech tree where Tityrus sings his love songs. The farmland comprises the middle ground with its small pastures marked off by hedge and stream. In the background are neighboring farmhouses, their chimneys smoking, and finally the hills whose shadows lengthen as evening comes on. The three levels of perspective are comparable to those of the Villa Albani panel, which Vergil's landscape also resembles in its joining together of the disparate features of a small but complete world. The framing panels of *Eclogue* 2 similarly present a step-by-step revelation of objects in a land-scape: grove, harvest field, orchard, and vineyard with an im-plication of distant fields, although there is here no horizon to mark the beginning of an exterior world. The landscape of the sixth poem comprises a cavern and forests, bounded by hills above which rises the evening star. In the seventh, Meliboeus is in the foreground, working his fields, close to the ilex which is the setting for the songs. Behind him we see the Mincio sliding through the pastures, and in the distance the vague suggestion of a humble farmstead. The scenes of the ninth poem do not range from foreground to background but are spread out in succession along the road that leads to the city in the manner of a horizontally composed frieze.

Although all of these landscapes are imaginary, their careful, deliberate organization makes us understand that they are real to the persons who live within them. To the reader, they should stand as representations of actual scenes. These are the land-scapes whose inhabitants are conscious of time and season, aware of living in nature and responsive to its demands. Such landscapes are consistent with a world in which history plays a role: where the real Rome is always in the background and the pastoral setting is only one location within the framework of a greater nature.

But in the visions of the *locus amoenus* there is no such reality, no organization of objects in receding perspective. Here, the juxtaposition of images obeys the laws of fantasy alone. The countless flocks, the summer pastures, the attendant nymphs that are Corydon's vision of pastoral felicity, do not exist within the context of an orderly nature but are images suspended in imaginative space. The unhappy lover's orchard is a refuge from experience. It does not open onto a prospect of fields and pas-tures but only onto a hostile reality that the lover sees with dim eyes. In the Gallus poem, the *locus amoenus* is placed at the center of three concentric panels of description. In all cases, the ab-sence of a logical perspective removes the *locus amoenus* from the limitations of the natural world but imposes upon it the limits of fantasy, the knowledge that such visions have no hope of real existence in nature. In these visionary settings, men have sought freedom from the responsibilities and emotional frus-

trations of their ordinary lives, yet the freedom is temporary
and as evanescent as the landscapes themselves.

Such juxtapositions and deliberate representations of fantasy
are a poetic technique that can never quite be achieved by the
resources of the landscape painter, yet there is one group of
scenes that approaches the tenth *Eclogue* in organization and
symbolic value: the series of three sacral-idyllic paintings from
the red room at Boscotrecase (Figures 8–10).

The foregrounds of these paintings show the idealizing
potential of sacral-idyllic landscape at its height. The attitudes
of the figures indicate contentment. Shepherds gaze contem-
platively into space; worshipers have reached their goal at the
shrines; a wayfarer rests and plays with his dog. Trees, shrines,
and statues create pleasing contrasts of lightness and solidarity.
A harmony of complementary shapes and subjects gives unity
to the design. The ideal quality of the foreground composition
is enhanced by the placement of its distinct figures against a
lighter background of monumental buildings and trees. Foreground and background are seen in differing perspective. There
is no logical continuity between the two, and thus the sacred
places seem detached from reality, existing within a rarefied
atmosphere of their own. A whitened area surrounding each
composition that sets it apart from its black border and gold
frame is interpreted by von Blanckenhagen to indicate that the
panels do not present such views as we see from a window; they
are not convincing *trompe l'oeil* impressions of reality, but images
of nature suspended in space, visions of an ideal, imaginative
world.[37]

These paintings draw their images from reality. Both the
sacred places in their foregrounds and the buildings in their
backgrounds are reminders of the actual countryside. By his
subtle use of unreal perspectives, inconsistent parallels, and
obliquely seen objects, the painter has transformed the interrelationship of these objects, creating for the spectator an
atmosphere of vision and enchantment: "A lost world of Theocritean shepherds and nymphs, of simple people in simple
worship, of distant shores and romantic isles is blended with

[37] See von Blanckenhagen, pp. 30–35.

familiar views of handsome buildings, votive gifts, statuettes, goats and sheep into an image of fairyland where nothing is quite real or even determinable, where nature has lost its threatening powers, but has kept its indefinable vastness and variety."[38] This world von Blanckenhagen compares with a philosophical country of the mind, a remote world difficult to achieve, a mirage at once close-by and intimate yet at the same moment untouchable and far away.

The interrelationship of visionary worlds in the Gallus poem is similar. Like the paintings, the poem is designed to illuminate a central image of a remote, ideal world, attainable only through imagination. But where the paintings create a harmonious, philosophical transition from reality to vision, the poem suggests discord, a broken, spasmodic play of wandering imagination. The contrasts between the landscapes are sharp. The symbolic value of wild Arcadia, with its evocation of irrational, extravagant love, jars against the lover's pastoral fantasies and also against the framing image of quiet rusticity, where the Eclogue Poet sings his song in the shade. Yet both the poem and the paintings succeed in informing us that their visions of the pastoral answer to man's desire to alter the nature of reality within the confines of an ideal world.

The many similarities of subject and organization between Vergil's landscapes and those paintings that were becoming fashionable in Rome and Campania suggest that the poet of the *Eclogues* was thinking in a manner shared with other persons of his time. From our discussion of these pictures we have seen that the use of perspective arrangements as a part of artistic planning and design may alternatively convey the impression of factual realism or of deliberate unreality. In the *Eclogues*, the contrasting of subjective and objective visions of nature, of landscapes of fantasy and landscapes of the real world, is a fundamental principle of poetic design. As we go on to study the characters of the pastoral singers we will see that such contrasts in the organization of landscape are associated with contrasts in point of view. Even within the boundaries of the pastoral, man experiences conflicts between the ideal world that answers

[38] *Ibid.*, p. 58.

to his desires and the real world in which he must live and play a responsible role.

The variety of nature is the basis for the complexities of the *Eclogues*. The poems have no consistent landscape. No one image stands out as typically pastoral. Their world is created as a microcosm of nature, offering the contrasts that nature offers to the eye. But in creating his varied landscapes, Vergil is also conscious of their symbolic potential, of parallels between nature and man. Like the faces of nature, the emotions of men are varied and inconsistent. The four modes of landscape in the poems have associations with patterns of conduct and thought: the farm with man's desire for order, the rustic world with his anxieties and uncertainties, the wilderness with his uncontrolled passions, and the *locus amoenus* with his fantasies and his urge for withdrawal. The cultivated field, the wilderness, and paradise are territories of the human mind. In the midst of his varied landscapes, the poet explores man's nature as an emotional and a historical being, and traces the conflicts of order and disorder that beset his affairs to their deep beginnings in human thought.

CHAPTER 4

Roman Realities and Poetic Symbolism in *Eclogue* 1

The first *Eclogue* measures the distance between modern man and the golden age, between Vergilian and Theocritean pastoral. Through its images of nature and its cognizance of historical forces, it shows the impossibility of maintaining an old pastoral ideal in a new world.[1] For Vergil, the departure from Theocritus is not a loss, but a rejection. Familiar Theocritean images of pastoral leisure and simplicity have become an illusory vision that must be supplanted by images more vital and more representative of the contemporary world.

In the central passage of *Eclogue*, Meliboeus, the farmer on his way into exile, describes the farm belonging to Tityrus, the newly manumitted slave:

> Fortunate senex, ergo tua rura manebunt
> et tibi magna satis, quamvis lapis omnia nudus
> limosoque palus obducat pascua iunco:
> non insueta gravis temptabunt pabula fetas,
> nec mala vicini pecoris contagia laedent.   [1. 46–50]

> (Fortunate old man, therefore your lands will remain your own, and large enough for you, even though bare stone and the

[1] Recent studies emphasize the juxtaposition of historical realities and "pastoral ideals." Viktor Pöschl, *Die Hirtendichtung Virgils* (Heidelberg, 1964), describes a symmetrical structure that clarifies the interdependency of the pastoral and Roman worlds, and discusses the poem's balancing of benevolent and destructive forces. Brooks Otis, *Virgil: A Study in Civilized Poetry* (Oxford, 1963), pp. 135–136, observes that Vergil's consistent allusions to Rome in bucolic language make us aware of the insistent influence of the historical world, while Charles Segal, "*Tamen cantabitis Arcades*—Exile and Arcadia in *Eclogues One* and *Nine*" *Arion* 4(1965):238–266, speaks of Vergil's idealization of the "eternal" world of pastoral, its beauty heightened by impending loss. Michael C. J. Putnam, *Virgil's Pastoral Art: Studies in the "Eclogues"* (Princeton, 1970), pp. 20–81, explores the paradox by which an ideal of intellectual freedom is made subject to the forces of politics and law.

marsh with its muddy reed may invade your whole pasture. No unfamiliar food will disturb the young unborn; no evil plagues from a neighboring flock will harm them.)

Here the virtues of the farm are almost negative. The land of Tityrus would seem to be poor land that wild nature might easily overwhelm. Swamps and stones impinge upon the pastures. Isolation alone can protect the flock. The subjunctive *obducat* suggests a constant threat of disorder. The meaning of the word and the context in which it appears are strikingly similar to those in a passage of the *De Rerum Natura* (5. 200–209).[2]

In support of his argument that the universe was not created by benevolent gods with human welfare in mind, Lucretius catalogues nature's flaws. The greater part of the world is a wilderness bristling with mountains and forests full of wild beasts, while cliffs and marshes and sea make still more regions inhospitable to human life. The burning heat of the tropics and cold of the polar zones are equally unendurable. Even in that small corner man has found habitable, nature threatens to create chaos:

> quod superest arvi, tamen id natura sua vi
> sentibus obducat, ni vis humana resistat
> vitai causa valido consueta bidenti
> ingemere et terram pressis proscindere aratris.   [5. 206–209][3]

---

[2] "Relegati paludes et silvas" is how Sallust (*Or. Lep.* 23) describes Sulla's veterans, whose hopes their commander had deceived with grants of unworkable land. Jachmann, "Die dichterische Technik in Vergil's Bucolica," *Neue Jahrb.* 49(1922):115–116, n. 5, suggests that this farm should be compared with that where Cato the Censor learned virtue through hard labor: "saxis Sabinis, silicibus repastinandis atque conserendis." H. Wagenvoort, "Vergil's *Eclogues* 1 and 9," in *Studies in Roman Literature, Culture and Religion* (Leiden, 1956), p. 247, suggests that the inferior quality of the land is intended to point up the owner's attachment to his home. Some scholars (such as Pöschl, p. 37, and Kenneth Wellesley, "Virgil's Home," *Wiener Studien, Donum Natalicium Albin Lesky* 77 [1966]:345) have even suggested that the poorness of the land should be taken as the reason why the farm has been passed over in the confiscations. The text is that edited by Cyril Bailey, *Lucretius De Rerum Natura,* 2d ed. (Oxford, O.C.T., 1922).

[3] See also Vergil 2. 411, where the verbal borrowing from Lucretius is very clear: "bis segetem densis obducunt sentibus herbae." The parallel uses of "obducat" were pointed out to me by Louise Holland.

(As for what is left by way of arable fields, even that nature by
her own force would invade with thornbushes did not human
force hold her in check, that force which is accustomed, for the
sake of keeping alive, to groan over the stout mattock and cut
through the earth with down-pressed plow.)

Obducat suggests invasion which man repels with his agricultural weapons. There is constant opposition of the *vis
natura* and *vis humana.* In his struggle for subsistence man
cannot escape from confrontation with the wilderness.

Lucretius' grimly realistic view of nature is echoed in
Melibeous' forthright description. Tityrus' farm is a place sal-
vaged from the continuing struggle between nature and man.
Yet Meliboeus also sees that the farm is bounded by streams
that offer refreshing coolness, and by hedges filled with a
pleasant sound of bees. Within these boundaries that signify
personal ownership,[4] the farm may appear ideal:

fortunate senex, hic inter flumina nota
et fontis sacros frigus captabis opacum;
hinc tibi, quae semper, vicino ab limite saepes
Hyblaeis apibus florem depasta salicti
saepe levi somnum suadebit inire susurro;
hinc alta sub rupe canet frondator ad auras,
nec tamen interea raucae, tua cura, palumbes
nec gemere aëria cessabit turtur ab ulmo. [1. 51–58]

(Fortunate old man, here among familiar streams and sacred
springs you will seek out cool shade. Here, as always, the
hedge by the neighboring boundary line, whose willow flowers
are tasted by the bees of Hybla, will often, with its soft whisper,
urge you to go to sleep. Here, beneath a high cliff, the leaf-
cutter will sing to the breezes. While all the time neither the
deep-voiced pigeons, your especial care, nor the turtledove will
cease to murmur from the airy elm.)

As an enclosed location, the farm world lacks the open freedom
of the Theocritean pasture. In order to protect the harmonious
design of his environment, man must have barriers against

---

[4] Jacques Perret, *Virgile: Les Bucoliques* (Paris, 1961), p. 23 *ad* v. 47: *"lapis,
palus, pascua:* These words help us to recognize the legal nature of Tityrus'
domain."

nature. No man is more conscious of this need than Meliboeus, for already in journeying from his own lost farm he has begun to experience the hardships of an unprotected life in nature. Although the goatherd cares anxiously for his flock, he must force them to suffer with himself:

> en ipse capellas
> protinus aeger ago; hanc etiam vix, Tityre, duco.
> hic inter densas corylos modo namque gemellos,
> spem gregis, a! silice in nuda conixa reliquit.   [1. 12–15]

(See, sadly I urge my goats onward. This one here I can barely lead, Tityrus. Just now, amid the thick hazels, she left behind her twin kids—the promise of my flock—to which she gave birth on bare, flinty rocks.)

Although the words *densas corylos* might suggest a protective pastoral enclosure, this hazel thicket has become a place of death.

At the end of the poem, this same harsh nature is again before us as Tityrus looks toward the hills that form his horizon, now casting long shadows over the valley. Like the streams and hedges of the farm, these hills may serve as a protective barrier, enclosing a small cluster of farms and houses, but they also mark the beginning of the great world. Beyond them lies Rome, the source of civil war, and further still the hard and inhospitable lands to which Meliboeus must travel in his exile.

The landscape of Tityrus' farm is a symbolic introduction to the new world of nature in the *Eclogues,* a world where man no longer lives in instinctive harmony with his surroundings, but must secure and defend the order of his life. This farm is the most complex of Vergil's agricultural images and is unique among literary landscapes of its time, unfolding, as I have said, upon three clearly delineated planes of perspective in such a manner that each further view expands and changes our understanding of those before it. Throughout the poem, the farm landscape is the only prospect seen directly and in detail, the center of the world the poet is creating, yet always we look obliquely beyond it to the suggestions of chaos on its borders. Thus the farm incorporates two modes of existence: it is at once a self-contained, harmonious microcosm, the symbol of a well-balanced life, and a location within the greater world of harsh, demanding nature. By his juxtaposition of order and disorder, Vergil is at once creating an image of the Italian countryside in the contemporary moment and transforming it into a symbolic statement concerning pastoral poetry. In its double perspective, the farm anticipates other aspects of the *Eclogues;* its security is associated with Tityrus and the poet's projected rebirth of the pastoral, its fragility with Meliboeus and the forces that trouble man's search for order. This ambiguity pervades the poem, as the characters' specific revelations of their fortunes provide the basis for the development of a poetic symbolism. Historical and poetic implications are intertwined, but such refinements are beyond the grasp of the characters who participate in historical circumstances they do not understand and in a literary design that eludes their comprehension.[5]

Consequently, despite the questions and answers of the dialogue, the speakers fail to understand one another. Each tells the other of events that have changed his life, but the disparity of their experiences draws the two further apart. Each pursues the line of discourse closest to his thoughts. Meliboeus wishes to solve the riddle of Tityrus' good fortune, for it seems somehow pertinent to himself, but he is less interested in the details of the old slave's adventures than in the contrast between Tityrus and himself. Tityrus asks no questions of Meliboeus; his eagerness to reveal his own marvelous discoveries wholly possesses his mind. At the end of the poem, there is no synthesis of the two versions of experience and no reconciliation of order and disorder. This failure of understanding, and the resultant inconclusiveness of the poem, signify that the full possibilities of Vergil's reawakening of the pastoral await further development.

[5] For surveys of the historical problems, see Karl Büchner, *P. Vergilius Maro: Der Dichter der Römer* (Stuttgart, 1961), pp. 161–164; Ernest Fredricksmeyer, "Octavian and the Unity of Vergil's First *Eclogue*," *Hermes* 94(1966):208–209, nn. 3, 4 (esp. for attitudes toward Octavian as the author of the land confiscations). Fredricksmeyer makes use of the characters' limited knowledge as a principle of interpretation in arguing that vv. 40–45 are the climax of the poem: the moment when Meliboeus realizes that the *deus* whom Tityrus praises and the Octavian who has evicted him are the same.

The opening lines contrast two versions of fortune. Tityrus enjoys rural leisure while his neighbors are driven from their fields and homes:

> Tityre, tu patulae recubans sub tegmine fagi
> silvestrem tenui Musam meditaris avena;
> nos patriae finis et dulcia linquimus arva.
> nos patriam fugimus; tu, Tityre, lentus in umbra
> formosam resonare doces Amaryllida silvas.   [1. 1–5]

(Tityrus, you lying here on your back, beneath the shelter of a wide-branching beech tree, you practice the songs of a woodland muse on a thin straw of oat. We are giving up the country and the sweet fields of our fatherland; we are fleeing from our fatherland. You, Tityrus, tarrying in the shade, go on teaching the forest to echo the name of lovely Amaryllis.)

The carefree attitude of the happy shepherd surprises Meliboeus.[6] Expecting that the other must soon share his exile (thus the plural verbs), he wonders why he remains undisturbed, with no apparent thought for the future, his mind absorbed in the heedless occupation of song. Thus his tone is slightly reproachful. His insistent *fugimus, linquimus*, point to the urgency of the moment. Tityrus is slow (*lentus*). His tree is providing a shield (*tegmine*) from reality. The *tenuis avena* implies that music is a trivial occupation for such a critical time.[7] In Tityrus, Meliboeus sees the wanton prolongation of what is irrevocably lost: love, leisure, kinship with nature. While Meliboeus has already found the countryside transformed into a world of experience, Tityrus lingers within the illusory fastness of a lost golden age.

The suggestions of a golden age grow stronger as Tityrus

---

[6] John Van Sickle, "Studies of Dialectical Methodology in the Virgilian Tradition," *MLN* 85(1970):890, suggests that Meliboeus is surprised by Tityrus' unconcern since he had imagined trouble for the whole countryside.

[7] Van Sickle (pp. 893–896) makes much of the contrast between "tenuis avena" and "calamus agrestis," Tityrus' own term for his musical instrument. The oaten straw is, he suggests, an "unpromising poetic tool," the reed, quite possibly "one that really works." Mr. Van Sickle has demonstrated the point quite cogently by presenting me with an actual oaten straw, a slender stalk about one-quarter inch in diameter, quite useless for producing any variety or modulation of sound.

begins to explain to Meliboeus how a god has given him leisure
and sanctioned the continuity of his peaceful world (6–10). He
speaks as a man to whom something miraculous has happened.
His animals are now free to wander and he to play as he wishes
upon his shepherd's pipe. To Meliboeus the story is also miraculous. He professes no envy, only amazement, before Tityrus'
good fortune (11–12), believing that his own disaster was, at
least, forewarned by the gods (16–17). He continues to question
Tityrus concerning the identity of the benevolent god.

The picture is not really so simple, and the difference between the two farmers is exaggerated in these opening lines.
If we accept the luxuriant shelter of the beech tree as the ideal
landscape of Vergilian pastoral, it must prove misleading. It
is, in fact, a rather conventional image, a reminiscence of the
Theocritean tree and stream, and thus of the traditional disposition of the mode in which Vergil has chosen to write.[8]
Already the contrast of Tityrus and Meliboeus shows a need
for reinterpreting the tradition. The remainder of the poem
will modify, if not entirely obliterate, the bland felicity of the
opening image.

Tityrus, like Meliboeus, is a man of the contemporary world.
His answers to Meliboeus' questions reveal a profound difference between his rural *otium* and the spontaneous freedom
of a golden age. First, this freedom is not even the familiar,
unquestioned leisure of the Theocritean herdsman, but a hard-
won gain. When Meliboeus asks for the name of the god who
has favored him, we learn that Tityrus is a former slave who, by
the profits of his peculium, has been able to purchase his
freedom. Peculium, as Varro explains it in the *De Re Rustica*, is
the right of pasturage an owner may grant to worthy slaves
(1. 2. 17).[9] Thus Tityrus' flock is his own. Beyond this, his
place on the farm is somewhat mysterious and hard to interpret

[8] Pöschl, pp. 10–11, discusses the formal acknowledgement of Theocritus
here and compares Vergil's description with the opening passages of *Idylls* 1
and 7. For discussion of the whole poem as a programmatic introduction to
the *Eclogue* book, see his p. 23.

[9] "Quibus dant domini ut pascant." In 1. 17. 7 he mentions this privilege as one
especially necessary for foremen. All the same, as Kevin White, *Roman Farming*
(Ithaca, N.Y., 1970), p. 351, has indicated, there is no suggestion that the
peculium was, in such instances, intended for the purchase of freedom.

in credible terms. Surely he could not afford to buy the farm, yet he speaks with a proprietor's voice. He could, of course, be a bailiff, still working for his old master; in that case his life would include little *otium*. Perhaps we should think of him as a tenant farmer, although the role is not usual for a freedman.[10] Quite deliberately Vergil seems to tease the reader with this question, thus making it plain that the position of Tityrus is one more suited to poetry than to life.

The journey to Rome does have a practical explanation, even if most slaves obtained their freedom by a shorter trip to the nearest municipium.[11] Tityrus has sought *manumissio censu:* a grant of freedom by the censor that could only be given at four-year intervals in Rome. By this method, the master ordered his slave to present himself to the censor to be enrolled on the citizen lists. This was, by all accounts, the most honorific form of manumission, since it carried an immediate grant of citizenship in addition to freedom.[12] The design of the poem requires

[10] White (pp. 350–360) gives a grim picture of the life of the free laborer; it was far worse, by all accounts, than that of the farm slave. There was little likelihood, he suggests, that manumitted slaves would remain on the farm. On tenancies see W. E. Heitland, *Agricola: A Study of Agriculture and Rustic Life in the Greco-Roman World from Point of View of Labor* (Cambridge, 1921), pp. 195–196.

[11] On forms of manumission see Susan Treggiari, *Roman Freedmen During the Late Republic* (Oxford, 1969), pp. 20–31.

[12] On the importance of this form of manumission see David Daube, "Two Early Patterns of Manumission," *JRS* 36(1946):58–60: "In manumission *censu*, the master's *iussum* was addressed to the slave, a direction to present himself before the censor. It formed no part of the legally relevant transaction; that was the affair of the censor alone. All that the master could do—and it was a great deal since the censor would not normally act otherwise—was to allow his slave to apply for incorporation. *Iussum* or *voluntas* in the texts concerning manumission *censu* designates not a declaration conferring liberty, but 'consent,' authorization, that is, to take the necessary steps to obtain admission to the community of citizens, to get registered at the census."

Technically, Tityrus might not yet be free, although he certainly believes that he is. According to Cic. *De Or.* 1. 183, there was some question as to the exact moment when a slave manumitted by *census* could call himself *liber:* at the time of enrollment, or only after the completion of the lustrum. Vergil has not chosen the most probable course of action for the late Republic, when local manumissions were much more common than those by census (Treggiari, pp. 25–27). But, although the census was never completed by a lustrum during the years 70–29 B.C., and thus there was technically no census, still censors were elected and entered upon office in 65, 61(?), 55, 50 and 42. T. R. S. Broughton, *The Magistrates of the Roman Republic*, vol. II (New York, 1952), gives the

that Tityrus should have visited Rome; but it is equally important that he should be able to consider himself a genuine
citizen of the Roman world.

Tityrus explains the cause of his journey in a single word:
Libertas. The word means both freedom and citizenship, but a
third meaning may be associated with the journey to Rome.
According to Servius, *Libertas* was the name by which Varro
called Juno Feronia, in whose temple freedmen received the
pilleus.[13] Her sanctuary at Tarracina contained a stone seat
inscribed with the verse: "Bene meriti servi sedeant, surgant
liberi" (Let well-deserving slaves sit down; let them rise as
free men). If we understand the Libertas of Tityrus as the
freedmen's goddess, we can better understand his personifica-
tion of this word with the verb *respexit*. He speaks of the goddess
as one who has given him personal attention:

> Libertas, quae sera tamen respexit inertem,
> candidior postquam tondenti barba cadebat,
> respexit tamen et longo post tempora venit.   [1. 27–29]

(The goddess of freedom, who, however late she has had com-
passion for an idle man after his beard fell whiter from shaving,
still has had pity, and after much time has arrived.)

---

censors for 42 as C. Antonius M.f.M.n; P. Sulpicius, P.f.-n. Rufus. Since Vergil
implies that Meliboeus lost his farm in the autumn of 42, we may assume that
Tityrus had been counted earlier that year. The failure to complete the lustrum
would not yet be known, and would not in any case affect his going to Rome to
be enrolled.

[13] Servius, *Servii Grammatici qui feruntur in Vergilii Carmina Commentarii*, ed.
G. Thilo and H. Hagen, vol. II, *Aeneidos Librorum VI–XII Commentarii*, ed. G.
Thilo (Leipzig, 1884: repr. Hildesheim, 1961), 279–280 *ad Ae.* 8. 564: "Mother
Feronia is a Campanian nymph and also a goddess of freedmen in whose temple
they received the cap of liberty on their shaved heads." The accuracy of the
information is borne out by several inscriptions (see n. 39 below). Franz Altheim,
A History of Roman Religion, trans. Harold Mattingly (New York, n.d.), p. 256,
traces the ceremony of the stone seat to the Greek custom of obtaining freedom
by sitting close to an altar. There is, of course, no evidence that such a ceremony
was ever practiced at Rome, and it would not, in any case, have had legal
validity as a form of manumission. But C. Koch, *Der römische Juppiter* (Frankfurt,
1937), p. 83, makes the plausible suggestion that the ceremony was a symbolic
manumission parallel to the legal act and made the freedman a client of the god,
even as he was already a client of his former master. For parallels to the use of
"respexit" here, see the discussion of "respicere" in Plautus in J. A. Hanson,
"Plautus as a Source Book for Roman Religion," *TAPA* 90(1959):79.

Libertas is one of the *divi praesentis* (41) Tityrus has encountered at Rome. It is not necessary to think he has journeyed to Tarracina or participated in the ceremony of the stone seat. Feronia had a temple at Lucus Feroniae not far from the city, and a shrine in the Campus Martius.[14] In both places she received offerings from freed slaves. The slave who obtained emancipation at Rome might well have visited her temple to make a small dedication in token of the freedom granted by the censor. Thus his momentous journey would be distinguished by ceremonies: the legal and the symbolic granting of freedom receiving the slave into membership in the Roman world.

Equally important is the fact that Tityrus has not always been in a position to make the journey of freedom, that Libertas has recognized him only after a length of time. The word has still a fourth meaning, for Tityrus' social servitude was at one time coincident with an amorous servitude. While he loved the demanding mistress Galatea, he could save no money to buy his freedom. The name Galatea recalls Theocritus. In *Idyll* 11, she is an unattainable sea-nymph whom the Cyclops, in his fantasies, imagines to be deliberately eluding him and leading him on. Polyphemus promises her simple things: cheese, flowers, fawns, bearcubs. In this harmless courtship, says the poet, he was well off. Had he been a city man, he would have spent gold (*Idyll* 11. 80–81). For Tityrus, the playful coyness of the sea nymph has been translated into flirtatious greed. His Galatea is a true daughter of the modern world—mercenary, an obstacle to freedom. Under her influence, Tityrus was no ideal shepherd, but like the city man Theocritus mentions, he does spend gold, squandering the profits from the sale of his goats and cheese with no care for saving from his peculium (30–35).[15] The pastoral world is hardly innocent when the

---

[14] For the discovery of an altar to Feronia at Lucus Feroniae and three inscriptions confirming her importance as a cult goddess for freedman see "Capena and the Ager Capenas," *PBSR* 30(1962):192. Livy 22. 1. 18 records a collection of money for a gift to Feronia taken by Roman freedwomen in 217 B.C. For discussion of the shrine in the Campus Martius and the festival of Feronia, see Warde Fowler, *The Roman Festivals of the Period of the Republic* (London, 1899), pp. 252–254.

[15] Segal thinks Tityrus has come to scorn his old life and to look down on country activities as a result of the new sophistication acquired in the city: "For him the country is a place of work and hard earned savings . . . and frustrations"

shepherd must choose between the purchase of freedom and the purchase of love.

From the rustic standpoint of Meliboeus, the splendid journey itself breaks the order of the pastoral world:

> Mirabar quid maesta deos, Amarylli, vocares,
> cui pendere sua patereris in arbore poma;
> Tityrus hinc aberat. ipsae, te, Tityre, pinus,
> ipsi te fontes, ipsa haec arbusta vocabant.   [1. 36–39]

(I wondered, Amaryllis, why you so sadly called on the gods, and for whom you left your apples hanging neglected on the tree. Tityrus was away from here. The very pine trees were calling you, Tityrus. The fountains and the orchards were calling after you.)

The description of nature's sadness recalls the universal mourning for the death of Daphnis in Theocritus. Here, where a mere journey takes the place of death, the mourning seems disproportionate to the event, and even grotesque with reference to the figure of the aging slave. As in the opening lines, Meliboeus seems reproachful, suggesting that Tityrus has neglected the world that loves him. But the journey to purchase freedom unavailable in pastoral isolation is a token of insufficiency in the natural world. As Tityrus says, he had no choice. Only his laziness kept him from making the journey sooner.

Servius suggests that Tityrus' two mistresses, Galatea and Amaryllis, are to be identified with Mantua and Rome, an idea most critics may dismiss as wholly irrelevant.[16] Yet the comment shows an awareness of the import of the passage. Tityrus believes he has changed from one mode of life to another, from

---

(p. 241). But the phrase "ingratae urbi" should indicate that the provincial town had been scornful of the old slave. Servius, *Servii Grammatici qui feruntur in Vergilii Carmina Commentarii*, ed. G. Thilo and H. Hagen, vol. III, *Servii Grammatici qui feruntur in Vergilii Bucolica et Georgica Commentarii*, ed. G. Thilo (Leipzig, 1887; repr. Hildesheim, 1961), 10 *ad* v. 34, thinks that the rustics who came to sell their produce were probably exploited and derided in these towns. In the great city of Rome, Tityrus has found an attitude more sympathetic to the country life.

[16] Servius, III, 9 *ad* v. 29. This is largely because he reads the love for Amaryllis as an *amor libertatis* and wishes to identify *libertas* and Rome.

a lazy, restricted provincial existence in slavery to a new life of freedom, oriented toward Rome. The new life that can only be won by breaking old pastoral limitations now appears as the most prosperous mode of existence in the pastoral world. For Tityrus the journey has been an educational as well as a practical experience, altering his entire vision of the world. The sight of Rome has dazzled the old shepherd. He describes it as best he can, attempting to make its grandeur fit his rustic terminology:

> Urbem quam dicunt Romam, Meliboee, putavi
> stultus ego huic nostrae similem, quo saepe solemus
> pastores ovium teneros depellere fetus.
> sic canibus catulos similis, sic matribus haedos
> noram, sic parvis componere magna solebam.
> verum haec tantum alias inter caput extulit urbes
> quantum lenta solent inter viburna cupressi.   [1. 19–25]

(That city they call Rome, Meliboeus, I used to imagine, when I was still an ignorant fool, was a city just like our city here where we shepherds often went to get rid of the weak offspring of the flocks. I knew that puppies looked like dogs and kids like the mother goats; in this way I always compared great things with small. But truly she raises her head as high above other cities as the tall cypresses among the bending vines.)

The description is labored;[17] its homely images verge on the comic, for Tityrus can still define his old assumptions more clearly than his new discovery. Still in the process of assimilating impressions, he lacks terminology to explain unexpected grandeur. Rome is not a larger copy of provincial towns and does not easily fit the pattern of relationships that govern the bucolic scene.

In the old time of ignorance, the farmer had believed in a homogeneous world. His *catuli* and *haedi* with their mothers

---

[17] Servius, III, 7 *ad* v. 19, thinks that the answer may be simple and garrulous: "He makes use of rustic simplicity so that the speaker may not maintain a complete sequence of narrative, but by long, indirect routes comes down to the questions asked." Pöschl, pp. 35–36, agrees, remembering that Vergil himself would know a country man's awe upon his first sight of Rome. Segal pp. 241–242, finds the phrases stilted and rhetorical, a mark of pretentiousness: Tityrus has brought back from the city some of its complexity and artificiality.

suggest an easy, unquestioning dependence of the provincial world upon the city. Now experience forces him to reckon with differences and contrasts. The terms he chooses—*cupressi* for Rome; *viburna* for the towns—aim to express a sense of order and proportion in Rome's pre-eminent grandeur, but they do not carry the idea very far.[18] Although the simile creates an effective visual image, it remains static. Tityrus desires to understand the relationship of city and country within the great pattern of nature, but understanding does not come easily to a rustic such as he. This same bafflement and exaggerated wonder characterize his actions.

Tityrus wants the new perspectives gained through experience to play a part in his life. His farmland is no longer isolated but has a place in the great world. As a symbol of his altered position, he has established a ritual of animal sacrifices honoring the god who gave him his freedom and sent him back to the farm:

> hic illum vidi iuvenem, Meliboee, quotannis
> bis senos cui nostra dies altaria fumant.   [1. 42–43]

> (Here I saw him in youthful shape, Meliboeus, the one for whom my altars smoke twice times six days a year.)

Such lavish sacrifice is an extravagance for the farmer, suggesting that Tityrus has given an exaggerated significance to the details of his journey to Rome.[19]

Among the gods the Romans worshiped, only two received a monthly sacrifice on fixed days: the Capitoline Jupiter and

[18] Servius, III, 8 *ad* v. 72, identifies the comparison as one of a kind used by Aristotle and Cicero. Tityrus wants to show that Rome differs from other cities not only in size, but also in genus, "as earth differs from the sky." Thus Vergil has made him compare the smallest and largest kinds of trees. E. E. Byers, "*Eclogue* 7: A Theory of Poetry," *Acta Classica* 5(1963):40, attempts to discover thematic subtlety in the comparison: "Rome must grow tall and straight as the cypress does; it is in the nature of other cities to bend low as the *lenta viburna* does."

[19] Van Sickle, pp. 900–903, discusses the equivocal nature of the sacrifice from a pastoral point of view. Thus "readiness to sacrifice for the sake of peace and prosperity shows a proper humanitarian consideration that should and does take precedence over feeling for beasts." But: "As for the future the promise of sacrifice is ominous, as if any birth and new productivity in this poetry might be subject to the same harsh service."

126   Vergil's *Eclogues*

the Lar familiaris. A lamb (or sheep) is the public sacrifice to
Jupiter on the ides of each month; it is also a proper sacrifice
to the Lares on great occasions, although the usual offerings are
a wreath and a bit of meal.[20] Tityrus implies that the altar, or
altars, to his god already existed at home before he made his
journey, but he has changed his mode of worship upon his
return. As a slave, he would have worshiped the Lares of his
master; as a freedman, he is entitled to a *lararium* of his own.

As Viktor Pöschl has pointed out, the farmer adopts the young
god as his Genius, the spirit that protects the master of the
house.[21] Ordinarily, the Genius is taken into the company of
the Lar. Such adoptions were not uncommon among great
Roman families. The Genius of the Julian family was Veiovis,
a god of their ancestral Bovilla. The Scipios are said to have
adopted Jupiter as their personal protector, and Octavian, after
considering the Julian Veiovis, finally chose Apollo for himself.

Just as the great families worshiped their Genii, so Tityrus
honors his *deus* as the founder and protector of his little farmstead. He is uncertain of the identity of his *deus*, but the depth
of his awe and the extravagance of his sacrifice suggest that he
has confused his benefactor with Jupiter himself. Thus he has
substituted the grander offering, the public tribute to the
protector of the city, for the traditional handful of meal that
a farmer should give to his Lar.

Still the question remains whether Vergil intends us to consider the *deus* as a god or as a person who seems godlike to the
farmer. In his echo ("erit ille mihi semper deus" [7] – Always
he will be a god to me) of the Lucretian praise of Epicurus

[20] For Jupiter: Ov. *Fast.* 1. 56: "idibus alba Iovi grandior agna cadit"; also
1, 587–588. For the general sacrifice to the Lares: Cato *Agr.* 143. For the offer
of a lamb to the Lares: *Rudens* 1208; Propertius 4. 3. 61; Tibullus 1. 1. 22, 1. 3. 34.
[21] Wagenvoort, pp. 245–257, takes the *deus* as an epiphany of the Lar familiaris. Pöschl, p. 44, points out that the Lar does not always occupy the *lararium*
alone but in company with the Genius, and thinks that Tityrus has added the
Genius of his benefactor, Octavian, to the number of his household gods. But
Gagé, *Apollon Romain* (Paris, 1955), p. 558, cites paintings from Pompeii and
Delos to demonstrate that the major gods of the Roman pantheon could also
make their way into *lararia*. For discussion of Jupiter and the Scipios, see
J. Hubaux, *Les grandes mythes de Rome* (Paris 1945), pp. 76–88, and L. R. Taylor,
The Divinity of the Roman Emperor (Middletown, Conn., 1931), p. 31. For the altar
dedicated by the *gens Julia* to Veiovis at Bovillae see *CIL* 14. 2387.

("deus ille fuit" [5. 8] that man was a god), he seems to hint at the latter. I do not think that he means us to think that Tityrus has encountered Octavian himself. Although the details of the journey as Tityrus relates them are elliptical—and Vergil seems to have made them deliberately ambiguous—there is no reason why a slave in the course of a journey for manumission should encounter one of the chief men of the Roman world. Certainly we cannot assume that Tityrus has gone to petition Octavian for the safety of the farm. He seems not to understand the confiscations, and it is likely that his farm has been passed over either by accident or because of its poor land and small size. All the same, since Octavian does figure indirectly in the poem as the source of Meliboeus' catastrophe, it is not unlikely that Vergil should contrive Tityrus' story to remind the reader of him.

Tityrus quotes the directive given him by the young god:

> hic mihi responsum primus dedit ille petenti:
> 'pascite ut ante boves, pueri; summittite tauros.'   [1. 44–45]

(He was the first who gave an answer to my questioning: "Feed your cows as before, boys; bring in your bulls to breed.")

The freedman is to continue caring for his peculium and to think of increasing the herd.[22] The plural address *pueri* is somewhat illogical, if we follow the conventional assumption that immunity from confiscation is being granted to one fortunate man. Rather, the *responsum* should be taken as a stock formula, such an answer as might be given to many newly manumitted slaves asking about their future: where to go and what to do. In Plautus' *Menaechmi* is an analogous situation. The slave Messenio, thinking himself liberated, begs to remain with his master:

---

[22] Büchner, p. 165, suggests that the directive should be applied to pastoral poetry, for which it expresses both continuity and new creation. Fredricksmeyer, p. 216, prefers to think that more than one farmer has been saved. Putnam's discussion, pp. 43–45, is excellent, pointing to a strange irrelevance in the oracle, a discrepancy between the georgic tone of the command and Tityrus' present *otium*. At the least, the *deus* is imperceptive. After the great changes of perspective that result from his Roman journey, Tityrus will never be the same as before.

salve, mi patrone. 'quom tu liber es, Messenio,
gaudeo.' 'crede hercle vobis. sed patrone, te obsecro,
ne minus imperes mihi quam quom tuos servos fui.
apud ted habitabo et quando ibis, una tecum ibo domum.'

[1031–1034]

("Greetings to you, my patron." "I rejoice, Messenio because
you are free." "I believe you. But patron, I beseech you, command me no less than when I was your slave. I will live with
you, and when you go off, I will go home with you.")

Like Messenio, Tityrus gains his freedom in a strange city, far
from home. Even admiration of Rome does not tempt him to
remain in the city—as did many slaves released from the farms[23]
—but instead he is grateful for the advice that has sent him
home to find new enjoyment in the life he knew before. Thus
the *deus* is the figure who has inspired his personal decision concerning the use of his freedom.

Like Libertas, the *deus* is one of the *divi praesentis* whose assistance can only be obtained in Rome. If we can momentarily exclude the supposition that this young god must be Octavian, in
person, and look for him among the youthful-appearing gods
who had Roman temples, other possibilities should appear. The
most appropriate is the mysterious Veiovis, the aforementioned
patron of the Julian family, of whom the one thing we know for
certain is that his cult image represented him as a youthful god
of the Apollonian type.[24] Veiovis had a shrine on the Tiber
Island, and a Capitoline temple located, as Vitruvius says, "inter
duos lucos" (between two groves).[25] This location seems to co-

[23] White, p. 351.
[24] According to Pliny *H N* 16. 23, the image was a very old one made of cypress
wood. The cult image found at the site is of Luna marble and portrays a young
god with flowing locks leaning against a treetrunk. See A. M. Colini, "Aedes
Veiovis inter arcem et capitolium," *Bull. Com. Arch.* 70(1942):16–17. Extensive
bibliography is in A. S. Pease, *Ciceronis de Natura Deorum*, II (Cambridge, Mass.,
1958), 1136–1137, *s.v. Veiovi*. For a possible connection between Veiovis and the
beardless Jupiter Anxur, Feronia's fellow deity at Tarracina (Serv. II, 279–280
2d ed. *ad Ae.* 8. 564), see G. Wissowa, *Religion und Kultus der Römer*, (Munich
1912), pp. 236–238; Altheim, pp. 257–266; and Koch, pp. 82–84, who suggests
that Jupiter Anxur is also a patron of the asylum.
[25] Thus Ov. *Fast.* 3. 429; Vitr. 4. 8. 4; Gell. 5. 12. 5. Romulus' inauguration of
the asylum is mentioned by Livy, 1. 8. 6: the place, he says, is now "saeptus as-
cendentibus." An association of Veiovis with the clientship has been proposed

incide with that of the asylum of Romulus, also situated "inter duos lucos." Consequently, several scholars believe that he was the patron deity of the asylum, and Franz Altheim thinks that he was the protector of the freedman's clientship, although there is no definitive evidence for this point. Still another theory, proposed by Louise Holland, is that the heavy traveling cloak over the arm of the cult statue and the location of the two places of worship ("on the island where the salt road crosses the river, and on the hill which guarded its approaches") indicate that Veiovis was a patron of wayfarers.[26] In this role, he would first have presided over the asylum, although other functions may have been given him later. Either as protector of clientship, or as a patron of wayfarers, the god of the asylum is a likely divinity for Tityrus to have visited in his Roman journey, and one from whom he might well have sought a directive for his future life.

The identification of the god as Veiovis gives help with the troublesome question of the monthly sacrifice of a lamb. This sacrifice is not the proper one for Veiovis, who, according to Ovid, receives a goat on his feast day, twice yearly at the most, and certainly not twelve times. But Ovid designates Veiovis as a little Jupiter, and his temple as that of Jupiter "not great":

> vis ea si verbi est, cur non ego Veiovis aedem
> aedem non magni suspicer esse Jovis?   [*Fasti* 3. 447–448]

(If the force of the word [ve] is diminutive, why should I not believe that the temple of Veiovis is the temple of a not-great Jove.)

---

on the basis of Dionysius of Halicarnassus 2. 10. 3: and man who offended against the clientship was put to death as a sacrifice devoted to "Jupiter of the infernal regions." But although Gellius calls Veiovis an infernal Jupiter (with the prefix "ve" expressing negation), Ovid sees him as a benevolent protector. Koch, pp. 61–69, argues for the latter view, believing that, in contrast to the impersonal Capitoline Jupiter, Veiovis is an Italic Jupiter whose cult maintains the flavor of personal associations between man and god. See also R. Syme (review of Koch), *JRS* 29(1939):109.

[26] Louise Holland, *Janus and the Bridge*, American Academy in Rome, Papers and Monographs 21(Rome, 1961), pp. 183–189. Veiovis is "a god similar to the *Lares Viales*, who certainly were road gods, and also had chthonic connections and were worshipped in groves. . . . It is tempting to see in Veiovis a god 'qui vias et semitas commentus est' (*CIL* 7. 271), and even some connection with *veho* or *via* in his name."

Although Ovid's meaning is etymologically inaccurate, it represents an apparently widespread popular belief.[27] Tityrus is no scholar or antiquarian; he would hardly question such a belief. Thinking of his *deus* as a benevolent young Jupiter, he offers him the sacrifice fitting for the greater god. His enthusiasm for his new-found freedom makes all things possible.

Thus the journey of Tityrus represents the orderly legal process by which a slave becomes a citizen and seeks his place in the Roman world. Although a unique and remarkable experience for the farmer, it is a journey that must have been made many times. For just this reason, however, the story of Tityrus can slip easily from historical reality into pastoral symbolism. As an old slave who has found a new life of freedom and Roman citizenship, Tityrus is analogous to the *Eclogues*, a Roman renaissance of the bucolic mode. His former life of inertia with its wasted love for Galatea, and fruitless trips to country towns represents a dull bondage to convention, an isolation from reality that can be found in the literary history of pastoral itself. Yet the positive aspects of this emancipation must be qualified. In his naïve wonder, Tityrus gives exaggerated importance to the benevolence of the city and is contented with total dependence upon Rome, a place he cannot easily explain or understand. Ironically, this dependence limits his effectiveness as a spokesman for the new Vergilian pastoral. No sooner has he heralded the instauration of a bucolic order than the revelations of Meliboeus show the same order swept away.

Like Tityrus, Meliboeus is a figure typical of the Roman world. The confiscations of the year 42 B.C. were only one of a series that had troubled Italy and Italian agriculture from the time of

---

[27] Holland, p. 187, argues convincingly that Veiovis cannot be a little Jupiter since the prefix "ve" never means "small" save in connection with a word that means "big." But in the present case, vulgar error may count for more than etymological truth. Tityrus does not make the proper sacrifice of a goat to Veiovis (*Fast.* 3. 443; Gell. 5. 12. 11) and the lamb belongs to Jupiter; thus he may have his ritual procedures mixed.

The sacrifice of a lamb to Jupiter by a private person in token of his role as protector and giver of good fortune is documented by *Captivi* 860–863: "Order a jug of pure water got ready quickly for a ritual, and have a good fat lamb brought in so you may offer a sacrifice . . . to me, by Hercules, for I am now your supreme Jupiter." Here Ergasilus, the parasite who brings good news, jokingly says he has *become* Jupiter and this is what the *deus* has become for Tityrus.

Sulla. If Servius and Donatus had never mentioned a particular set of historical circumstances for this poem, scholars might never have felt so certain of the exact year and place to which it belongs. Even if Vergil's own experience of the confiscations may have prompted the poem, its significance should, I think, be seen in relationship to the general problems of the late Republic, rather than to those of a single year.

Although historians speak of the abusive character of Octavian's partitions—the near mutinous demands of the soldiers, the commander's inability to make payment for the land, the greed of the possessors—we must remember that the simple policy of land distribution was not a political or social evil. The legend that attributes the custom to Numa sees land grants idealistically as a contribution to the stability of civilization. As Livy presents them in the early books of his history, plebeian demands for land, although politically troublesome, have some claim to social justice. To Scipio Aemelianus, who first proposed a program of land distribution in the second century, and then to the Gracchi who made it their cause, the resettlement of small farmers on the *ager publicus* was an effort to lessen overcrowding and poverty in the city and restore Rome to her old status as the center of an agrarian world.[28]

In a study of the army and the land in the late Republic, P. A. Brunt has shown that the grants generals made to their soldiers partook of some of these aims. The greater part of the army came from the farms and had no other occupation to which to return at the end of military service. Under Sulla the practice of land distribution would seem to have taken an abusive turn, although the soldiers were perhaps as greatly exploited as the citizens.[29] It was the Sullan veterans who gave rise to hatred of

[28] App. *BCiv.* 5. 14 says that Octavian was aware of the injustice done to the Italians and of the detriment to his own position but was rendered helpless by the demands of soldiers whose five-year term of recruitment was nearing its end; see also Dio Cass. 48. 6–8; Varro *Rust.* 1. 10. 2; Cic. *Rep.* 2. 16; 2. 26; D.H. 2. 7. 4.; 3. 1. 4; Plutarch *Publ.* 21. 10; Festus 476L; Pliny *H N* 18. 7; Livy *Ab Urbe Condita* 2. 41. 3–4.

[29] P. A. Brunt, "The Army and the Land in the Roman Revolution," *JRS* 59(1962):69–86, esp. p. 82 on the success of land distribution as a solution to agricultural problems. Brunt makes it clear that a large number of the veterans were always country men, versed in no skills but agriculture, who hoped to go home to a secure livelihood on lands of their own. See also App. *BCiv.* 2. 140.

the soldier colonist with legends of his greed and his stupid mismanagement of the land. Such prejudice is reflected in Meliboeus' castigation of the soldier as *barbarus* and *impius*, although the epithets are more indicative of Meliboeus' strong emotions than the character of the unknown *miles* himself.[30] In the turning out of the dedicated farmer, Meliboeus, we see the ironies of social justice gone awry, and of Rome's violation of that life that is her own ideal.

If Tityrus speaks for a new version of the pastoral founded upon the interdependence of country and city, Meliboeus defines the world that must be its substance. While Tityrus is talking of Rome and his journey, Meliboeus thinks of the animals and the land. For this reason, many readers have preferred him to the more optimistic Tityrus. The true appreciations of order in the farm and countryside are given to Meliboeus.

Unlike Tityrus, Meliboeus has always known freedom in the country. His earliest speeches — the descriptions of Tityrus beneath the beech tree and of nature's mourning for the absent herdsman — show a slight Theocritean coloring, almost a belief in a magical sympathy between nature and man. But these are backward glances, and Meliboeus, like Tityrus, is now a character in transition. Hardship and uncertainty are shaping him into a responsible herdsman who shares the pain of his animals as he makes his way through a hard world of nature. Thus he too is becoming a character of a type hitherto unknown in pastoral verse.

With this new vision of the realities of nature, Meliboeus shows us the appearance of Tityrus' farm. His descriptions do not exaggerate.[31] The farm is no lush paradise, but a small tract

---

[30] Servius, III, 16 *ad* v. 70, thinks that the soldier is "impius" either because of his seizure of the land or because he has been fighting in a civil war. He takes the phrase as implied criticism of Octavian: "Here Vergil strikes at Octavius Augustus; but he follows the truth, for as a soldier he offended against *pietas* by bearing arms and conquering others." App. *BCiv.* 5. 14 comments on the soldiers' avarice — their seizure of land portions larger than their allotments and of the best land. He mentions criticisms of Octavian by neighbors of the dispossessed who protested that this kind of colonization was worse than proscriptions.

[31] The description of the farm has two stages: vv. 46–48 show the land itself, and vv. 49–58 what the farmer has made of it. Thus Perret, p. 23 *ad* v. 27, comments: "The unpleasant landscape of vv. 45–47 transforms itself sharply into

amidst rocks and marshes. In his mention of Tityrus' isolation from the contagion of neighboring herds, he may refer ironically to the depopulated countryside around, but he sees in the farm the virtues of familiarity and a working harmony between nature and man. Practically speaking, the farm is efficient; a number of activities are combined within a small space. To Meliboeus this efficiency is manifested in an aesthetic order. Intermingled sounds blend separate activities into an harmonious whole. The leaf-cutter sings at his work;[32] the bees lull the herdsman to sleep; the birds respond to his care. Such harmony is the result of human organization of nature. The happiness of the farmer's life lies in making the best out of little.

As he speaks of the farm he has just left behind him, Meliboeus continues to think of the relationship between nature and man. His greatest regret is that he will not see the cycle of the seasons bring his work to fruition:

> impius haec tam culta novalia miles habebit,
> barbarus has segetes. en quo discordia civis
> produxit miseros: his nos consevimus agros!
> inscre nunc, Meliboee, piros, pone ordine vitis.   [1. 70–73]

(The disrespectful soldier will have these lands, newly plowed this year; the barbarian will have these seeded fields. See how discord makes citizens wretched. For these men have we sown our fields! Graft your pears, now, Meliboeus; tie up your vines in their rows.)

In this bitter recollection of the homely annual tasks of the farmer, Meliboeus reveals an emotional investment in the arts and tasks of agriculture. In the same spirit as Varro, he sees the farmer as a creator of order, tempering his humble duties with a sense of unity and design. It is this Roman concept of order that has been broken in the aftermath of civil war.

------

a paradise." Doubtless, as Pöschl has suggested (pp. 45–47), Vergil intends to recall the harvest scene of *Idyll* 7, but it is a mistake to consider the tone and extent of idealization in the two passages as precisely the same.

[32] The *frondator* is probably not, as generally thought, a pruner of the vineyard, but a worker cutting leaves to store for winter fodder. See Pliny 18. 34 and White, pp. 284, on problems of winter feeding. Thus his presence suggests the end of summer and the farmer's need to organize and provide for exigencies.

Pausing briefly to compare Vergil's two farmers with the herdsmen of Theocritus, we might first be struck by how much more we learn about them. The dialogue reveals a turning point in the life of each man. Each has a personal history that he brings into the poem; past and present are of equal importance to the image of the pastoral life. The Greek names of the farmers — the chief element of unreality in their portraits — show a debt to pastoral tradition, but the personal histories are Roman. Both the old slave who has bought freedom and the dispossessed citizen farmer are the product of Roman customs and institutions and could be found in no other region of the world. The meeting of Tityrus and Meliboeus is a symbolic meeting of regeneration and loss. In it we see a balance of forces that stands for the strengths and weaknesses of the Roman world, and also for the problems of the poet attempting to translate this world into new patterns of bucolic verse.

In Vergil's remolding of the pastoral from dream into reality, an inversion of the values of innocence and experience has occurred. In Theocritus, the happy rustic is the inexperienced rustic whose simplicity remains untouched by the great world. In the first *Eclogue,* pastoral felicity belongs to the experienced man who has recognized the deficiencies of his rustic isolation and whose life seems enriched by knowledge of the great world.

When the great world impinges upon the pastoral, innocence is no longer to be desired. Innocence has kept Meliboeus isolated until the shock of bitter experience drives him into the great world unprepared. Now the innocent rustic can only look backward, remembering a portent he had failed to heed and wishing he had foreseen his fate. Yet before the poem's conclusion, the positions of Tityrus and Meliboeus undergo further change. The problems of Meliboeus show that the experience of Tityrus has been one-sided for he has seen only the benevolent aspect of the great world. In the security of his freedom, Tityrus settles back into the easy complacency of a sentimental pastoralist, becoming, in some respects, the dreamer that he had first seemed to Meliboeus. Thus it is Meliboeus who has most to reveal of the relationship between the pastoral world and the great.

Tityrus believes that he has gained a vision of world order.

His devotion to the young god leads him to think of a world where all creatures, animal and human, live undisturbed in their own proper homes:

> Ante leves ergo pascentur in aethere cervi
> et freta destituent nudos in litore piscis,
> ante pererratis amborum finibus exsul
> aut Ararim Parthus bibet aut Germania Tigrim,
> quam nostro illius labatur pectore vultus.   [1. 59–63]

> (Not before the slight deer come to feed in the air, and the seas abandon the fishes, unprotected on the shore; not before the time when exiled peoples wander over each other's lands, when the Parthian drinks from the Rhone and the German from the Tigris, will his countenance slip away from my heart.)

If Tityrus thinks of his protector as Jupiter, the most powerful of the gods, this cosmic vision is easily understandable. In the security of his farm and his freedom, he can readily believe that the order of his own life typifies the order of the universe.

As Pöschl observes, this passage, so atypical of the pastoral, constitutes the climax of the *Eclogue*.[33] The boundaries of the limited rural scene open to reveal a prospect of Roman imperium, a view of the great world. But while Tityrus' speech shows an ideal similarity between the peaceful farm and its universal context, Meliboeus' answering speech shows the opposite:

> At nos hinc alii sitientis ibimus Afros,
> pars Scythiam et rapidum cretae veniemus Oaxen
> et penitus toto divisos orbe Britannos.   [1. 64–66]

> (But we others will go from here to thirsty Africa, and some will reach Scythia and the swift, chalk-white Oaxus and Britain, totally cut off from the rest of the world.)

Tityrus speaks the *adynaton* in enthusiasm and security, but for Meliboeus its images of discord are a prophecy of bitter truth. Ernst Fredricksmeyer has described very precisely the relationship between the two speeches: "A fate which Tityrus considers an *adynaton* as suffered by barbarians, Parthians and Germans,

---

[33] Pp. 63–64.

Rome's fiercest enemies [61–62], is about to come true for Roman citizens."[34] At the poem's point of widest focus, pastoral images have entirely dissolved into images of a nature harsh and strange: parching deserts, the chalky Oaxus, remote Britain. To these orderless places the exiles will bear their grief.

For Meliboeus, the world is an image of chaos that precludes all order he has ever known. It is a confusion of goings and comings: his arrival at the far corners of the earth, and the arrival of the soldier at his home. He cannot think of the soldier as a fellow Roman, but *barbarus* and *impius*, akin to the peoples in strange, hostile lands. In the figure of the soldier, Meliboeus sees the epitome of the world of experience.

The bitterness of Meliboeus' new discoveries now colors his reflections upon the pastoral life. In his period of innocence, he had embodied the ideals of agriculture: order and discipline. We see him now in the tension of a moment when the order that was second nature to him is at variance with the structure of human life. He labors under the first shock of innocence coming to experience: the feeling that no order is present anywhere in the world. As Meliboeus anticipates his exile and wanderings, order becomes something other than a lost ideal. It is the illusion with which human activity mocks itself. The farmer has seeded his land, grafted his trees, clipped his vines, yet produced no indissoluble bond between nature and himself. Although he is driven away, the coming of the soldier will not stop the harvest. The earth will not grow infertile, but will continue to bear for the soldier (70–71). This is what is hardest to endure.

This expression of disillusionment should be compared with that earlier passage where Meliboeus speaks of the groves, pine trees, and fountains that lamented the absence of Tityrus. Such a magical sympathy between nature and man is the ideal in which the farmer wishes to believe. Instead he must accept the knowledge of an impersonal nature, responding to one man as readily as to another. Her very reliability has turned to

[34] P. 213.

cruel irony. The processes of growth are oblivious to human justice. Thus nature comes to resemble history and seems to ally with history against man. As he entertains a last, vivid recollection of the green cavern, pastures, and rocky hillsides that he and his goats will not see again (75–78), Meliboeus relinquishes the last vestige of his identification with pastoral order: his songs ("carmina nulla canam" [77]). An impersonal, unsympathetic world gives no cause for singing. The poem supplies no solution for this dilemma. It ends on a note of ambiguous silence.

The invitation offered by Tityrus only contributes to this ambiguity. It is curiously tentative:

> Hic tamen hanc mecum poteras requiescere noctem
> fronde super viridi: sunt nobis mitia poma,
> castaneae molles et pressi copia lactis.   [1. 79–81]

> (Here, all the same, you would be able to rest for a night with me. I have mellowed apples, soft chestnuts, and a stock of cheese.)

Poteras suggests that the invitation is already too late. Meliboeus has already begun to urge his goats onward (74), he has already said farewell to his life in nature (75–78), when Tityrus offers the comforts of his farm. With a glance at the growing shadows of the mountains, he underlines the desirability of this refuge:

> et iam summa procul villarum culmina fumant
> maioresque cadunt altis de montibus umbrae.   [1. 82–83]

> (Now already the rooftops of distant farmhouses are smoking, and larger shadows fall from the high mountains.)

Pöschl has rightly seen a quality of hostility in these shadows and speaks of a contrast between the comfortable farmstead and the unfriendly world beyond the mountains.[35] But it is not just the great world that is unfriendly. The shadows fall

---

[35] Pp. 62–63. There is, he thinks, a contrast between the peacefulness of the evening and the hardships of Meliboeus. But H. Holtorf, *P. Vergilius Maro: Die grösseren Gedichte*, vol. I: *Einleitung, Bucolica* (Freiberg, 1959), p. 128, and Putnam, pp. 65–67, recognize the ominous gravity of the shadows.

over the valley where the farmers are talking, darkening that same world that looked so pleasant and inviting under the sun. The farmhouses and evening fires are a protection against the immediate environment as well as against the remote and unknown. For the wanderer who has already experienced hardship in this environment, nature is no less unkind or impersonal than history, and the coming darkness carries the threat of their combined forces.

The theme of loss that has characterized part of the dialogue is re-echoed by the might-have-been in Tityrus' invitation.[36] The casual, offhand tone of *poteras* is consonant with the fact that the consolations offered Meliboeus are material and temporary, lasting only one (*hanc*) night. Tityrus is not, as some have suggested, thoughtless and callous. He is powerless. He cannot reverse his fellow farmer's losses; he cannot restore the rightful owner to reap the harvest of the farm. Cheese and apples are poor substitutes for the *patria*. Above all, Tityrus cannot give back the lost vision of innocence that would restore the coloring of paradise to a dismal world.

Thus there is no true communication between the speakers; one represents pastoral freedom and the opportunity for creation — a poetic tradition renewed and ready to assume new forms; the other, that sound yet deeply emotional feeling for order that constitutes the Roman's vision of an ideal natural world. The two are driven apart; the rightful content slips away from the form, and the creation of the promised new Roman bucolic remains incomplete.

Lest this separation seem final and the poem imply total failure, Vergil has created a parallel in the lives of the farmers that they themselves are unable to see. Like Tityrus, whose wish for freedom was satisfied only after much time (*longo post tempore*), the exile longs for a return from his wanderings that can come only with the passage of time:

> en umquam patrios longo post tempore finis
> pauperis et tuguri congestum caespite culmen,
> post aliquot, mea regna, videns mirabor aristas?   [1. 67–69]

---

[36] Perret, p. 26: "mais il est trop tard."

(Shall I ever, after long time, stand in wonder before my father's lands and the roof of a poor man's hut, heaped with turf? Shall I wonder, seeing my own kingdom, after the ears of grain have dwindled to a few?)

The phrase *longo post tempore,* now repeated by Meliboeus, expresses man's perseverance in his quest for the right place in nature. Although a successful journey of experience has fulfilled this quest for Tityrus, it has left him with incomplete knowledge. Here his symbolic relationship to the new pastoral concludes, for he remains satisfied with a vision of order that is pertinent to himself alone. With Meliboeus there begins a new and more difficult journey into nature, but with the prospect of greater experience, and perhaps a more complete knowledge. The meeting of Tityrus and Meliboeus signifies the opening of a new relationship between nature and history, but it is a beginning only.

Tityrus' imperfect recognition of the *deus* is symptomatic of his limited comprehension of the new world he has encountered. From the beginning, the reader senses a strange importance in this figure so vaguely seen through the old shepherd's eyes. Veiovis, the protector of the asylum, is not a very important god, but the grateful enthusiasm of Tityrus has exaggerated his importance and almost made him into a pastoral god. This youthful figure with his somewhat imperceptive comment on the continuity of the pastoral life ("pascite ut ante boves" [45], is unlike any deity worshiped in the country before. He has nothing in common with Pan, the familiar protector of shepherds and carefree inventor of pastoral song whose noonday sleep must not be disturbed by shepherds' voices. He is a god from the city whose presence in the pastoral world needs justification.

"Erit ille mihi semper deus" (Always he will be a god to me [7]) is Tityrus' exclamation. As I have suggested, the reader cannot ignore the literary resonance of this phrase, which echoes Lucretius' expressions of reverence for Epicurus:[37]

---

[37] Pöschl, pp. 29–30, finds images of Epicurean tranquillity throughout the poem, but in his discussion of Tityrus' magnification of the *iuvenis* (pp. 16–19), he cites the transformation of men into godlike benefactors in Hellenistic cult and popular tradition. Karl Galinsky, "Vergil's Second *Eclogue:* Its Theme and

"deus ille fuit, deus, inclute Memmi" (That man was a god, a god, my famous Memmius [5. 8]); "quo magis hic merito nobis deus esse videtur" (Thus the more deservedly should he seem to us a god [5. 19]). There are many analogies between the forms of reverence felt by the sophisticated philosophical poet and the rustic farmer. To Lucretius, the godlike Epicurus is a liberator of the mind, as the god of Tityrus is a liberator of personal identity. Because of Epicurus, Lucretius achieves the knowledge of natural law that enables him to live at peace with the world. Because of his *deus*, Tityrus achieves *otium*. Both figures have an inspirational value for their worshipers. All of these analogies are based upon Tityrus' feelings, and the scholars who have noticed the Lucretian tone of the passage have taken it to indicate Vergil's favorable disposition toward the *deus*.

If we press the comparison further, we can discover other, less favorable analogies. The ideal Epicurus is a god who preaches withdrawal, the contemplation of frantic human activity from a safe intellectual distance. His attitude toward the political world is despairing. He offers salvation only to those who imitate him.[38] The gods that he himself worships are remote and impassive, incapable of concerning themselves with the order of the universe or with the affairs of men. Finally,

---

Relation to the *Eclogue* Book," *Classica et Mediaevalia* 26(1968):172–174, believes the *deus* is ideal and the poem an Epicurean triumph of song. H. J. Rose, *The Eclogues of Vergil* (Berkeley, 1942), pp. 66–67, thinks Vergil has used the Lucretian suggestions metaphorically to suggest (with qualifications) "that Octavian is a very remarkable man indeed." B. J. Farrington, "Vergil and Lucretius," *Acta Classica* 1(1958):46, contrasts the Epicurean philosopher with the godlike Platonic statesman whom Vergil would have known through Cicero: "The salvation of society would come when the philosopher was king, not when he led his followers into the garden. . . . This claim of divinity has been made for Octavius in *Eclogue* 1."

[38] Lydia Lenaghan, "Lucretius 1. 921–950," *TAPA* 98(1967):242–243, distinguishes between Epicurus and the Epicurean gods: "Unlike a true Epicurean god . . . he was extraordinarily moved by the unhappiness of man, who, despite nature's generousity in providing for most of his wants and the consequent availability of safety, persisted in being miserable." Although the *deus* in the poem is in a position to follow the lead of Epicurus and show pity, the plight of Meliboeus shows that he has not yet effectively done so.

Epicurus is only a mortal man, whom another, enthusiastic mortal has elevated to the rank of a god.

Although the youthful god whom Tityrus worships is not a mortal man, he is a god with whom a mortal man has chosen to identify himself. Before making his choice of Apollo as patron, Octavian, as some of his early coinage shows, had considered an alliance with Veiovis, the Latin Genius of the Julian family.[39] Although Tityrus has not seen and probably not heard of Octavian, he has taken for his patron the very god whom Octavian had chosen to present his ideal face to the world; and, furthermore, through his confusion of the *deus* with Jupiter, Tityrus has given him a significance far greater than that he conventionally possessed. Meliboeus also has not heard of Octavian, but, as we clearly know, Octavian is the man responsible for his loss.

Although the god who sponsors Tityrus' *otium* is Roman, the role that the old man gives him is one appropriate to the idyllic Theocritean world, a world that has been called Epicurean in its emphasis on withdrawal from the complexities of history and society. Tityrus' unquestioning faith in the perfect *deus* is bound up with his inaccurate confidence in a harmonious and orderly world.

As a historical figure, Octavian, the destroyer of Meliboeus, is mortal and far from ideal. The image of the benevolent *deus* is an image divorced from reality, a reality that Veiovis' mortal counterpart, Octavian, must face. Like the ideal and real images in the pastoral visions of the farmers, the ideal and the real aspects of the Roman leader need to be reconciled. Here, again, the poem offers no immediate solution for the problem it has posed.

The loss of the golden age has appeared in a historical and a

---

[39] *CIL* 14. 2387 (Dessau 2988): "Vediovei patrei genteiles Juliei/Vedi [ovei] aara leege Albana dicata." For a description of the archaic altar and discussion of Bovillae and its relationship to the Julian family, see A. Dobosi, "Bovillae, Storia e topographia," *L'Ephemeris Dacromana* 6(1935):240–367. For Octavian and the Veiovis type on coins see Harold Mattingly, "Vergil's Golden Age: Sixth *Aeneid* and Fourth *Eclogue*," *CR* 48(1934):162, and J. Liegle, "Die Münzprägung Octavians nach dem Siege von Actium und die Augusteische Kunst," *JDAI* 56(1941):94–95.

literary aspect. It has ceased to be a matter of legend and become a real event in men's lives. An awakening to the world of experience offers freedom from illusion and from man's static bondage to the past. Yet human nature is prone to illusions and persists in creating new visions of unreality to replace those outgrown. Despite his Roman images and Roman ideologies, Vergil has not yet released his pastoral from its Theocritean model.

CHAPTER 5

❧ The Frustrated Shepherds:
❧ Character Patterns in
❧ the Rustic Poems

A critic speaks of unsuccessful song in the *Eclogues* as song that awakens no echo in nature: "the song that falls lifeless." Thus, "song that is worthy the name is always that with power to influence nature, especially the power of awakening echoes."[1] The songs sung without skill are scattered to the winds and convince no one of their unity or of their kinship with nature. Such wasted song is attributed to Damoetas in *Eclogue* 3 by an insulting rival: "non tu in triviis, indocte, solebas/stridenti miserum stipula disperdere carmen?" (Haven't you been spending time at the crossroads, you ignorant singer, dismembering a wretched song on a squeaky reed-stalk? [3. 26–27]). In their singing contest, neither Damoetas nor his rival Menalcas gains the victory. Baffled by their asperity, their judge dismisses them with uneasy compliments. But not all the unsuccessful singers are so boorish, nor are their songs without charm. Many of the most fanciful, idyllic pictures of pastoral life are created

---

[1] Marie Desport, *L'incantation virgilienne: Essai sur les mythes du poète enchanteur et leur influence dans l'oeuvre de Virgile* (Bordeaux, 1952), p. 38. Mlle Desport thinks unsuccessful song rare in the *Eclogues*, believing that all pastoral singers have the power of musical enchantment, although to greater or lesser degrees. Her statements have recently been qualified by scholars who emphasize the negative elements and theme of failure inherent in the Orpheus myth. Thus Michael Putnam, *Virgil's Pastoral Art: Studies in the "Eclogues"* (Princeton, 1970), p. 13: "The poet may be forced to acknowledge in himself the tense union of reason and emotion which is his heritage from Orpheus." John Van Sickle, "Studies of Dialectical Methodology in the Virgilian Tradition," *MLN* 85(1970): 884–889, associates "Arcadian" poetry with rhetorical success or the power of influencing (men rather than nature) while the Orphic strain is bound to failure through passion.

by singers who either fail to convince an audience or fall short of the purpose for which they sing.[2]

The theme of unsuccessful song pervades the *Eclogues*. In the first poem a cessation of song marks the exile's departure for a life of wandering in inhospitable lands. But in the ninth, an unhappy shepherd pleads for silence within the pastoral world. Age, he says, has taken his memory for songs. He has, indeed, lost all faith in song, for he recalls how even the master poet Menalcas failed to preserve his homeland:

> sed carmina tantum
> nostra valent, Lycida, tela inter Martia quantum
> Chaonias dicunt aquila veniente columbas.   [9. 11–13]

(Amid the weapons of Mars, Lycidas, our songs have just so much force as people say of the doves of Chaonia when an eagle comes among them.)

The disillusionments depicted in these poems are extremes, but they frame a number of other, explicitly dramatized failures of song. In the second poem, Corydon loses faith in his singing. In the eighth and tenth, the songs themselves express defeat. In the third and seventh poems, braggart singers over-estimate their poetic skill, leaving their hearers unimpressed. With the exception of the fourth and sixth poems, whose chief speaker is the Eclogue Poet himself, only the fifth portrays genuinely successful song, and even here, hints of restlessness precede the songs. Finally, the Eclogue Poet expresses his own doubts concerning the efficacy of pastoral verse. It is clear that the unsuccessful singers and the reasons for their failure are a major issue in the interpretation of the *Eclogues*.

In considering Vergil's rustic characters, we should be mind-

---

[2] P. Maury, "Le secret de Virgile et l'architecture des Bucoliques," *Lettres d'humanite* 3(1944):77–79, points to failure in most of the love songs. The lovers are illustrations of psychological and emotional chaos. Both peace and order are wasted on them; their loves belong in an iron, not a golden, age. More recently, Charles Fantazzi, "Virgilian Pastoral and Roman Love Poetry," *AJPhil* 87(1966): 17–18, argues that the love songs are unsuccessful because expressions of passion become trivial in the face of bucolic nature. In the opinion of Karl Galinsky, "Vergil's Second *Eclogue*: Its Theme and Relation to the *Eclogue* Book," *Classica et Mediaevalia* 26(1968):188–189, *amor* is the enemy of *otium* and destroyer of the healing power of song.

ful that we are not dealing with such flexible, many-sided personalities as we find in narrative fiction,[3] but rather with individuals of set disposition whose idiosyncrasies designate them as symbolic types. What really happens in the *Eclogues* is not the development of character but the exploration of themes, a result of confessional monologues by or dramatic encounters between persons who do not change but merely reveal themselves more fully. Whatever circumstantial changes do appear to influence the characters, such as those in the lives of Tityrus and Meliboeus, have always taken place before the poems begin. Like Tityrus and Meliboeus, most of the herdsmen are capable of no more than one point of view.

Their ideas are fixed or move in circles, ending often at the point where they began. At the conclusion of his song, Corydon still suffers the noonday heat of passion. Damoetas and Menalcas extend their quarrel into their songs. Moeris insists on making progress toward the city with his burden, and Gallus turns away from Arcadia toward a hard world of love. Each character tends to reiterate rather than expand his thoughts, and repetition enforces the symbolic pattern. If we compare the several roles of Corydon, Damon, and Gallus, the rejected lovers; of Menalcas, Damoetas, and Thyrsis, who fail in contests; of Meliboeus and Moeris, the deprived and discouraged farmers, we find a pervasive network of thematic similarities that provides the basic principle of design for the *Eclogue* book.

The themes encountered in later poems are implicit within the first *Eclogue*. At the end of this introductory piece, pastoral poetry faces a pair of critical alternatives. Innocence has disappeared from the pastoral world. Nature has become insufficient to protect human freedom. The ideals represented by Tityrus and Meliboeus are conflicting. Is it better to withdraw, as Tityrus has done, into a state of bucolic unconcern and seek

[3] Recent criticism has emphasized interpretation of these characters, often positing dramatic changes in them during the course of their songs. Brooks Otis, *Virgil: A Study in Civilized Poetry* (Oxford, 1963), pp. 127–128, sums up this attitude: "Something decisive happens . . . even if the happening is chiefly subjective or psychological. . . . Emotion does not resolve about a single spot, but actually progresses towards a climax. . . . They are serious lovers or sufferers whom we can take seriously because we empathetically follow their feelings and participate in their tragedy."

for the personal satisfaction of *otium* within narrow confines, or should one preserve amidst chaos the life adapted to the cycles and realities of nature, carrying the lost ideal of order out into the greater world?[4] As creatures of history, Tityrus and Meliboeus have no choice in their destinies, but as the poems continue and the shadow of history is temporarily lifted, characters assume greater independence of action, and the contrast between the initial speakers hardens into a polarity of purpose. On the one hand is the dream of withdrawal: the creation of a self-pleasing imagined order within a world of recovered innocence; on the other, the search for a broader perspective that allows for reconciliation with the world of experience. The making of poetry is the means of approaching these ideals, but the theme—much broader than a poetic credo—is that of man's responses to the vicissitudes of his life. Different kinds of character and differing poetic structures distinguish the explorations of these contrasting ideals. The monologue poems—2, 8, and 10—are poems of withdrawal, poems that are, despite their charm, regressive, negative, dominated by the *locus amoenus:* the symbol of pastoral illusion. The dialogue poems—3, 5, 7, and 9—are dynamic, oriented toward the realities of nature and ultimately toward an interrelationship of the complementary orders of poetry and nature.

Eclogues 2, 8, and 10

Corydon's failure is apparent from the first lines of *Eclogue* 2. Vergil terms his words *incondita* ("ill-composed"), his purpose a *studium inane* ("meaningless desire"). *Inanis* is a word Cicero sometimes uses to denote unsuccessful verbal or intellectual effort.[5] Here it indicates not only Corydon's failure as a lover, but also his intellectual failure. Although his courtship song celebrates the pleasures of an ideal bucolic life, it is full of

---

[4] For a slightly different view of the conflicts and ambiguities at the conclusion of the poem, see Putnam, pp. 74–78.

[5] *Brut.* 8. 34; *Tusc.* 3. 18. 42; 5. 41. 119; *De Or.* 1. 6. 20: "nisi res est ab oratore percepta et cognita, inanem quandam habet elocutionem et paene puerilem."

logical contradictions and excessive self-aggrandizement.[6] At one moment the singer is master of a thousand flocks, wealthy in milk and cheese; at another, he is a humble goatherd in a little hut, driving his animals with a slender reed. He is renowned for his mastery of music, the owner of a much-envied pipe; he is the lover of country Amaryllis; and finally the companion of the nymphs.

Such inconsistencies in the song, such rapid turnings from homely rusticity to elegance and refinement, and at last to dreamlike fantasy, have led many to think Corydon a pathetic figure, crazed by passion.[7] Among many critics who have attempted to resolve the contradictions of this poem, only a few have acknowledged the dominant elements of comic frustration in Corydon. H. J. Rose finds him ludicrous, because he is pretentious and aspires to a grandeur beyond his reach, imitating in his courtship song the Polyphemus of Theocritus: "He is for a moment no longer poor Corydon, the slave herdsman, but the amorous giant, scorned, not by a brat from the city, but by Galatea the mermaid."[8] But it is impossible to assess verisimilitude in the portrait of a rustic whose song is interwoven with allusions to literature no herdsman could know. Even in adopting the convenience of discussing Corydon as a person, we must constantly remember that he is an abstraction or a theory character: a representation of the ideal of pastoral withdrawal.

There is no realistic basis for the boasts and promises of Corydon's song, which — as he must himself admit (56–59) — spring only from fantasy, altering the true face of nature to produce a kind of golden world.[9] Such songs do not suit the life of a country man, who, as the Eclogue Poet observes (69–73), should be passing his time in useful work. Still Corydon's song

[6] Bibliography and a more extensive discussion are in Eleanor Winsor Leach, "Nature and Art in Vergil's Second *Eclogue*," *AJPhil* 87(1966):441–442; also Jacques Perret, *Virgile: Les Bucoliques* (Paris, 1961), pp. 29ff.

[7] E.g., Georg Rohde, *De Eclogarum Vergilii, Forma et Indole* (Berlin, 1925), pp. 9–11; Otis, pp. 121–124; Galinsky, pp. 162–168.

[8] *The Eclogues of Vergil* (Berkeley, 1942), p. 34; also Fantazzi, pp. 171ff.

[9] Putnam's more sympathetic interpretation attributes the discrepancies to the speaker's conscious shifting from reality to unreality, pp. 92ff.

is a subtle composition. Its contradictions and obvious inappropriateness to the station of its singer constitute more than an
amusing play upon character. The shifting, illogical images,
the pretensions and incongruities are part of an experiment in
pastoral verse. In its praise of the rural life, it combines almost
every conceivable style of bucolic description. The love song is a
literary pastiche.

The lonely, despairing lover who wanders in midday heat is a
figure from an epigram of Meleager.[10] The rich master of the
flocks recalls Polyphemus of the *Idylls*. Corydon compares his
own beauty and musical accomplishments with those of Daphnis,
the ideal herdsman. A rustic quarrel about a shepherd's pipe
and a catalogue of simple love-gifts recall Theocritus' more
naturalistic imagery, while the flower-bearing nymphs are
reminiscent of Moschus and the later Alexandrian pastoral. The
garland of carefully culled flowers is commonplace in Greek
poetry and particularly associated with the highly artificial pastoral epigrams of Meleager. When the plants and flowers are
intertwined with fruit, the image resembles those graceful,
elegant garlands that often festoon a painted colonnade in
Roman mural decoration.[11] Other rustic details—the cook stir-
ring up salad and the homely shepherds' huts—have no apparent literary source but seem drawn from Italian country life.
Throughout this dazzling array of images, the reader is not so
much invited to identify specific literary echoes as to recognize
a highly contrived, synoptic reminiscence of Greek pastoral
poetry.

The artistic pretensions in the courtship song show them-

[10] *Anth. Pal.* 12. 127. Borrowings from the Greek anthology are discussed by
Jean Hubaux, *Le réalisme dans les Bucoliques de Virgile* (Paris, 1927), p. 19.

[11] Edwin Pfeiffer traces the history of the *topos* with charts to clarify Vergil's
innovations in *Virgils Bukolika: Untersuchungen zum Formproblem* (Stuttgart,
1933), pp. 60–62. Phyllis Williams Lehmann, *Roman Wall Paintings from Boscoreale in the Metropolitan Museum of Art* (Cambridge, Mass., 1953), pp. 9–11,
describes the decoration of the peristyle of the villa: "all the gifts of an abundant nature were woven together into multicolored festoons. . . . Quinces,
pears, grapes and pomegranates; apples, plums, nuts and lemons, oleanders
and lilies, poppies and sheaves of grain, pine cones and tendrils of ivy, all the
produce the benevolent gods might grant to an industrious household made up
the heavy swags." Such painted garlands, as Mrs. Lehmann explains, reflected
the practice of hanging real garlands between colonnades.

selves in Corydon's metaphors for poetry and poetic inspiration. In his midday wanderings, he sings in company with the cicadas:

> at mecum raucis, tua dum vestigia lustro,
> sole sub ardenti resonant arbusta cicadis.   [2. 12–13]

(In chorus with me, while I trace out your footsteps under a burning sun, the vine orchards resound with hoarse cicadas' voices.)

The shrill sound of the cicada is Callimachus' figurative description of his artful, highly polished style (*Aetia* 1. 29–30). The allusion anticipates further echoes of Alexandrian diction such as the terms in which Corydon speaks of his own imagination:

> heu heu, quid volui misero mihi? floribus Austrum
> perditus et liquidis immisi fontibus apros.   [2. 58–59]

(Alas, alas, what have I brought upon my unhappy self? Senselessly I have let the south wind loose among my flowers and the wild boars in my clear running fountains.)

Fountains and flowers are traditional Alexandrian metaphors for the sources and products of poetic inspiration.[12] In the *De Rerum Natura,* Lucretius makes them symbols of his aspirations toward sublimity: "I am pleased to come to untouched fountains, and to drink; I am pleased to cut new flowers and to seek for my head an outstanding crown from regions where the muses have never before found ornaments for the temples of a human poet" (1. 927–930). In his use of such images, Corydon betrays a hint of aesthetic self-congratulation, a confidence that his visions, however fragile, are at least sensitive and refined.

Yet Corydon's cicadas are hoarse, as if he did not quite understand the significance of the Alexandrian metaphor. His attempts at elegance are interspersed with lapses into homely rusticity.[13] The addition of nuts and plums turns the traditional flower garland into a kind of living-room decorator's piece. Such failures of image and tone give the song a comic never-

---

[12] See Lawall, *Theocritus' Coan Pastorals: A Poetry Book* (Cambridge, Mass., 1965), pp. 102–105.
[13] Perret suggests a lack of perspective: "He is a country man who has been foolish not to restrain his imagination" (p. 32).

never quality that is far more effective as parody than a straight-forward exaggeration of Alexandrian elegance and artificiality could be. The song is inappropriate to its singer because it serves Vergil's purpose rather than Corydon's; it is a *reductio ad absurdum* of the pastoral tradition that preceded the *Eclogue* book.

As a dreamer in quest of an elusive world of innocence, Corydon represents this tradition. Unlike Meliboeus, he does not see the image of such a world in another man's unapproachable felicity, but rather within his own imagination. Although he is a humorous version of the unsuccessful lover, Corydon is certainly to be distinguished from the Cyclops, in whom the comic element verges upon the grotesque. What is comic here is the more delicate situation of a character striving against impossibilities with a refined gesture of intellect. Although Corydon acknowledges his practical failure in foreseeing his inevitable rejection by Alexis his habits of thought do not change. The madness many critics have seen in him should not be ascribed to his dedication to passion but rather to his way of envisioning a world where passion might flourish.

In his moment of disillusionment, Corydon allows that he is only a rustic:

> rusticus es, Corydon; nec munera curat Alexis,
> nec, si muneribus certes, concedat Iollas.   [2. 56–57]

> (You are a country man, Corydon; and Alexis does not cherish your gifts; nor, should you wage a contest of gifts, would Iollas give in to you.)

This humility is not to be taken too seriously. Although Corydon speaks in apparent self-deprecation, his words show a self-consciousness like that which Cicero once deplored in the orator Lucius Cotta who cultivated a rural accent to identify himself with the high-minded ethic of old Rome.[14] *Rusticitas* is proof of innocence, and thus one of the desiderata of pastoral. Corydon looks affectionately at his own limitation, for it is no less than an

---

[14] *De Or.* 3. 42: "L. Cotta gaudere mihi videtur gravitate linguae sonoque vocis agresti et illud, quod loquitur priscum visum iri putat, si plane fuerit rusticanum."

indirect boast of superiority to the crass, mercenary Iollas who can outdo him in gifts. While attempting to lure a "city brat" to the country, Corydon shows pride in his freedom from the taint of a baser world.

He displays his pride most clearly in defending his rural identity against Alexis' supposedly urban point of view:

> quem fugis, a! demens? habitarunt di quoque silvas
> Dardaniusque Paris. Pallas quas condidit arces
> ipsa colat; nobis placeant ante omnia silvae.
> torva leaena lupum sequitur, lupus ipse capellam,
> florentem cytisum sequitur lasciva capella,
> te Corydon, o Alexi: trahit sua quemque voluptas. [2. 60–65]

(From whom are you fleeing, mad one? Gods also have lived in the forests and so did Dardanian Paris. Let Pallas cherish for herself those cities she founded; may the forests please us before all things. The fierce lioness pursues the wolf; and the wolf, the goat; the playful goat pursues the flowering clover and Corydon pursues you, o Alexis. His own kind of pleasure lures each one.)

This outburst of self-justification implies a traditional bucolic separation of city and country, for which Corydon finds sanction in myth. His mention of Dardanian Paris suggests that he sees himself as a kind of hero in bucolic disguise, but he fails to flatter himself by the comparison, for Paris was also a character whose pastoral breeding made him unfit for life in the larger world when inexperience gave excuse for folly in love.

By likening his pursuit of Alexis to the single-minded appetite of animals seeking their natural food, Corydon tries to show that his passion is an inevitable part of life amidst nature. The comparison is witty but sophistical, and debases the concept of natural simplicity. Love in the world that Corydon thinks of—the world of Trojan Paris—is an unmitigated *voluptas*, for which innocence provides only the thinnest excuse. Corydon's wooing is hardly on a higher plane than the despised Iollas'; his seductive pastoral vision is not truly the landscape seen by a country dweller, but rather the urban sophisticate's self-indulgent dream of paradise.

Still, the song of Corydon would not appear so futile were it not for its proximity to the sober, orderly farm world of *Eclogue* 1 and the Eclogue Poet's own picture of Corydon's home on the farm with its vineyard and hard-working plowman coming home from the fields. These disciplined images show that Corydon has spun his fancies at the expense of reality and point to another meaning for his *rusticitas.*

It is not his rural surroundings that make this unsuccessful lover *rusticus,* but rather a self-imposed limitation of perspective, a stubborn refusal to accept the realities of an experienced world. Corydon's limitations do not, like those of the farmers in *Eclogue* 1, derive from events beyond his knowledge or control. Unlike these persons, Corydon possesses a measure of pastoral self-determination but uses it in scorn of all things unsympathetic to his personal vision. As he sings of the superiority of the country with its homely huts and Pan-like singers, he betrays his awareness that the golden world is past while insisting that fantasy can rebuild it. His *rusticitas,* or limitation, is an aggrandizement of fantasy. The world Corydon cherishes and proffers to Alexis is no more than a projection of his own ideas, and to these he is bound.

The poem displays conflict between an aspiring poet and his limitations, between a free world of ungoverned imagination and the rational restrictions of nature. Alexis himself is relatively unimportant, a vague symbol of the great world that Corydon does not care to understand. Although he sees himself in competition with an insensitive society where true merits cannot be recognized and love follows gifts, Corydon is also proffering a gift—a gift of imagined innocence that has little value for the farm or the city. His pleasurable fancies are created in defiance of real nature. Not only are his innocence and pastoral idleness the opposite of rational, civilized life, but also they are incapable of development and growth. In the long run, he cannot convince even himself of the value of his offerings. Anticipating Alexis' scorn of the products of imagination, he admits that he cannot make the imaginary into reality.

But even in admitting his failure, Corydon refrains from serious criticism of himself. If the real world must defeat him, he rationalizes this defeat by turning nature itself into a symbol of insensitive restriction. The wild boars have invaded his fountains. He is *rusticus*, and has this accident, rather than any inherent flaw, to blame.

As a symbol of that search for innocence that men pursue both vainly and in misguided ways, Corydon introduces a pattern that is to assume major importance in the *Eclogues*. He is the type of the frustrated shepherd, a character who lets imagination obliterate reality, who imposes his own desires upon nature and is dissatisfied with nature's inability to meet his desires. For such characters, true nature seems harsh and brutal, full of boars to muddy the fountains and winds to blight the flowers.

The second poem parodies Alexandrian pastoral, and the eighth returns to this style. Both are love poems, and the fact that Vergil deals with pastoral love most extensively in these overtly traditional compositions indicates that he is less interested in the subject for its own sake than for its usefulness in establishing a particular perspective within the bucolic mode.

The unhappy lover—who should not be confused with the Damon who sings his song[15]—is another Corydon in his feelings of superiority to a harsh world that has injured him. He is not merely rejected, but actually deceived; he believes himself a victim of experience. The girl and the emotion that have misled him become *indignus amor* (unworthy love). His deception proves that the gods do not listen to human appeals. The marriage of his beloved Nysa and Mopsus may be called a violation of natural order;[16] yet a nature that permits such monstrous happenings is no longer a measure of order.

> Mopso Nysa datur: quid non speremus amantes?
> iungentur iam grypes equis, aevoque sequenti
> cum canibus timidi venient ad pocula dammae.   [8. 26–28]

---

[15] Putnam, p. 254, suggests that "Tityrus" of v. 55 should be taken as the singer's name and makes the interesting suggestion that the poem should be seen as "an inversion of an epithalamion in pastoral terms."

[16] Otis remarks on the lover's confusion between Nysa and his personal interpretation of the world: "In reality, it is not Nysa's character but the lover's world that has been turned upside down" (p. 107). There is nothing in the poem to indicate that Nysa has consciously deceived the lover or, indeed, that his relationship to her—save for the meeting in childhood—has ever been closer than romantic idealization of a woman seen at a distance. His belief that she might have been married to him is pure fantasy.

(Nysa is given to Mopsus: what may not lovers expect? Now griffins will be joined with horses, and, in the age after this, the timid deer will come to drink with the hounds.)

The lover's standards are easy to recognize: simplicity, rusticity, and protection from experience. His love for Nysa goes back to a remembered moment in childhood:

saepibus in nostris parvam te roscida mala
(dux ego vester eram) vidi cum matre legentem.
alter ab undecimo tum me iam acceperat annus,
iam fragilis poteram a terra contingere ramos.   [8. 37–40]

(Amidst our rows of trees, I saw you as a small girl with your mother, collecting apples wet with dew. [I was your guide.] Already I had reached the year that comes after eleven, and already I could touch the breakable branches from the ground.)

The orchard is enclosed and fertile, a rustic paradise. The boy who bends the branches to offer the fruit is a giver of nature and love. Although the apples are a promise of amatory experience, he expects that such experience will always remain as innocent and undisturbing as in childhood. All that is hostile to his expectations and to the integrity of his memories must be wrong.

Unlike Corydon, who confesses rusticity only as a last resort, the lover is militantly rustic and militantly uncouth. Much more than Corydon, he resembles Polyphemus. To him, rugged, uncultivated looks denote honest innocence. When Nysa fails to agree, she betrays the shallow prejudice of a woman blind to hidden worth:

o digno coniuncta viro, dum despicis omnis,
dum tibi est odio mea fistula dumque capellae
hirsutumque supercilium promissaque barba.   [8. 32–34]

(O woman, joined to the man you deserve, while you look down on everything: while my shepherd's pipe is loathsome to you and my goats, my shaggy eyebrows, and my unkempt beard.)

Like Corydon, this lover cherishes his limitations and cannot forgive Nysa for not cherishing them too.

Experience for this goatherd is the world beyond the apple orchard that has turned the illusion of love into *malus error*. Since the lover has been constantly trusting and innocent, his failure must be laid to the passion that seized him in spite of himself. So love now seems alien and wild (42–45), the unjust teacher who showed Medea how to murder her sons:

> saevus Amor docuit natorum sanguine matrem
> commaculare manus; crudelis tu quoque, mater.
> crudelis mater magis, an puer improbus ille?
> improbus ille puer; crudelis tu quoque, mater.   [8. 47–50]

> (Savage love taught the mother to stain her hands with her children's blood; so you too were cruel, mother: was the mother more cruel or was Love the more wicked? Love was a wicked boy, but you, also, mother, were cruel.)

For *mater*—Medea—we may substitute Nysa.[17] The circular, repetitive thought betrays confusion. When the lover speaks of *Amor*, it is not clear whether he means Nysa's love for her husband, which is the source of her treachery, or his continuing love for Nysa. But like Medea's children he suffers from a marriage. He sees himself, like them, as the defenseless victim of experience, an experience that has left its accustomed sphere of tragedy to invade the pastoral world. By comparing his misfortunes with those of tragic figures, the lover begins to give a heroic coloring to his self-pity.[18]

This exaggeration is possible because the lover has already ceased to live in the real world. Unlike the second *Eclogue*, this poem has no farmyard, no stable image of real nature to counter

---

[17] Karl Büchner, *P. Vergilius Maro: Der Dichter der Römer* (Stuttgart, 1961), p. 210, thinks that the lover mistakenly regards Nysa as a *coniunx:* thus for him she would be parallel to Jason. The jingly confusion of the expression betrays the speaker's confused state of mind. F. Klingner, *Virgil: Bucolica, Georgica, Aeneis* (Zurich, 1967), p. 141, takes the theme of *Mutter und Kindermord* as a perversion of world order anticipating the *adynaton* of vv. 52–56.

[18] Rohde, p. 22, remarks that the lover has forgotten he is a shepherd and speaks with the dignity appropriate to a figure in the *Aeneid*. Otis, p. 109, characterizes the song as "intense tragedy." Klingner, pp. 135–139, thinks Vergil has added both epic and tragic notes not in Theocritus.

the ramblings of fantasy. Instead, the lover forms a world out of projected self-pity, dreaming of a mythical Arcadia where love blends into the landscape:[19]

> Maenalus argutumque nemus pinusque loquentis
> semper habet, semper pastorum ille audit amores
> Panaque, qui primus calamos non passus inertis.   [8. 22–24]

> (Maenalus has always his shrill-sounding groves and his speaking pine trees; and always he hears the love songs of the shepherds, and he hears Pan who first could not let the reeds lie idle.)

Into this imaginary world the lover has withdrawn to contemplate his undeserved failure and cast invidious accusations at the real world. Only before a sympathetic audience can he preserve his vision of the apple orchard, holding the fictionalized beauty of a lost past against the injustice of a cruel present.

At the moment dramatized by this song, even the vision of lost beauty is about to disappear. To be rid of love, he must be rid of himself, love's victim. The only further retreat from experience is the final retreat of death. Death is the only means to recapture lost innocence, the only possible compromise with nature. Even the lover's memories of the innocent world have become agents of cruel deception. Nysa's marriage has revealed that a static and unrenewable image of the ideal cannot always produce illusions to shield the lover from experience. In destroying himself, he will therefore destroy his enemy, the deceptive memory of the past. As he casts off the identity that experience has tainted, the lover will triumph over all that is hostile to his illusions of a complete and perfect self.

Like Corydon, the lover uses his rustic innocence to excuse the failure of his private imaginative world, but he exceeds Corydon in his dedication to that beauty he considers too great for the insensitive world of experience to value. When other fictions have failed him, he creates one last supreme fiction: his death will rectify the abuses and imperfections of nature. His helpless innocence has elicited nature's cruelty; by removing

---

[19] Fantazzi, p. 180, and Perret, p. 88, regard the Arcadian pretensions of the song as a failure, believing that Arcadia should be a country of happy love. But Galinsky, p. 179, suggests that the key to Vergil's meaning lies in the fact that Pan himself was overcome with love for Syrinx.

nature's victim, he will banish disorder from the world. The *extremum munus* (final service, 60) he has to offer is not simply his song—as critics have thought—but his magnanimous death that must either transform all nature into a golden age, or else precipitate universal destruction:[20]

> nunc et ovis ultro fugiat lupus, aurea durae
> mala ferant quercus, narcisso floreat alnus,
> pinguia corticibus sudent electra myricae,
> certant et cycnis ululae, sit Tityrus Orpheus,
> Orpheus in silvis, inter delphinas Arion.
> omnia vel medium fiat mare. vivite silvae:
> praeceps aërii specula de montis in undas
> deferar; extremum hoc munus morientis habeto.   [8. 52–60]

(Now let the wolf run far from the sheep, the hard oaks bear golden apples, and the alder blossom with narcissus; let the tamarisks sweat rich drops of amber from their barks; let screech owls contend with swans and Tityrus become an Orpheus—an Orpheus among the forests and an Arion among the dolphins—or else let all things become deep sea. Farewell and prosper, forest world. Headlong I will go, down into the waves from the brow of an airy cliff. Accept the last offering of a dying man, forest world.)

The heroic death of Daphnis and the threatened suicide of the comic lover in *Idyll* 3 are the precedents here; yet the dramatic plunge into the sea recalls the legend of the Leucadian lovers' leap that Menander associates with Sappho.[21] Tradition says

---

[20] Otis, p. 107, misses the point here in saying that the lover bids the world turn topsy-turvy since he is dying. To him the world is already topsy-turvy, and he bids it set itself right upon his death. Rohde, p. 42, and Klingner, p. 141, comment on the golden-age coloring of the images, but Fantazzi, p. 181, considers them a caricature of the golden age.

"Omnia vel medium fiat mare"—which Otis, p. 117, takes as a part of the *adynaton* ("he sees the Arcadian woods merging into the sea, i.e., his own death") —is, I think, another comic touch. We should assume that the lover has wrongly interpreted *Idyll* 1. 134: πάντα δ' ἔναλλα γένοιτο. For the ἔναλλα ("changed"), the lover substitutes ἐνάλια ("sea"), thus his last words envisage a cataclysm that is entirely unwarranted. See John Conington, ed., *P. Vergili Maronis Opera: The Works of Vergil*, I (London, 1898), 99; Klingner, p. 142.

[21] A. S. F. Gow, *The Idylls of Theocritus*, II (Cambridge, 1952), 30–31, and R. M. Ogilvie, "The Song of Thyrsis," *JHS* 82(1962):109, take the ἔβα ῥόον of *Idyll* 1. 140 to refer to a real stream and death by drowning, while Lawall, pp. 25–26,

that this plunge will cure, not kill, a lover. If such is the case, then his tragic vision is converted to comedy, and his golden age is prophetic of the miraculous restoration of his innocent world. Even death would at last become mere illusion. But the gesture exceeds the norms of pastoral, and the lover's expectations remain unclear. Only by jeopardizing his abused life for the sake of order and beauty can he live up to his illusions of heroic innocence.

Comparison of *Eclogues* 2 and 8 shows an intensification of the conflict between reality and illusion. In Corydon's song, an obvious discrepancy between nature and the imaginary *locus amoenus* amuses the reader and embarrasses the singer himself; but in the lover's song, illusion has obliterated reality, and this is the ultimate danger when the ideal of innocence is taken too seriously. At this point, nature loses all restorative potential through alliance with the chaos of human experience. No objective standards measure the lover's vision of nature; his only measure is himself. Where Corydon is able to divorce himself from his fictions, the lover has no identity outside the insubstantial fantasies he has created and his fictions provide the cause of his self-destruction. Death or complete transformation are the only alternatives for a singer whose improbable existence is wholly compounded of illusions.

Eclogue 10 is designed to make the conflicts of illusion and reality clearer through one final recurrence of the figure of the frustrated shepherd. The protagonist in this poem is a person much closer to the reader, a man from the historical world. In creating his fictional rustic lovers, Vergil has not hesitated to

---

prefers Acheron, the river of Hades. Ogilvie also finds reminiscences (1. 77, 7. 74) of the version of the story that made Daphnis fall to his death from a cliff (Σ Theoc. 8. 93 [K]). All the same, the death of Daphnis is quiet and undramatic. In contrast, the proposed death of the goatherd in the *Komos* 25–26 seems to be a comic allusion to Daphnis' fall from a cliff, and this is what the lover imitates. Servius, *Servii Grammatici qui feruntur in Vergilii Carmina Commentarii*, ed. G. Thilo and H. Hagen, vol. III, *Servii Grammatici qui feruntur in Vergilii Bucolica et Georgica Commentarii*, ed. G. Thilo (Leipzig, 1887: repr., Hildesheim, 1961), p. 102 *ad* v. 59, links the lover's suicidal plunge with the Leucadian leap, a traditional recourse for those wishing to gain affection from a scornful beloved. At times the idea is comic: the object not to die, but to be cured. See L. C. Palmer, *Ovidii Heroides cum Planudis Metaphrasis* (Oxford, 1873), pp. 433–435.

take poetic liberties. Their songs are literary set pieces that far exceed the limits of a convincing rustic decorum and link these impractical dreamers with the pastoral tradition. But the fictional basis of the tenth poem is less unrealistic, for the singer is a Roman poet, conceivably familiar with the pastoral tradition.

The last of the seekers after innocence, the elegiac poet Gallus is a man of sophistication and worldly experience; yet he too demands of the pastoral an image of that simplicity lost in an allegedly unjust world.[22] Like the unhappy lover, he withdraws to Arcadia, cherishing his sense of injured merit in a wild, cold landscape. Like Corydon, he attempts to refashion nature into a paradise of love. Gallus' claim to innocence is the wrong he has suffered. His passion is rewarded by infidelity; his military life keeps him in inglorious bondage, while another soldier defeats him in love. These wrongs are neither fictional nor illusory, but common dangers of the experienced world. Still, Gallus exaggerates their importance. As self-pity leads him to echo the complaints and fantasies of the awkward rustic lovers, Gallus, despite his sophistication, becomes a comic figure. He is, nonetheless, a better informed and more self-conscious dreamer than the rustics. When he speaks of his *locus amoenus,* he speaks with the knowledge that it is a world of escape.

Consequently, in the tenth poem, Vergil makes the pastoral withdrawal of Gallus a literary issue and uses literary terminology in defining a contrast between the elegiac and the bucolic

---

[22] To many the tenth *Eclogue* has seemed to constitute the triumphant climax of an idealized Arcadian vision. Bruno Snell, *The Discovery of the Mind: The Greek Origins of European Thought* (New York: Harper Torchbooks, 1960), pp. 295–299, and C. P. Segal, "*Tamen cantabitis Arcades*—Exile and Arcadia in *Eclogues One* and *Nine*," *Arion* 4(1965):260–266, understand the welcoming of a poet exiled from reality within the confines of a "gentle Arcadia" as Vergil's final affirmation of the value of poetry; also Klingner, p. 174. John Van Sickle, "The Unity of the *Eclogues:* Arcadian Forest/Theocritean Trees," *TAPA* 98(1967):501, sees this Arcadia as the climax of Vergil's transformation of Theocritus. But scholars thinking primarily of the discrepancy between bucolic and elegiac themes and styles comment on Gallus' lack of rapport with a pastoral landscape and pastoral characters: Maury, p. 104; Büchner, pp. 223–224; Perret, pp. 107–108; Otis, p. 141; Fantazzi, pp. 182–184; Galinsky, p. 188; Putnam, pp. 342–394: "Virgil can only accept the final antagonism that exists between "pastoral" (both as a poetic style and as a mode of life) and the realities of the Roman social and creative world around him."

poet. He announces that he will sing of the *sollicitos Galli amores* (Gallus' troubled thoughts of love [6]). *Amores* means not only the feelings of passion, but also love poems. Gallus speaks of carving his *amores* into woodland trees. The elegiac poetry of Gallus is the symbol of his sophistication, the definition of the role he plays in the historical world, and thus of the character he brings to the bucolic.

In this *Eclogue*, bucolic poetry no longer passes for a spontaneous emotional utterance but is acknowledged as a definite literary mode. Swept away by an enthusiasm for nature, Gallus considers changing himself into a bucolic poet.

> ibo et Chalcidico quae sunt mihi condita versu
> carmina pastoris Siculi modulabor avena.
> certum est in silvis inter spelaea ferarum
> malle pati tenerisque meos incidere amores
> arboribus: crescent illae, crescetis, amores.   [10. 50–54]

> (I will go revise all those poems I wrote in Chalcidicean verse, recasting them to the rhythms of a Sicilian shepherd's oaten straw. I am certain I would prefer to endure the life of the forest, among the caves of the wild beasts, and would prefer to cut my love songs into the bark of tender trees. The trees will grow, and you too, my passions, will increase.)

By this gesture the poet thinks to free himself from artificiality. While Euphorionic verses symbolize his civilized life, Sicilian song seems natural and spontaneous, the transformation of an old life into a new. By letting his *amores* grow with the trees, Gallus implies a desire to transcend the uncertainties of human emotion by an alliance with nature's stability and dynamic life. The fantasy is ludicrous, not only in its extravagant enthusiasm, but also in its flaunting of the discipline of literary art. He forgets that the *avena* is a fragile straw; that such an instrument can no more make a pastoral poet than growing trees can turn elegiac *amores* into pastoral verse. Such fantasies are far more artificial than the composition of Euphorionic verses; yet, superficial as they are, they are consistent with the demands Gallus makes of the pastoral as the vehicle for the transformation of a reality that cannot be changed.

These points have often been discussed by critics who think

that Gallus' inability to find satisfaction in the pastoral is attribut-
able to his natural commitment to urban poetry. The elegist
cannot genuinely conform to a pastoral point of view. Critics
have also suggested that Vergil intends a graphic demonstration
that the bucolic and elegiac genres do not easily mix. It might
follow that *Eclogue* 10 is a mockery of Gallus' attempts to compose elegiac poetry in the bucolic mode.

The kind of poems Gallus actually wrote is a matter of much
speculation here. Servius testifies that Vergil has incorporated
quotations from Gallus' own love poems into the structure of
the amorous complaint;[23] the verses so designated are not bucolic, however, but those in which the lover laments his bondage
to the service of Mars. Still, one is greatly tempted to regard
Vergil's picture of Gallus in Arcadia as a scene from his own
poems, to see him amidst a world of his own creation, with
Vergil as the critic of his interpretation of pastoral verse. The
evidence to confirm or contradict such speculation will never
be definitive, but it is not necessary to establish the historical
probability of this theory to see that it describes what Vergil
has done in this *Eclogue*. The poem need not be explained as a
commentary on the real works of Gallus, for it is sufficiently
important as a commentary on bucolic withdrawal and on the
Eclogues themselves.

To Gallus the pastoral world is a novel solution for the injustices of the actual world. Despite his poetic distinction, his
approach to pastoral is naïve. He treats its most conventional
patterns — the same patterns Vergil has already thoroughly ex-

---

[23] Servius, III, 124 *ad* v. 46: "Hi autem omnes versus Galli sunt, de ipsius
translati carminibus." The first question is how extensively this comment should
be applied to the speeches of Gallus in the poem. Franz Skutsch in *Aus Vergils
Frühzeit* (Leipzig, 1901) and *Gallus und Vergil* (Leipzig, 1906) proposes that the
poem is a catalogue of Gallus' elegiac-bucolic themes. Rose, p. 113, objects on
the grounds that no elegiac poet could write in the bucolic mode, save from a
city-dweller's point of view. E. Breguet, "Les Elégies de Gallus d'après la Xe
Bucolique de Virgile," *Rev. Et. Lat.* 26(1948):204. 214, insists that 42–49 are the
only verses properly elegiac and must be taken as the limit of the quotation.
Klingner, pp. 169–171, has reaffirmed Skutsch's position that the whole of
Gallus' monologue is a catalogue of the poet's elegiac themes, but Putnam,
pp. 366–383, has made the controversy seem somewhat academic with his
illumination of the interweaving of elegiac and bucolic words throughout the
monologue.

plored—as a unique personal discovery. His actions follow old literary formulas. Within the fictional structure of the *Eclogue*, Gallus becomes both an interpreter and a composer of pastoral. In so doing he sums up that ideal of pastoral withdrawal whose futility Vergil has already exposed. For this reason he exposes himself to comic scrutiny.

The elegiac poet approaches his new subject by a well-worn literary path. Echoes of the Alexandrian pastoral, present in the second and eighth poems, appear here with new vigor as Gallus throws his entire personality into the acting of a traditional role: the imitation of the dying Daphnis.[24]

> illum etiam lauri, etiam flevere myricae,
> pinifer illum etiam sola sub rupe iacentem
> Maenalus et gelidi fleverunt saxa Lycaei.
> stant et oves circum; nostri nec paenitet illas,
> nec te paeniteat pecoris, divine poeta:
> et formosus ovis ad flumina pavit Adonis.   [10. 13–18]

> (Truly the laurels wept for him, and even the tamarisks; even pine-bearing Maenalus wept for him as he lay beneath a lonely cliff, and the cold rocks of the Lycean river shed tears. The sheep stand around—they are not ashamed of us, and you, divine poet, should not be ashamed of the sheep; even the beauteous Adonis kept sheep by the river.)

Verses 13–15 are flowing and lyrical, but their rhythm halts abruptly with the monosyllabic *stant*. The mellifluous tone disappears and with it the image of nature's sympathy. The sheep display no emotion, but merely stand looking on. Only the unreasoning elements of nature are paying the traditional due of tears. Shepherd and elegiac poet are all the same to them.

With the poet's parenthetical *nostri nec paenitet illas*, the lyrical scene turns to burlesque. These words make it clear that Gallus is no Daphnis; his dramatic outburst of grief invites comparison with a character whose history is, ironically, far more complicated than his own. While Daphnis, who had be-

---

[24] The conventional nature of Vergil's use of the Daphnis legend here is pointed up by the fact that he has already, in *Eclogue* 5, created a strikingly original variation upon Theocritus; see, e.g., Maury, pp. 102–103; Otis, p. 141.

trayed his pastoral love in the world of experience, returned
to face death resolutely in his natural homeland, Gallus has
never been in Arcadia before.[25]

Gallus, says the poet, should not be ashamed of the sheep,
for the beautiful Adonis once led sheep to the river. But in
the first *Idyll*, Daphnis mentions Adonis with scorn: "Adonis,
too, is in his bloom; he herds his sheep, kills hares, and hunts
all manner of beasts" (109–110). Adonis is not, like Daphnis,
a shepherd dedicated to nature, but a shepherd made effemi-
nate by Venus, a mock-shepherd. The allusion points to Gallus'
awkwardness in the role in which Vergil has cast him. But it
is not only because he belongs to the great world that he is not a
convincing imitator of Daphnis. Where Daphnis was punished
by the nature he loved and wronged, Gallus creates his own self-
punishment. Unlike Daphnis, he is not giving up love, but in-
dulging it. His death is only a metaphor for erotic suffering.[26]

In the first *Idyll*, Daphnis is visited by shepherds and deities
who cannot understand why love has condemned him to death.
Here the gods and citizens of Arcadia come in procession, but
none can comprehend passion that provokes such excesses of
grief. All ask questions: " 'unde amor iste' rogant 'tibi?' "

---

[25] Interpretation of Gallus' woes as comic has not been extremely popular,
however; see H. Holtorf, *P. Vergilius Maro: Die grösseren Gedichte*, vol. I: *Einleitung, Bucolica* (Freiburg and Munich, 1959), pp. 241–242; Segal, p. 260;
Klingner, p. 167, also suggests that "Virgil beginnt mit einer unbeschwerten
Travestie."

As Gow, pp. 1–3, observes, the Daphnis legend is obscure and it is hard to
tell how closely Theocritus followed any given version. Thus Lawall, pp. 20ff.,
sees Daphnis as a chaste nature hero, the equivalent of Hippolytus, who chose
to die rather than yield to love. But the following authors argue for the Sicilian
version in which Daphnis, betrothed to a nymph, was seduced by a princess
and punished for his infidelity by death: Ogilvie, pp. 106–110; F. J. Williams,
"Theocritus *Idyll* 1. 81–91," *JHS* 89(1969):121–123; E. A. Schmidt, "Die Leiden
des verliebten Daphnis," *Hermes* 85(1968):539–552. Schmidt, pp. 551–552,
suggests that Vergil's "indignus amor"—a love unworthy because unreturned
—is Vergil's approximate translation of the δυσερώς ἔρως—forbidden love—
of Daphnis in the *Idyll*.

[26] Probus, in Servius, III, 348 *ad* v. 18, points out that Adonis is not traditionally a shepherd. This artificial role has been created for him by Alexandrian
pastoral, Bion's *Lament*, and Moschus 3. 69. Ogilvie, pp. 109–110, suggests that
Daphnis' death is not voluntary but must be attributed to some accident contrived by the nymphs.

(21). While Daphnis' death violates the familiar laws of love and nature, Gallus' sorrow is even more foreign to the natural world. Apollo reminds him that his case is hopeless:

> 'Galle, quid insanis?' inquit. 'tua cura Lycoris
> perque nives alium perque horrida castra secuta est.'
>
> [10. 22–23]

> ("Gallus, why are you raving?" says he; "your cherished Lycoris
> has gone after another; gone off through the snows and through
> war's bristling camps.")

Pan asks the question that the raving Corydon asked himself:

> 'ecquis erit modus?' inquit. 'Amor non talia curat,
> nec lacrimis crudelis Amor nec gramina rivis
> nec cytiso saturantur apes nec fronde capellae.'   [10. 28–30]

> ("Will there be no limit?" he says. "Love cares nothing for such
> grief; cruel Love no sooner has his fill of tears than the grass
> of running streams, the bees of clover or the goats of leaves.")

The phrase *Amor crudelis* recalls the unhappy lover's bitter accusations of love's savagery, but Pan attempts to explain, not to condemn. The ways of Love are those of a constantly hungry nature. He will never be appeased by human grief. In taking his sorrows to nature, Gallus has merely exposed their unnatural exaggeration. To all but himself, he is a comic figure.

But even if Gallus' self-indulgence is the opposite of Daphnis' resigned acceptance of death, the two are similar in their desire to play a heroic role. Adam Parry has said that the first *Idyll* places Daphnis amidst nature as the only remaining world where contemporary man can be a hero.[27] Such a world is what Gallus seeks: a new and sympathetic environment where all aspects of his personality—the lover, the soldier, and the poet—may find fortunes more in keeping with his sense of natural desert. The lover will find pastoral maidens to soothe his rejection; the poet will turn to pastoral song; the soldier will overcome passion's fury in the pursuit of wild beasts. Unhappy love has made Gallus see the real world as an inhibition of his

[27] "Landscape in Greek Poetry," *YClS* 15 (1957):11–12.

talents and energies. Yet the new world that reflects his desire is also a mirror of his disorder. Gallus is incapable of escaping from himself.

Unlike Daphnis, who taunts the gods that question him, Gallus does not defend himself against the criticisms of the Arcadians. Holding fast to his melancholy self-pity, he begs them to remember him permanently through song:

> tristis at ille 'tamen cantabitis, Arcades,' inquit
> 'montibus haec vestris; soli cantare periti
> Arcades. o mihi tum quam molliter ossa quiescant,
> vestra meos olim si fistula dicat amores!'   [10. 31–34]

> (But he spoke sadly: "No matter, Arcadians; you will sing of this to your mountains, you who alone are skilled in song. O, how peacefully my bones would rest if someday your pipe would rehearse my love songs.")

Karl Büchner has rightly seen in these verses the longing to achieve a secure heroic image ("The song of heroic love is always safer in the Arcadian-bucolic world, and this will be a greater consolation to him after death"),[28] but contrary to the general opinion, these words promise Gallus no sympathy from the Arcadian world. Quite aware of his status as an outsider, he wishes that he had been an Arcadian, imagining the pleasant life he might always have known. As his vision grows, it absorbs him more fully; the tense of his verbs changes from wistful pluperfect to imperfect, and the Arcadian woodlands become an enchanting *locus amoenus:*

> certe sive mihi Phyllis sive esset Amyntas
> seu quicumque furor (quid tum, si fuscus Amyntas?
> et nigrae violae sunt et vaccinia nigra),
> mecum inter salices lenta sub vite iaceret;
> serta mihi Phyllis legeret, cantaret Amyntas.   [10. 37–41]

---

[28] P. 224. He believes that the *amores* are Gallus' own poems, while Putnam, p. 361, suggests that the tradition of pastoral involves singing of another's love. Servius, III, 124, thinks Gallus is asking the Arcadians (i.e., Vergil) to compose a new song in his honor; thus Vergil claims to surpass Gallus even in the writing of love poetry: "et allegoricos ostendit Vergilius quantum ei praestat amorem eius canendo."

(Surely a Phyllis or an Amyntas would love me; which ever one my passion fancied [what matter if Amyntas is dark? the violets are dark and the deep-blue berries] would recline with me among the willows beneath the pliant vine. Phyllis would twine my garlands and Amyntas would sing.)

This vision resembles the imaginary paradise of Corydon.[29] For the lover weary of emotion, the sum of felicity is to be no more than a conventional rustic swain. Such painful subjects as faith and infidelity have no place in the willow bower of shifting fancies where Gallus may be as capricious as Lycoris is now. But here even Lycoris might rest contented with simple love:

hic gelidi fontes, hic mollia prata, Lycori,
hic nemus; hic ipso tecum consumerer aevo.   [10. 42–43]

(Here are cold fountains, here soft meadows, Lycoris, here a grove; here might I be wasted away for my very span of life with you.)

Once the name of Lycoris has brought reality into the dream world, the whole insubstantial structure vanishes, returning the dreamer abruptly to the hard present where he is a soldier in camp while Lycoris travels over cold mountains, far from the imaginary Arcadia as well as from her native land. Unlike Corydon, Gallus does not make his courtship the excuse for his fantasies but knows they are for his pleasure alone.

Thus his pastoral vision gives way to a second, of a very different kind. Dwelling no longer on the world that might have been, Gallus attempts to make himself a part of the Arcadian landscape. The tense of the verbs changes once more—from imperfect to future—as he begins to imagine a life of action, in keeping with the uncivilized Arcadian milieu.[30] His description rises to a heroic pitch as he throws himself into the excitement of the boar hunt:

[29] Thus the very conventional nature of the passage; the offhand references to Phyllis and Amyntas; the repetition of the dark-light *topos* that Corydon uses in 2. 15–18. For further comment see Klingner, p. 169; Galinsky, pp. 186–187; Putnam, pp. 364–365.

[30] "What he conceives of as an Arcadian simplicity . . . is a kind of hardy primitivism . . . which he hopes will serve as an antidote for his passion and a reintegration of himself" (Fantazzi, p. 184).

interea mixtis lustrabo Maenala Nymphis
aut acris venabor apros. non me ulla vetabunt
frigora Parthenios canibus circumdare saltus.
iam mihi per rupes videor lucosque sonantis
ire, libet Partho torquere Cydonia cornu
spicula — tamquam haec sit nostri medicina furoris.

[10. 55–60]

(Accompanied by the Nymphs, I will wander over Maenalus,
or else I will hunt the fierce boar. Freezing cold will never keep
me from surrounding the Parthenian marshes with dogs.
Already I see myself moving among the cliffs and through the
echoing groves; perchance hurling my Parthian spear tipped
with Cydonian horn — these pastimes may be like medicine to
my passion.)

The pursuit of the wild boar has its traditional symbolic value:
the struggle against erotic desires. This image can hardly be
separated from its mythological associations with Meleager and
Adonis; thus we may suspect that this wild hunt is not only a
symbolic substitute for erotic fulfillment, but also a courtship of
defeat.[31] Declaring that the rigors of nature — the *frigora* already
associated with Lycoris' infidelity — will not keep him back from
the chase, Gallus shows traces of the mad impulse toward self-
destruction that is so often the means of destroying a frustrated
love. In his search for a *medicina furoris*, he has come closer
to Daphnis, but is still far from the quiet resolve with which the
ideal shepherd hero turns toward death.

Once more the vision fails suddenly. Gallus finds that Arcadian nature can no longer amuse or distract him;

iam neque Hamadryades rursus nec carmina nobis
ipsa placent; ipsae rursus concedite silvae.   [10. 62–63]

(No longer do wood nymphs please me, nor even my own songs;
go away from my mind now, forests.)

In recognizing the failure of his imaginings, Gallus knows that
he, not nature, is to blame. He has sought consolation in Ar-

---

[31] Snell, p. 298, cites Euripides *Hippolytus* 215ff. For Hippolytus and Daphnis,
see Lawall, p. 19; and Büchner, p. 226, for hunting as a philosophical remedy
for love.

cadia only because this wild region reflected his self-pity and
grief. His visions were no more than a pastime; the comforts of
nature have wrought no change in him. At last, he admits to a
perpetual condition of disorder springing from the very nature
of love:

> non illum nostri possunt mutare labores,
> nec si frigoribus mediis Hebrumque bibamus
> Sithoniasque nives hiemis subeamus aquosae,
> nec si, cum moriens alta liber aret in ulmo,
> Aethiopum versemus ovis sub sidere Cancri.   [10. 64–68]

> (My energetic strivings cannot alter Love, not if I drink from the
> freezing waters of the Hebrus, enduring watery winters and
> Scythian snows; not if I drive a sheep flock under the sign of
> Ethiopian Cancer, where the dying bark grows brittle high on
> the elm.)

The snows and the desert, representing the realities of rejection and passion, define the extremes of the lover's experience
within the territory of his inner world. They are his true images
of nature. In these descriptions, Gallus repeats the wanderer's
complaint voiced by Meliboeus in *Eclogue* 1. More than ever,
wandering defines the human condition, but it is no longer the
act itself that condemns human life to chaos, but rather the
nature of the wanderer. Like Meliboeus, Gallus is a victim of
discord, but his suffering comes from internal rather than external strife. The soldier's most violent war is that of *Amor*, beside which the wars of Rome fade into insignificance: "omnia
vincit Amor: et nos cedamus Amori" (Love conquers everything; and I, too, may surrender to Love [69]). Disorder and
chaos are no longer bound to historical causes, places, and times.
Gallus takes his chaos with him, transcending place and time.

Although Gallus and Daphnis are opposite in their relationship to the pastoral, yet the soldier approximates in his final
gesture the steadfast character of the heroic shepherd. His
resolution to abandon pastoral consolations for the world of
experience and his commitment to the chaos of love are equal
to Daphnis' return to the world of his former innocence. A final
reminder of Daphnis echoes in Gallus' words of farewell to his

Arcadian refuge: *omnia vincit Amor*. It is the way of the modern hero to suffer an unending but noble defeat.

Even if Gallus possesses none of the qualities of pastoral poet or pastoral hero, it is not his innate deficiencies that ultimately cause his failure, but Vergil himself. If we were to consider Gallus' Arcadian visions as an independent poem, they would not seem so egregiously unsuccessful. Their interweaving of bucolic imagery and elegiac themes is hardly awkward; in fact it is graceful and charming. The presence of a sophisticated elegiac speaker with his momentary faith in the efficacy of pastoral retirement gives new life to conventional images.

Yet here, as in the second *Eclogue*, the placing of the *locus amoenus* within the more vital and dynamic context of Vergilian nature renders it fantastic and improbable, conventional and outworn. The Arcadian Gallus is a comic shadow of the figure whose real identity is only to be found in confrontation with his proper environment: the heroic world of love and war. Within the structure of the *Eclogue* book, Gallus' pastoral failure provides a final clarification of the futility of the dream of withdrawal.

In contrast with Tityrus' isolated and naïve contentment, the pastoral withdrawal of the unhappy lovers is plainly escapist. Turning toward nature as a refuge from experience, they are oblivious to those aspects of the pastoral image that link it with the great world. Perforce their dreams must reconstruct nature in accordance with an inner model, excluding all that is not conducive to self-gratification. While nature is dynamic, such dreams remain static, incapable of reconciliation with the exigencies of human life. Within the visionary *locus amoenus*, the Roman love of nature grows pale, losing that vital sense of human and environmental cooperation, that makes a real world compatible with an ideal. Instead of merging with reality, these dreams are pathetically shattered. The lovers lose faith in their ideals of innocence even as they have already lost faith in the experienced world. Such disappointments ought not to surprise the Roman reader whose ideology conditions him to uneasiness in natural isolation.

Yet the lovers are essential to the design of the *Eclogue* book, for they are the figures who most consistently remind us of the pastoral impulse wherein all poems of nature have their necessary beginning. Through the experience of broken illusions that leads to an inevitable rejection of the pastoral they warn us of the dangers of following this impulse to its extreme.

Eclogues 3, 5, 7, and 9

The dialogue poems are less restricted in subject than the monologues, and consequently less similar in organization and theme; yet, as a result of the shifting relationships between their speakers, they too may seem to follow a loosely consecutive pattern. Beginning, in the third poem, with invidious discord, the songs and conversations move toward a more sympathetic and harmonious form of communication in the ninth, where the speakers are united by common love of the pastoral world. Each poem is organized to emphasize contrasting points of view, embodied in the contrasting temperaments of its characters. While each contains one person who expresses the negative perspectives of rural isolation and lost innocence, his ideas are countered by those of another more confidently and optimistically reaching toward the world of experience. The rustic settings of the poems are a factor of their attention to the realities of nature. Thus while the lover's songs create a divorce between nature and poetic vision, the dialogues suggest reconciliation. From time to time they provide glimpses of an ideal correspondence between the order of poetic creation and the order that man establishes through his affectionate cultivation of the natural world.

In the third *Eclogue*, as in the second, is a character who self-consciously acknowledges rusticity while courting the approval of a personage belonging to the great world. "Pollio amat nostram, quamvis est rustica, Musam" (Pollio appreciates my muse, rustic though she may be [84]), sings Damoetas, and his rival Menalcas answers scornfully with a word on Pollio's *nova carmina* (modern poetry). But, unlike Corydon, Damoetas does not associate rusticity with isolation and failure; rather, it is his bid for recognition from the great world. While Corydon sings, half to himself, of a personal, imaginary world, Damoetas strives to dazzle his audience with a showy glamorization of the pastoral. Menalcas, his critic, is more homely and countrified, and his response to Damoetas' pretensions is sarcastic and derogatory. The form of the poem is Theocritean. The borrowings are easy to recognize.[32] A rustic quarrel leads to a song contest. The chief models are the most naturalistic of the *Idylls*, 4 and 5. But although Vergil has combined elements, even translated lines, from both poems, his composition differs greatly in theme and tone. While the Theocritean poems dramatize amatory quarrels, the hostility between Vergil's characters stems from poetic ambition.

Neither herdsman is the master of his flock. Menalcas tends the goats belonging to his father and stepmother, while Damoetas tends another man's sheep. Hired shepherds appear in the *Idylls*, and are sometimes suspected of being bad shepherds who neglect or abuse their charges,[33] either through other preoccupations, as Corydon neglected his vine trimming, or wantonly, as a kind of joke. Damoetas keeps the flock of Aegon, who has gone courting, and Menalcas accuses him of overmilking the sheep:

> hic alienus ovis custos bis mulget in hora,
> et sucus pecori et lac subducitur agnis.   [3. 5–6]

> (This stranger guardian milks the sheep twice an hour; the sweet liquid is filched from the flock, the milk from the mouths of the lambs.)

---

[32] Traditionally the poem has been considered as one of the earliest *Eclogues*, strongly reminiscent of Theocritus. For comparison with Theocritean sources see G. Jachmann, "Die dichterische Technik in Vergils Bukolika," *Neue Jahrbuch* 49(1922):101–112; Büchner, p. 170; Klingner, pp. 50–59. Jachmann found differences from Theocritus in the "Arcadian" or elevated quality of the songs, and Büchner, pp. 174–175, sees Vergil in the process of developing his own style as he idealizes his images of the countryside. Two recent studies have offered highly idealistic interpretations of the poem's symbolism and its relevance to the poetics of the *Eclogues*: Charles Segal, "Vergil's *caelatum opus:* An Interpretation of the Third *Eclogue*," *AJPhil.* 88(1967):280–283; Joseph Veremans, *Éléments symboliques dans la IIIᵉ Bucolique de Virgile: Essai d'interprétation* (Brussels, 1969).

[33] *Idyll* 4. 3–4. Vergil has exaggerated the Theocritean herdsman's accusation of milking the animals on the sly in the evening.

To Menalcas, Damoetas is an exploiter insensitive to the welfare of the flock.[34] Vergil's inflation of a comical Theocritean motif into a suggestion of outright abusiveness is typical of his new tone in this poem. Throughout their quarrel, the herdsmen hint darkly at violations of the order of nature, that result either from wanton destructiveness or from a seeking for material gain.

In answer to Menalcas' accusation of thievery, Damoetas mentions an unspeakable deed that took place before the eyes of the goats at a shrine of the nymphs. An act of sexual perversion such as that openly mentioned in *Idyll* 5. 8–9 seem implied, but the prurient secrecy of this allusion increases its sense of grossness. Menalcas accuses Damoetas of cutting the new shoots of a vineyard ("mala vitis incidere falce novellas" [11]), a criminal act according to laws of the Twelve Tables, and a perverse violation of nature's promise and growth. Damoetas, in turn, recalls how Menalcas broke the bow and reed pipes that Daphnis had given to Micon (12–15), pointing to his insidious jealousy of a younger rival's success. In reply, Menalcas returns to Damoetas' thievery, accusing him of lifting a goat (16–20). Damoetas retorts that the goat was rightly his; he had won it in a song contest, but the niggardly owner withheld the prize (21–24). Menalcas is derisive: Damoetas is an inept pretender to music, incapable of winning an honest prize (25–27).

Although the sharpness of these insults and accusations recalls Theocritus, the explicit bawdiness of the older poet is absent from their language. The peccadilloes, with the exception of the secret deed of verses 7–9, are mercenary rather than sexual. But the open ribaldry of Theocritus' quarrel scenes keeps them from unpleasantness. Here there is no bawdy humor to temper the attacks, but only an unmitigated asperity. The rivalry of Damoetas and Menalcas is one of jealousy and insidious meanness. Their world does not seem to be a free and generous countryside, but sordid and oppressive.

The parsimony of Damon who grudged a prize is equaled by the owners of Menalcas' flock. The father and stepmother —

---

[34] Büchner, p. 170, thinks Menalcas the more aggressive but is considering his role as leader in the quarrel rather than the deeds to which his rival refers.

another distortion of nature—who count over the goats twice a day complete the picture of material obsession. Under such circumstances, even the herdsmen's praises of their animals have an avaricious, calculating sound. When Damoetas stakes a heifer who gives milk twice daily and nurses twins, he demands to know what Menalcas will offer: "tu dic mecum quo pignore certes" (You say with what pledge you are rivaling me [31]). Although Menalcas has provoked the contest with his insult to Damoetas' music, the latter's opportunistic interest in prizes appears to equal his artistic pride.

The singers' attitudes toward the prize cups they offer are telling. Menalcas first stakes his cups to avoid putting up a valuable animal:

> verum, id quod multo tute ipse fatebere maius
> (insanire libet quoniam tibi), pocula ponam
> fagina, caelatum divini opus Alcimedontis.   [3. 35–37]

> (Indeed, I will stake something that you, yourself will confess far superior [since you please to be so foolish], these beechwood cups, the enchased work of heavenly Alcimedon.)

To compensate for his inability to match Damoetas' heifer, Menalcas praises the cups highly, yet gives little indication that he truly appreciates their symbolic value. Where the goatherd in Theocritus' first *Idyll* speaks with almost reverent admiration of the beauty of his carved bowl (τέρας κέ τυ θυμὸν ἀτύξαι [1. 56]), Menalcas' praises are rather commercial. He calls the cups an *opus caelatum* (a work of engraving or enchasing), but *caelatum* is properly used to describe the decoration of precious metals, not the humbler art of wood carving.[35] Perhaps the word should be seen as an appeal to Damoetas' mercenary tendencies; perhaps Menalcas is attempting to inflate the value of the cups. Otherwise the goatherd gives only a summary sketch of the cups' decoration and has even forgotten the name of one of the carved figures. Like Theocritus' goatherd, he

---

[35] Quintillian 2. 21. 9: When Ovid (*Met.* 8. 668–669) uses *caelatus* to describe an object made of baser materials ("caelatus eodem argenti crater") he is speaking ironically to show that Philemon and Baucis, the owners of the vessel, could not afford *opera caelata*.

swears that the cups have never touched his lips. But the goatherd has kept his unsullied (ἄχραντον [1. 60]), as if he reverenced a beauty too great for common use, while Menalcas has kept his cups hidden away (*sed condita servo* [43]) like a miser's gold.[36]

Damoetas thinks it a bad bargain to stake his heifer against the cups, for he also has two by the same maker.

> Et nobis idem Alcimedon duo pocula fecit
> et molli circum est ansas amplexus acantho,
> Orpheaque in medio posuit silvasque sequentis;
> necdum illis labra admovi, sed condita servo.
> si ad vitulam spectas, nihil est quod pocula laudes.   [3. 44–48]

(That very same Alcimedon made two cups for me, and around their handles twines the soft acanthus. In the middle he placed Orpheus with the woodlands coming after him. And not yet have I touched them to my lips, but I keep them buried away. If you look at my heifer, you will see that there is nothing to praise in the cups.)

The phrase *idem Alcimedon* suggests that the works of this artist are no great rarity.[37] In repeating Menalcas' words "necdum illis labra admovi, sed condita servo," Damoetas seems to mock the parsimony of his rival. Although he implies that his Orpheus cup is better than Menalcas' Conon, his final words show disappointment and scorn of such prizes. But his boasting gives Menalcas a chance to close the bargain and dismiss the heifer: "Numquam hodie effugies; veniam quocumque vocaris" (Today you shall not escape; I will respond

[36] Most critics believe that the descriptions of the cups are on a higher artistic plane than the surrounding dialogue; e.g., Perret, p. 39; Klingner, pp. 52–53. Segal, "Vergil's *caelatum opus*," pp. 285–292, makes them the focal point of the poem: a symbol of Vergilian pastoral and of the poem as a work of art. Veremans, pp. 53–61, gives them a mystical association with the consecration of a poet.

[37] Servius, III, 36 *ad* v. 44, finds scorn in Damoetas' tone: "And it is as if he had said: Do you think you are the only person who has [such] cups? For whom, indeed, has Alcimedon not made one? You don't touch yours out of esteem for their value, but I, because I think they are trashy." At the opposite extreme is Veremans, pp. 16–17, who suggests that Damoetas does not want to give up his cup because it is too precious.

howsoever you challenge me [49]).[38] When the singing is over, Palaemon, the judge, seems unaware that the cups had been offered and assumes the prize was a heifer ("et vitula tu dignus et hic"—both you and he deserve the heifer [109]). Or perhaps he considers both contenders unworthy of the cups.

In fact, the cups ought not to change hands, since the decoration of each is particularly suited to the personality of its owner. The figures on Menalcas' cup are related to the agricultural life. Menalcas shows a restrictive, somewhat depressive view of the country. He is cautious, and rather parsimonious. Taking a self-righteous pride in his humble perspectives, he regards Damoetas as a braggart, as well as an exploiter and violator of the integrity of nature. By contrast, Damoetas is confident and boastful, scornful of his rival's narrower view. The Orpheus cup, with its image of the master singer, is appropriate to his pretensions, for his stealing of the begrudged prize shows his aggressive determination to be in control of his world.

The personalities of both herdsmen are a debasement of the symbolic value of the cups, whose ideal implications are left to the reader. The carved figures represent the two interpretations of nature vital to the *Eclogues:* the agricultural and the poetic. The scientists provide systems and methods to guide man's work in nature, while the image of Orpheus leading the forests presents an analogous but loftier concept of order created through imaginative art. These orders are complementary and should not be at variance, but the quarreling herdsmen have made them a subject for discord. Appropriately, both believe that real animals are a more valuable prize. Indeed, the cups symbolize all that is lacking in these rustics whose conversation makes disorder its theme and takes no account of the beauty of the natural world.

Their insensitivity appears greater by contrast with Palaemon, the first speaker to describe nature with observant appreciation. To his mind the contest is in keeping with the atmosphere of a fertile spring:

---

[38] Servius, III, 36 *ad* v. 49: "You are looking for excuses not to contend; it's not because you think the cups are worthless."

Dicite, quandoquidem in molli consedimus herba.
et nunc omnis ager, nunc omnis parturit arbos,
nunc frondent silvae, nunc formosissimus ánnus.   [3.55–57]

(Speak out, since we have taken our places in the soft grass. Now every field, now each tree brings forth new life. Now the forests grow leafy, now is the most beautiful time of the year.)

At once we might see that Palaemon will never influence the inimical rivals or settle their quarrel. He is, as Gunther Jachmann has suggested, a rather sentimental rustic whose idealism makes him either deliberately or absent-mindedly oblivious to the hostility that has provoked the contest. Yet his brief description of springtime restores an absent perspective to the poem. Like the symbolic figures on the cups, it calls up a better world than that represented by the herdsmen and assures us that this real and living nature is the true, if neglected, subject of pastoral song.[39]

As Palaemon describes the amoebean dialogue, the form for the contest, he emphasizes its capacity for balance and harmony: "alternis dicetis; amant alterna Camenae" (You will sing by turns; the muses love alternating stanzas [59]). But the amoebean is also an opportunity for rivalry, and the singers choose to exploit it. Jachmann has rightly observed that the topical linking of the strophes does not appear natural and effortless, as in Theocritus, but artificial and strained. In fact, the singers do not attempt to complement one another or to embroider each other's themes. The song divides into three sections: love (60–84), poetry (84–91), and the pastoral life (91–103). As it continues, Damoetas and Menalcas become increasingly adept at using their pastoral descriptions as vehicles of bitter personal abuse.[40]

---

[39] Jachmann, p. 106. See Perret, p. 40; Segal, "Vergil's *caelatum opus*," pp. 293–294; John Van Sickle is less positive: "It is the season, if not yet the decisive moment for new art" (p. 499).

[40] On the amoebean form as a reflection of harmony between man and nature, see Desport, p. 39, Jachmann, pp. 103–105. The sectional divisions are Büchner's (p. 172). The first and third sections are further subdivided: 68–71, courtship and gifts; 72–75, vacillations of love; 76–79, bitter love; 80–83, love's deterioration; 92–95, danger; 96–99, daily life; 100–103, failure of animals to flourish. Segal, "Vergil's *caelatum opus*," p. 296, makes the divisions rather

Damoetas begins in a pretentious, self-conscious manner, with an echo of the *Phaenomena* of Aratus; a strange choice for the man who scorned the astronomical cup):[41]

> Ab Iove principium Musae: Iovis omnia plena;
> ille colit terras, illi mea carmina curae.   [3. 60–61]

> (In Jove is the source of the Muses. All things are full of Jove's power. He watches over the earth; my songs are his personal care.)

This identification with the chief of the gods is the *credo* of a self-styled master poet. Menalcas implicitly censures such boasting, choosing Phoebus as the more appropriate patron of his song. But Damoetas continues to speak as a connoisseur of pastoral living, slightly superior to the ordinary conventions of the pastoral world. He is sought by an enamoured Galatea (64–66), and her praises of him go up to the ears of the gods (72–73). His love gifts have a mythological cast; they are the *aëriae palumbes* (air-dwelling doves) of Venus. Menalcas' topics are comparatively understated. His love gifts are golden apples plucked from a tree; he speaks of animals and the hunt, and his descriptions of love are awkwardly ludicrous:

> At mihi sese offert ultro, meus ignis, Amyntas,
> notior ut iam sit canibus non Delia nostris.   [3. 66–67]

> (But my flame, Amyntas, puts himself so much in my way that already my dogs know him better than Delia, goddess of the hunt.)

While Amyntas has the role of the heroic hunter and pursues the boar, his lover stays behind keeping the nets (74–75).

The search for subjects culminates in references to the patronage and favor of Pollio, and here the singers' rivalry takes an explicitly unpleasant turn. Damoetas' boast that his

---

different to show an alternation of elevated and low themes that echoes the elevated and low discourse of the opening section: 60–63, traditional poetry; 64–83, shepherds' love; 84–91, modern poetry; 92–99, pastoral themes; 100–103, animal love.

[41] Servius, III, 37 *ad* v. 60.

rustic muse finds favor with Pollio is in keeping with his desire
to appear superior to the ordinary pastoral world.[42] Menalcas'
answer, "Pollio et ipse facit nova carmina" (And Pollio himself
composes modern songs [86]), is intended to discourage. The
sophisticated urban poet can hardly have real interest in a
rustic muse. Thus Menalcas continues with a mocking figurative
description of his ambitious rival "pascite taurum,/iam cornu
petat et pedibus qui spargat harenam" (Feed up this bull, that
he may straightway strike out with his horn and scatter the sand
with his hoofs [86–87]). Like the young bull already imitating
the actions of mature warrior bulls, the aggressive young poet
plans to invade the sophisticated literary world.

Ignoring the irony, Damoetas goes on with his flattery.
Association with Pollio is an entry into the golden age:

> Qui te, Pollio, amat, veniat quo te quoque gaudet;
> mella fluant illi, ferat et rubus asper amomum.   [3. 88–89]

> (Let the man who adores you, Pollio, come where he may also
> delight in you; let honey flow for this man, and let the sharp
> thorns bear incense.)

The phrase "veniat quo te quoque gaudet" is, I think, an overt
request for an invitation to meet Pollio. For this ambitious rustic
singer, the golden age is not to be found in the country. It
centers about Pollio in the urban world. In revealing his eagerness for this world, Damoetas betrays his impatience with the
limitations of pastoral, and belittles the very muse upon whom
he pins his hopes for attention and favor.

Still mocking Damoetas' pretensions, Menalcas makes a comment on poetic ineptitude:

> Qui Bavium non odit, amet tua carmina, Maevi,
> atque idem iungat vulpes et mulgeat hircos.   [3. 90–91]

---

[42] Others give a more positive interpretation to the herdsmen's attitude.
Putnam, pp. 129–130, suggests that Pollio is being given a place of honor equal
to that of Jupiter and Apollo. Veremans, pp. 26–29, links *nova carmina* and
aurea aetas as symbols of a "monde merveilleux" of poetry and love toward
which the singers' ambitions tend. It is a world above rusticity into which the
singers have not yet been initiated.

(Whoever doesn't hate Bavius, let him adore your songs, Maevius; and let that same man yoke foxes and milk the he-goats.)

Abuse of tasteless, incompetent poets is a part of the contemporary literary scene in which Damoetas aspires to have a place. In a mincing, mock-elegant style, Menalcas parodies the clichés of criticism. Bavius and Maevius are urban poetasters and Damoetas no better than their kind, those who make fools of themselves by attempting the impossible in ignorance of the realities of nature. The man who milks he-goats is an awkward city slicker in the country, but not unlike the country bumpkin in the sophisticated world. In Menalcas' eyes, the rustic poet is hardly improved by his aspirations toward worldly success.

From this point on the descriptions of the pastoral world become harsh and unpleasant.[43] There are warnings of danger for the unwary:

> D. Qui legitis flores et humi nascentia fraga,
>   frigidus, o pueri (fugite hinc!), latet anguis in herba.
> M. Parcite, oves, nimium procedere: non bene ripae
>   creditur; ipse aries etiam nunc vellera siccat.
> D. Tityre, pascentis a flumine reice capellas:
>   ipse, ubi tempus erit, omnis in fonte lavabo.
> M. Cogite ovis, pueri: si lac praeceperit aestus,
>   ut nuper, frustra pressabimus ubera palmis.   [3. 92–99]

> (D. You boys who gather flowers and berries born from the earth, get away from here, O boys; a cold snake hides in the grass.
> M. Careful, sheep, don't go too far: the bank is not to be trusted. The ram himself is even now drying his fleece.

---

[43] Servius, III, 42, *ad* vv. 93ff., sees a double meaning in the harsh images but explains them as a political allegory concerned with Mantua and the soldiers. Klingner, p. 57, refers the *frigidus anguis* back to the poetasters, Bavius and Maevius; Putnam similarly suggests: "If there is bad poetry, there is also evil in the land" (p. 130). Most critics think the song produces a kind of harmony between the speakers: Büchner, p. 172; Fantazzi, p. 177; Segal, "Vergil's *caelatum opus,*" pp. 303–304; but Maury, p. 82, describes the song as an extension, on a higher plane, of the personal animosity and jealous vanity of the quarrel, while Putnam, p. 134, finds its subjects expressive of uncertainty and pessimism.

> D. Tityrus, chase the browsing goats back from the river. I
> myself, when the time has come, will bathe them in the
> fountain.
> M. Pen in the sheep boys: if the summer's heat prevents their
> milk, as it did not long ago, we will press their udders in
> vain with our palms.)

These warnings continue the literary quarrel. The cold snake
is Menalcas, whom Damoetas pictures as an envious carper at
his innocent poetic ambitions (*qui legitis flores*), while the fool-
hardy ram is Menalcas' image of Damoetas, whose self-con-
fident aspirations have already led him onto uncertain ground.
The river is a well-known figure for the poet's verbal outpour-
ings.[44] Thus Menalcas is like the browsing goats; he must not
wander near this stream alone but wait for Damoetas to dip him
into the fountain of inspiration. But Damoetas, like the sheep in
summer, must be restrained, lest his energetic ambitions cause
his verse to run dry. Finally Damoetas' image of a lean bull in
a rich field pining for love (100–101) is a mockery of Menalcas'
meager efforts in pastoral verse, while Menalcas' complaint that
an evil eye has bewitched his flock (102–103) implies that
Damoetas is destructively jealous of him.

The series of insults ends with the famous riddles which may
also—at least in part—be related to the quarrel. In a mocking
tone, Damoetas promises Menalcas the name of his patron
Apollo if he can tell him where the sky is only twelve feet wide.
The answer might be where Menalcas himself stands, for his
perspective is narrow and countrified. In the same vein, Menalcas' riddle (Where are flowers inscribed with the names of
kings?) embodies the pretensions of Damoetas who seeks a
heroic, commanding role in the pastoral world.[45]

The invidious quarrel of the herdsmen has robbed the pastoral world of its beauty and tranquillity. As a vehicle for per-

[44] E. g., Hor. *Ser.* 4. 11; 10. 62: "quale fuit Cassi rapido ferventius amni
ingenium."

[45] The answer to the second is well known. A good answer to the first is proposed by M. C. J. Putnam, "The Riddle of Damoetas," *Memnosyne* 18(1964):
150–154. Amaltheia, the constellation of the kids. This answer may be linked
with Damoetas' first strophe, since Amaltheia appears in Aratus 156ff. and is
associated with the infancy of Jove, as Menalcas' riddle is associated with Apollo
and Hyacinthus.

sonal abuse, the image of nature has been twisted into sinister, unlovely forms. The acts of destruction first mentioned by the herdsmen and their mercenary quibbling over prizes are only a preface to the wanton perversion of pastoral song that makes the quarrel end more bitterly than it began. It is only fitting that no prizes should be awarded to singers who have distorted their subject to serve their own hostile ends.

In Servius' opinion the final words of Palaemon—"claudite iam rivos pueri; sat prata biberunt" (Close off your streams, boys, the fields have drunk enough [111])—suggest either boredom or exasperation, as though he had said "I am satiated with listening." The word *rivos* echoes the herdsmen's contentious references to the stream of poetry and implies that the two singers are more nearly equal than they wish to believe. Still Palaemon maintains his idealism, accompanying his decision by a gentle rebuke.[46]

> Non nostrum inter vos tantas componere lites:
> et vitula tu dignus et hic, et quisquis amores
> aut metuet dulcis aut experietur amaros.   [3. 108–110]

> (It is not for me to resolve such great quarrels as yours. Both you and he are worthy of the heifer, and whoever may fear sweet loves or experience bitter ones.)

The contest was undertaken for the ignominious purpose of settling a quarrel, but it has failed to achieve even that. Both contestants are at fault. In their aggressive, envious encounter, both show a fear of *dulces amores*, and increased bitterness is the result.

The third *Eclogue* adds another dimension to the failure of pastoral song. Like Corydon and the unhappy lover, the quarreling singers are out of harmony with their world. In his criticisms of Damoetas, Menalcas is a defender of the integrity of the country life, but his honest rusticity is warped by petty denigration of his rival. Damoetas, whose higher poetic aims are represented by Pollio and the Orpheus cup, shows traces of a more expansive perspective, but his songs express no more than

---

[46]Servius, pp. 43–44 *ad* v. 111. Perret, p. 44, interprets the lack of a decision correctly as a depreciation of the efforts of the singers.

a conflict between his ambitions and his rustic environment. Menalcas must bear the brunt of his restless pretensions. For Damoetas an illusion of experience is as dangerous as the illusion of innocence to Corydon. Here, as in the first *Eclogue*, Vergil has juxtaposed two potentially ideal representatives of the pastoral life: the farmer and the singer. The two should be parallel, but human weakness has placed them in conflict and created opposition in place of harmony.

In the fifth *Eclogue*, a subtle contrast between the singers is ultimately subordinated to a contrast of their songs. Here the bolder, more ambitious singer has composed a lamentation for death and the failure of order,[47] while his quieter yet more authoritative comrade sings a new song of triumph and rebirth. As Damoetas has broken the decorum of pastoral with his craving for the world of Pollio, so these songs continue the movement toward the historical world. But here the great world is no longer glamorous and alien, an object for hungry ambition, but, rather, a world as fragile and susceptible to catastrophe as the pastoral itself. The two worlds are linked by a common concern for the loss of order, a common hope for tranquillity and renewal. Only through this humane perspective can the previous political and aesthetic separation of the two spheres be bridged and the ideal qualities of the pastoral be reshaped as a model for the entire world of man.

The apotheosis of the ideal shepherd Daphnis is an old Theocritean subject made new.[48] Vergil's fictional Daphnis is not a beautiful, ineffectual Adonis figure, a hero of pastoral withdrawal, but an inspirational leader who brings peace and harmony to the agricultural world. His influence is manifested in the spirit and character of the pastoral singing, which grows

[47] Van Sickle, p. 503, sees a static quality in Mopsus' song. The poet is "content to embroider on Daphnis as Theocritus left him, which is to say dead: a completed, closed tradition in literature." But Menalcas "goes beyond Theocritus to speak of a Daphnis resurrected."

[48] Northrop Frye, "Literature as Context: Milton's *Lycidas*," in *Milton's Lycidas: The Tradition and the Poem* ed. C. A. Patrides (New York, 1961), pp. 200–201, speaks of the dying, resurrected nature god as the archetypal figure of pastoral elegy; yet it remains that the resurrection had no place in pastoral poems before *Eclogue* 5. Frye associates pastoral rebirth with rituals of Adonis, yet there is no suggestion of rebirth in Bion's *Lament for Adonis*.

progressively more confident, dynamic, and original as the *Eclogue* continues. Accordingly, the interrelationship of the pastoral singers also undergoes a striking change, from petty bickering in the opening verses to harmonious agreement at the end.

This *Eclogue*, like the third, takes the form of a singing contest with its invitation and exchange of songs, but no judge is chosen and no prizes set. The invitational speeches are more courteous than those in the earlier poem. Still, the idiosyncrasies of the singers are in evidence and make the scene subtly comic.[49]

Menalcas begins, proposing, with the faintly patronizing tone of an elder poet, that they should settle in a grove of elms and hazel and that Mopsus should pipe while he sings the verses (1–3). The suggestions are clearly unwelcome to Mopsus, who answers politely but evasively, hinting at a preference for a nearby cave:

> Tu maior; tibi me est aequum parere, Menalca,
> sive sub incertas Zephyris motantibus umbras
> sive antro potius succedimus. aspice, ut antrum
> silvestris raris sparsit labrusca racemis.   [5. 4–7]

> (You are the elder; it is fair for me to obey you, Menalcas, whether we sit down under the shadows wavering with the west wind's motion, or perchance if we sit within the cave. See how the woodland grapevine sprinkles the cave with its scattered clusters.)

In the end Mopsus has his way. Menalcas chooses the cavern and allows Mopsus to sing first. His remarks display a measure of artistic vanity. When Menalcas pays a traditional compliment by comparing his skill with that of Amyntas, he is petulant: "quid, si idem certet Phoebum superare canendo?" (What of that? Amyntas tries to outdo Phoebus in singing [9]). Although Menalcas displays an appreciative familiarity with his works

---

[49] Putnam, *Virgil's Pastoral Art*, pp. 166–171, emphasizes the hints of a poetics in this debate. The cave is traditionally associated with poetic inspiration, but not a traditional pastoral singing place. Mopsus must reconcile this setting with bucolic themes. Menalcas does not understand the younger shepherd's insistence upon a "new" song, a song so unusual it has been written out on bark: "a practice repugnant, or at least foreign, to the shepherd's oral art" (p. 169).

(10–12), Mopsus insists upon airing a new song, one that pleases him so greatly he has inscribed it on the bark of a tree (13–14). He adds a spiteful word for Amyntas: "tu deinde iubeto ut certet Amyntas" (Then call Amyntas to contend with me [15]).

Thus it is in spite of the prickly self-assertion of Mopsus that the songs reach a new height of pastoral accord. After Mopsus has completed his song, the exchange of comments is friendlier. He is gratified by praise (45–52) and by Menalcas' choice of a song to complement his own (53–55). When this song is finished, all pettiness vanishes; the speakers are drawn together by their common involvement in the songs. Their last dialogue is purely laudatory, culminating in a spontaneous exchange of pastoral gifts. Menalcas gives the pipe on which he learned his first songs (85–87), and Mopsus gives a shepherd's staff:

> At tu sume pedum, quod, me cum saepe rogaret,
> non tulit Antigenes (et erat tum dignus amari),
> formosum paribus nodis atque aere, Menalca.   [5. 88–90]

> (But you take this staff, which, often as he used to beg me, Antigenes has never carried [and he was worthy to be loved]. The staff is beautifully formed, with a balance of wood knots and brass, Menalcas.)

As Servius suggests, the design of the staff combines the natural (*nodis*) with art (*aere*).[50] The new harmony between the singers also represents a tempering of nature by art, and reinforces a thematic change from chaos to order that takes place in the content of the songs.

The two songs differ in their degree of originality and in their modes of perceiving the world. Although Mopsus' lament for Daphnis is newly composed, it develops the old theme of lost innocence, exploring the traditional kinship between nature and the ideal shepherd. The animals grieve for the death of Daphnis, refusing water and food. Pales and Apollo abandon the fields, as Justice fled at the close of the golden age. The most original element of the song is its ambiguously symbolic language: its combination of the *flora* of Theocritean pastures with cultivated Vergilian fields and its interweaving of alien,

[50] Servius, III, 64 *ad* v. 90.

mysterious images suggesting that Daphnis is a character belonging not merely to the pastoral, but also to a greater world. Echoes of the first *Eclogue* make the death of Daphnis a new Roman loss of the golden age. These many suggestions are juxtaposed without explanation; at the end of the song their meaning remains unresolved.

The composition of the song is symmetrical. It opens and closes with strong echoes of Alexandrian tradition, but its central passages incorporate images that defy traditional interpretation. In the first lines, the old pastoral is dominant:

> Exstinctum Nymphae crudeli funere Daphnin
> flebant (vos coryli testes et flumina Nymphis),
> cum complexa sui corpus miserabile nati
> atque deos atque astra vocat crudelia mater.   [5. 20–23]

> (The Nymphs wept for Daphnis, cut off by a cruel death [you hazel trees and rivers are witnesses for the Nymphs]; when, embracing the pitiful body of her son, his mother berated the gods and cruel stars.)

By his mention of the weeping nymphs and Daphnis' grieving mother, the singer echoes the pastoral laments of Bion and Moschus. The Daphnis of Theocritus' first *Idyll* dies neglected by the nymphs.

In the *Idyll*, wolves and jackals howl for Daphnis and the cattle weep. Domestic and wild nature are united. The union is preserved here, but with a stronger expression of emotion in civilized nature. Instead of sentimental tears, there is a halt in the order of rural life:

> non ulli pastos illis egere diebus
> frigida, Daphni, boves ad flumina; nulla neque amnem
> libavit quadripes nec graminis attigit herbam.
> Daphni, tuum Poenos etiam ingemuisse leones
> interitum montesque feri silvaeque loquuntur.   [5. 24–28]

> (In those days, no men drove well-fed cattle to the cool stream, Daphnis; nor did any animal taste the river or touch a blade of grass. Daphnis, for your death they say that the lions of Carthage groaned, and the mountains and the wild beasts and the forests.)

The phrase *illis diebus* suggests a definite historical time, a designated period of mourning that differs greatly from the vivid yet timeless moment of the *Idyll*. The Carthaginian lions intrude upon the homogeneity of the bucolic world, directing our attention beyond the stricken pastures toward a universal nature.

A similar suggestion is in the lines that follow (29-31). Daphnis taught men to yoke Armenian tigers; he established the rites of Bacchus and wound soft leaves about the pliant spear.

Now the Vergilian Daphnis is clearly distinguished from his Theocritean predecessor. No longer an ineffectual idealist in an isolated world, the shepherd has become a tamer of the wilderness and a teacher of society. The spear (*hasta*) wreathed with branches belongs less to a warlike Bacchus than to Bacchus the giver of peace and fertility.[51] Thus Daphnis the victor brings civilized order in the wake of his triumph over the wild.

The comparison of Daphnis and the nature god continues in the next lines with images of order and fruitfulness:

> vitis ut arboribus decori est, ut vitibus uvae,
> ut gregibus tauri, segetes ut pinguibus arvis,
> tu decus omne tuis.   [5. 32–34]

(As the vine is an ornament to the trees, and the grapes to the vine; as the bulls are the pride of the herds and the crops of the rich fields, so were you among your own people.)

Although Daphnis has subdued savage nature, his true home is the organized community of Roman agriculture: the world of vines, crops, and herds that formed the background of *Eclogue* 1. The poet's series of images delineate the interdependencies of the agricultural world, which are now the interdependencies of a leader and his people. But despite their laudatory and affectionate coloring, the images betray a certain passivity. The tree supports the flourishing vine; the herds submit to the

---

[51] The warlike Bacchus and the military associations of the thyrsis are described in Macrob. *Sat.* 1. 19. 19. For the multiple nature of Bacchus and his role as giver of fertility see A. Bruhl, *Liber Pater* (Paris, 1953), pp. 3ff. For his role as champion of Italian liberty in the last century of the Republic see *ibid.*, pp. 42–45, 119–122; Robert Rowland, "Numismatic Propaganda under Cinna," *TAPA* 97(1966):417.

pleasure of the bull. In historical terms this passivity may be described as the dependence of a people upon their leader for a definition of identity and purpose. In pastoral terms it is the passivity of innocence.

Not because of sympathy, but rather on account of dependency, the order of the agricultural world has failed with Daphnis' death:

> grandia saepe quibus mandavimus hordea sulcis,
> infelix lolium et steriles nascuntur avenae.   [5. 36–37]

> (From the furrows to which we have often entrusted the swelling grain, unlucky cockle weeds and barren oats are born.)

The image of the sown fields recalls the first *Eclogue* ("his nos consevimus agros [1. 72]"), but this time nature has ceased her productivity in response to human catàstrophe. The origin of the image seems to lie in rural superstition. According to Pliny, the farmer believed that his grain sprouted oats and cockles when the seed was corrupted in the earth.[52] The notion fits this metaphorical context, where the image of cultivated nature is rapidly becoming parallel to that of the ordered state. A leader is a figure in whom expectations are planted, the person who brings his nation's hopes to fruition. Again we sense the note of passivity in a world that pities itself for hopes grown fruitless and is bewildered by the chaos that follows upon the leader's death.

As if to emphasize how far this lament has departed from the old Theocritean pattern, Vergil's singer completes the description of chaos by a return to the language and imagery of the *Idyll*:

> pro molli viola, pro purpureo narcisso
> carduus et spinis surgit paliurus acutis.   [5. 38–39]

> (In place of the gentle violet and the purple narcissus, the thistle and the thorn bush spring up with sharp spines.)

---

[52] Pliny *HN* 18. 17. 44. A proverbial use of the idea may be found in two passages: Cic. *Fin.* 5. 30. 91; Ennius *Praecepta* frg. 2 (Vahlen, p. 165): "ubi videt avenam lolium crescere inter triticum seligit, secernet, aufert in operam addit seduto quae tanto cum studio servit."

In contrast to the homely farm plants, these are literary and pastoral, the same that Theocritean Daphnis mentions in his farewell to the world: "Now violets bear ye thorns, and ye thorns bear violets, and let the fair narcissus bloom on the juniper" (1. 132–133). This inversion of nature is the gentle curse of a dying nature hero whose beloved world cannot help him survive. But in the *Eclogue* the violet and the narcissus have not simply changed their places, they have disappeared. It is as if the old curse had at last been fulfilled in the more significant catastrophe of the new Daphnis' death.

As I have already said, this Daphnis has little in common with the Theocritean hero who withdrew from the world of experience to recapture his kinship with nature in death. That Daphnis was a famous singer, and his failures, like those of Orpheus, suggest the fragility of art when embodied in a mortal form. Although this Daphnis loves song (54–55), he is no singer. His only verses are those of his own epitaph:

> 'Daphnis ego in silvis, hinc usque ad sidera notus,
> formosi pecoris custos, formosior ipse.'   [5. 43–44]

(In the forests, I am Daphnis, renowned from here to the stars; the keeper of a beautiful herd, more beautiful myself.)

As a leader Daphnis must be remembered. He epitomizes the ideal qualities of the Vergilian responsible shepherd. But such a figure can not die unobtrusively in harmless seclusion. His death has cruelly awakened his world from innocence to experience.

The several new details of the lament may in part be explained as allusions to the death of Julius Caesar which, in some cases, are quite explicit. The mourning of Daphnis' mother is that of Caesar's divine mother, Venus. The groaning of the Carthaginian lions recalls Caesar's special patronage of that city, which he had restored and recolonized under her ancient name. The agricultural images might suggest Caesar's relationship to Italy, which supported him in the face of senatorial Rome. Daphnis' *tumulus* in the forest suggests Caesar's monument in the Forum, erected by his supporters shortly after his death.[53]

[53] My opinion of this identification is close to Büchner's (pp. 198–199). Although one may argue against the association of Daphnis and Caesar, it is hard

These few allusions are enough to indicate the song's involvement in the historical world. At the same time it is clear that Daphnis and Caesar are never completely identified. To the singer Daphnis remains no more than the ideal figure of the pastoral world. Only the reader bothers with the allusions and with the reconciliation of the great disparity between the two very different figures that the poem compares.

Such a comparison demands simplification of material on both sides. Of the old Theocritean Daphnis little remains save his role as a magical hero of the pastoral living in kinship with nature. Likewise Caesar loses his political ambiguity and his association with civil war. Instead of a dangerous elder statesman he becomes a youthful, promising leader, cut off in his prime. The point of the comparison is not that either loses his identity to the other. Rather, each contributes to the building of a new figure, a fictional character whose identity is greater than the sum of the elements in his background. The new Daphnis represents the best of both worlds. He is a leader more ideal than any historical figure, and a shepherd of far greater consequence than any before.

In this context we must read the central passage of the lament, the passage whose metaphorical significance is the most puzzling aspect of the poem:

> Daphnis et Armenias curru subiungere tigris
> instituit, Daphnis thiasos inducere Bacchi
> et foliis lentas intexere mollibus hastas.   [5. 29–31]

> (Daphnis taught the yoking of Armenian tigers to a chariot, and the performance of Bacchic dances, and the way to wind the pliant spear with soft leaves.)

Attempts to refer these details to specific events in the career of Caesar are generally unconvincing. Certainly the Bacchic

---

to imagine how a Roman in 41, or even 37, could read the apotheosis song *without* thinking of Caesar. For references see D. L. Drew, "Virgil's Fifth *Eclogue*, A Defence of the Julius Caesar-Daphnis Theory," *CQ* 16(1922):57–64; Suet. *Jul.* 84. Drew, pp. 59–62, also compares Daphnis' *tumulus* with the monument erected to Caesar in the Forum (Suet. 85) and Caesar's triumphs with the triumph of Bacchus. Less reliable, I think, is his suggestion that the failure of the crops may refer to the clouding of the sun mentioned by Plutarch.

dances cannot be taken literally.[54] The Armenian tigers do not seem to single out any one conquest of Caesar's. The most plausible explanations are found in the nature of Bacchus himself. Like Daphnis he belongs to the natural world, but like Caesar he is a conqueror and civilizer. Thus he helps to reconcile the two disparate individualities in the background of the poem. Beyond this, he has another significance related to the thematic development of the poem.

In Cicero's *De Natura Deorum*, the Stoic speaker explains the apotheosis of minor deities as a tribute rendered to outstanding benefactors of mankind: "A custom common to the life of men allows that certain men who excel in their gifts to others and in their reputation should raise themselves of their own accord into Heaven" (2. 62). Romulus is among those so honored, and also Liber, whose gift to man was a knowledge of the use of the vine.

In the *De Legibus*, Cicero also mentions the apotheosis of Bacchus when he praises certain rituals of initiation whose influence has not only bettered civilization but also inspired men with hopes of happiness after death:

For although your city of Athens seems to me to have originated many outstanding and godlike practices and to have given them a place in human life, nothing is better than those mysteries by which we are refined from our rustic, savage life and molded toward humanity. As these mysteries are called initiations, so do we learn from them the true beginnings of life, and we receive not only the principle of living with joy, but even of dying with a better hope.   [2. 14. 36]

In Menalcas' song Daphnis will follow the model of Bacchus, taking his place among the gods as a figure toward whom man directs his aspirations for a better life. In Mopsus' lament this

---

[54] Servius, III, 57 *ad* v. 29. Most scholars agree that Caesar's importation of Bacchic rituals cannot be correct. For a summary of opinions, see Bruhl, pp. 124ff., who finds Drew's proposal concerning Caesar's triumph (with elephants as Dionysiac animals) convincing. He does not accept Maury's belief that Vergil was interested in mystery cults, but stresses the influence of Bacchus as a civilizing god (see also Putnam, *Virgil's Pastoral Art*, pp. 174–175). It is remotely possible that Vergil is remembering that Caesar's victory at Munda fell upon March 17, the date of the Liberalia, as the author of the *Bell. Hisp.* records (31. 6).

promise goes neglected, and Daphnis remains a defeated earthly hero whose death has reversed his beneficent influence and rendered nature passive and helpless. Such helplessness is the inevitable consequence of mourning for lost innocence. Although Mopsus' new song has gone boldly beyond the limits of the pastoral in establishing the relevance of a traditional theme to the affairs of the great world, still it has produced only a pessimistic vision of a world united by destruction.

In seeking to remedy this helplessness and restore order through the human activity of song, Menalcas attempts a higher task than his companion:

> nos tamen haec quocumque modo tibi nostra vicissim
> dicemus, Daphninque tuum tollemus ad astra.   [5. 50–51];

(However, I, in my turn, will answer you as best I can, and I will lift up your Daphnis to the stars.)

As he creates a vision of Daphnis on Olympus, and of his renewed influence upon the countryside, the singer goes beyond tribute to become an imitator of the ideal shepherd. Like Daphnis he calls for peace amidst civilization. Where Daphnis established the rites of Bacchus, Menalcas in turn gives Daphnis rites of his own. His song restores the power death had taken from the hero, making him once more able to fulfill his thwarted promise of giving order to the world.

The new order, spontaneous and magical as it may seem, is in fact one that places restraint upon nature, demanding conformity to the ideal set by the god:

> nec lupus insidias pecori, nec retia cervis
> ulla dolum meditantur: amat bonus otia Daphnis.   [5. 60–61]

(Let the wolf plot no treachery against the flock, nor any nets think of snaring the deer. The good Daphnis loved harmony.)

In *otium* is another echo of the first *Eclogue*. As before, *otium* is a gift that the historical world may bestow upon the pastoral, but this *otium* belongs to everyone, not just to a single fortunate shepherd. Historically, *otium* may suggest the clemency of Caesar that had disappeared from Rome in the bitter struggles that followed his death.[55] The allusion implies reproach and seems to urge that apotheosis, rather than revenge, is a fitting tribute to a historical leader.

The meaning of Daphnis' apotheosis for the shepherd world is expressed obliquely, through a description of rituals to be established by the shepherds themselves:

> sis bonus o felixque tuis! en quattuor aras:
> ecce duas tibi, Daphni, duas altaria Phoebo.
> pocula bina novo spumantia lacte quotannis
> craterasque duo statuam tibi pinguis olivi,
> et multo in primis hilarans convivia Baccho
> (ante focum, si frigus erit; si messis, in umbra)
> vina novam fundam calathis Arusia nectar.
> cantabunt mihi Damoetas et Lyctius Aegon;
> saltantis Satyros imitabitur Alphesiboeus.
> haec tibi semper erunt, et cum sollemnia vota
> reddemus Nymphis, et cum lustrabimus agros.   [5. 65–75]

(Be kind and propitious to your followers! Behold four altars: two, Daphnis, to you and two to Phoebus. Every year I will dedicate to you two cups foaming with new milk and two bowls of rich olive oil. There will be feasts that revel in abundant wine— before the hearth when it is cold, and when it is harvest time, in the shade—and I will pour a new nectar, Arusian wine, into the cups. Damoetas and Lyctean Aegon will sing for me, and Alphesiboeus will imitate the leaping Satyrs. These rites will be yours, both when we pay our solemn vows to the nymphs and when we purify the fields.)

Pierre Grimal has identified Menalcas' four festivals with the state religion. The summer celebration he believes is the *Ludi Apollinares* which followed close after Caesar's birthday and included theatrical games. The winter would be the feast of Caesar's divinity established in January 42. The spring festival is either the Vinalia Priora or the Cerealia, and the autumn is the Fontanalia.[56] But specific identifications are less important

---

[55] The disorders that followed upon Caesar's death were in violation of an amnesty granted by the Senate to the murderers. See Cic. *Att.* 14. 6. 2, 9. 2, 14. 3, 15. 4. 3; *Fam.* 12. 1. 2; App. *BCiv.* 2. 13. 5. As Perret, p. 64, observes, *otium* is a word that spans the poetic and political worlds.

[56] Pierre Grimal, "La Ve Eglogue et la culte de César," in *Mélanges d'archéologie et d'histoire Charles Picard, Rev. Arch* ser. 6, 30 (1948):406–419.

than the concept of a pattern of ceremonies reflecting the pattern of human activities in nature, an idea implicit in the whole Roman tradition of seasonal festivals. These rituals for Daphnis, well integrated into the cycle of rural life and the seasons, form a contrast with the lavish animal sacrifices that Tityrus had vowed to his *deus*. Here, in place of conspicuous extravagance is a simple tribute that utilizes the products of man's work in nature — milk, oil, and wine — and draws the rural community together in a spirit of festivity. Daphnis assumes an active role in the order of the world he protects. The chaos and disharmony of his untimely death yield to a traditional pattern symbolizing the unity of the natural and civilized worlds.

The new world under the guardianship of Daphnis has a homely dignity that contrasts with the more flamboyant visions of the golden age elsewhere in the *Eclogues*. It is neither a *locus amoenus* nor a world of spontaneous growth and relaxed labors, but one where human activity is ennobled by simple, instinctive piety:

> dum iuga montis aper, fluvios dum piscis amabit,
> dumque thymo pascentur apes, dum rore cicadae,
> semper honos nomenque tuum laudesque manebunt.
>
> [5. 76–78]

> (So long as the boar loves the ridge of his mountain, so long as the fish loves his stream, so long as the bees feed on thyme and the grasshoppers on dew, always your honor, name, and praises will remain.)

The shepherds' devotion to Daphnis is equal to the love that creatures feel for their homelands, for a nature whose order is manifested in her ability to provide for her own. The promise of eternal remembrance clearly recalls Tityrus' *adynaton* in *Eclogue* 1:

> Ante leves ergo pascentur in aethere cervi
> et freta destituent nudos in litore piscis,
> ante pererratis amborum finibus exsul
> aut Ararim Parthus bibet aut Germania Tigrim,
> quam nostro illius labatur pectore vultus.   [1. 59–63]

> (Not before the slight deer come to feed in the air, and the seas abandon the fishes, unprotected on the shore; not before the

time when exiled people wander over each other's lands, when
the Parthian drinks from the Rhone and the German from the
Tigris, will his countenance slip away from my heart.)

The new formula shows the weakness of the old. Where Tityrus
speaks in grandiose language, calling up names that reach far
beyond the limitations of his experience, Menalcas defines his
concept of world order in simple, familiar terms that carry
great conviction. His images of a stable, beneficent nature
convey a spirit of vital interdependence that makes the organization of natural life a model for the most idealistic ordering of
the historical world.

In the final words of his song, Menalcas reiterates his suggestion of mutual dependencies, of mutual giving and response:

> ut Baccho Cererique, tibi sic vota quotannis
> agricolae facient: damnabis tu quoque votis.   [5. 79–80]

(Just as to Bacchus and Ceres, the farmers will make vows to
you each year: by giving fulfillment, you will hold them to their
vows.)

Damnabis expresses a strong bond between man and deity,
giving a formal, legalistic definition to the interdependence
pictured just before.[57] As nature is to her creatures, so is Daphnis to the shepherds. By the fulfillment of his duties as guardian
and benefactor, Daphnis will bind his followers in gratitude,
thus holding them to their vows. Such mutual obligation is
necessary to make the experienced world ideal. It is based
upon a realistic acceptance of nature and of the duties nature
creates for man, and is thus a far greater tribute to Daphnis
than that passive grieving after lost innocence that brings chaos
to the natural world. Only through man's resolve to imitate
the ideal qualities of the lost leader can the promise of Daphnis
become other than a futile, disappearing hope.

Through its interpretation of apotheosis, the poem com-

---

[57] Servius, p. 63 *ad* v. 80, explains the legalistic tone of this word in its applica-
tion to obligations between man and god: "Id est cum deus praestare aliqua
hominibus coeperis, obnoxios tibi eos facies ad vota solvenda, quae ante quam
solvantur, obligatos et quasi damnatos homines retinent." Se also Ter. *Phorm.*
422; Nep. *Timol.* 53; Hor. *Sat.* 2. 3. 68; Livy 5. 25. 2, 7. 28. 4, 10. 37. 16, 27. 45. 8,
39. 9. 4.

pletes that interweaving of pastoral and history that earlier *Eclogues* have demanded yet failed to achieve. Here apotheosis carries a double significance: it is at once an ambiguous historical gesture—expedient rather than ideal—and a response to man's enduring desire for regeneration.[58] The pastoral makes us see the human meaning that underlies the political gesture and urges an acceptance of its ideal significance upon the historical world. In allowing his shepherds to sing of rebirth, Vergil fulfills the promise of regenerating the pastoral first suggested by Tityrus' acquisition of *otium* and *libertas*. But the two worlds that unite in this poem are not just the simple, rustic country and the sophisticated city that Tityrus, Corydon, and Damoetas portray. Rather they are two parts of one world of nature, so closely bound up together that they cannot be separated. The events of history have given their shape to the contents of pastoral, but only the pastoral can interpret the lasting significance of these events.

The fifth *Eclogue* is the only one where the speakers comment extensively upon each other's songs. From their mutual praises spring the agreement and conciliation that mark the dramatic and symbolic progress of the poem. At the close of Mopsus' lament, Menalcas compares his singing to the restorative comforts of nature:

> Tale tuum carmen nobis, divine poeta,
> quale sopor fessis in gramine, quale per aestum
> dulcis aquae saliente sitim restinguere rivo.   [5. 45–47]

> (Such is your song to me, godlike poet, as sleep in the grass to worn-out men; such a solace as the sweet waters in the leaping river give to thirst in summer heat.)

Through its articulation of grief and fear, the lament gives consolation. Mopsus' song has captured the freshness and vitality of a living nature, a counter to the weariness of human emotion and the discord of the civilized world. Such praise is bucolic, but what Mopsus says to Menalcas at the conclusion of the apotheosis song strikes a higher note:

[58] For historical analysis of the apotheosis of Caesar see L. R. Taylor, *The Divinity of the Roman Emperor* (Middletown, Conn., 1931), pp. 58–180.

Quae tibi, quae tali reddam pro carmine dona?
nam neque me tantum venientis sibilus Austri
nec percussa iuvant fluctu tam litora, nec quae
saxosas inter decurrunt flumina vallis.   [5. 81–84]

(What thing shall I give you? What gifts can repay such a song?
For I have never heard anything so pleasing: neither the
whistle of the south wind's approach, nor the sea coast pounded
by waves, nor any stream rushing through its stony channel.)

In the second *Eclogue*, the south wind, *Auster*, was the harsh
breath of reality withering a fragile garden of imagination.
Now imagination has risen above nature's reality, creating its
own dynamic transformation of the world. The images Mopsus
chooses are heroic, rather than pastoral, recalling those brief
glimpses of a wild but majestic nature often found in Homeric
similes.[59] The poet's vision need no longer be protected from
the strength and energy of real nature. The delicate garden of
innocence has given way to a vital and challenging world of
experience.

The idealistic union of nature and human emotion persists,
in lesser form, in Corydon's songs of the seventh poem where
the rustic horizon has closed in, for the first time wholly ob-
literating the great world. Of all the *Eclogues* this has most
frequently been designated an *ars poetica*, and understandably
so, since the differences between the two singers are sharper
than in other contest poems.[60] These distinctions appear the
more striking because the singers are first introduced as equal
in background, age, and skill:

ambo florentes aetatibus, Arcades ambo,
et cantare pares et respondere parati.   [7. 4–5]

---

[59] *Iliad* 2. 145ff., 2. 208ff., 2. 393ff., 4. 422ff., *etc.*
[60] See E. E. Beyer, "Vergil: *Eclogue* 7: A Theory of Poetry," *Acta Classica*
5(1962):38–47; Perret, pp. 77–84; Viktor Pöschl, *Die Hirtendichtung Virgils*
(Heidelberg, 1964), pp. 93–154; H. Dahlmann, "Zu Vergils siebentem Hirten-
gedicht," *Hermes* 94(1966):228–229; Klingner, pp. 118–125; Putnam, *Virgil's
Pastoral Art*, pp. 222–254. There is some disagreement on the meaning of the
contest; Beyer, Perret, Dahlmann, and Putnam emphasize the development of
a Vergilian ideal in Corydon's songs, while Pöschl and Klingner give more
weight to the balancing of antithetical points of view.

(Both in the flower of their age; Arcadians both; equally ready to sing and to answer in song.)

The significance of Arcadian singing is clarified by the Greek historian Polybius, a native of that land who writes of his country as a place so harsh and demanding that its people could only make their labors endurable by cultivating the arts of song.[61] From early youth, the young men of Arcadia were trained to perform in contests and to entertain one another at banquets with original compositions. The designation *Arcades* suggests detachment and formality as well as a certain degree of polish conducive to the theoretical consideration of song. The seventh *Eclogue* portrays a moment when pastoral singing is not made a vehicle for personal longings or aspirations, but is intended purely for the enjoyment of its audience.

The introductory narrative enforces this point. The Arcadian singers have appeared near the farmland of Meliboeus, a poor Italian farmer, hard pressed by his double responsibilities of herding and planting. Daphnis has joined the young herdsmen beneath a rustling ilex and urges Meliboeus to take time to hear their contest (9–13):[62]

'huc ades, o Meliboee; caper tibi salvus et haedi;
et, si quid cessare potes, requiesce sub umbra.
huc ipsi potum venient per prata iuvenci,
hic viridis tenera praetexit harundine ripas
Mincius, eque sacra resonant examina quercu'.   [7. 9–13]

(Come here, o Meliboeus, here is your goat, safe, and your kids, and if you can stop your work for a little, rest in the shade. Here the bullocks will come by themselves through the fields to drink. Here the Mincio covers over its green banks with tender reeds, and the buzzing swarm resounds from the sacred oak.)

By capturing Meliboeus' strayed kid, Daphnis offers the farmer a momentary freedom from his responsibilities. For the farmer,

---

[61] *The Histories* 4. 21. 2.

[62] Pöschl, pp. 93–100, discusses the "magical," "Arcadian" quality of the setting, while Putnam, *Virgil's Pastoral Art*, pp. 224–230, stresses the contrast between this ideal world and Meliboeus' everyday world of hard work.

the contest is a great event (*magnum certamen*), and he accepts the offer of relaxation and entertainment ("posthabui tamen illorum mea seria ludo" — I decided to place my duties second to their sport [17]). Here, as in Polybius' Arcadia, song tempers the hardships of a difficult life.

The difference between the singers begins to appear with their opening stanzas.[63] Corydon addresses the *Nymphae Libethriades* and prays for skill as a poet. Should he fail, he will hang up his pipe on a shrill-sounding pine (21–24). Thyrsis calls upon the *pastores Arcades*, demanding the honors due a promising poet. He mutters against a rival who jealously disparages his growing talent (25–29). Not only is the one singer modest, the other brash and self-aggrandizing, but also the one establishes ideal standards while the other binds himself to standards that are purely human.

The songs of Corydon and Thyrsis are imaginary, descriptive compositions. Through vignettes centered about the topics of piety, love, relaxation, autumn, and the woodland, each builds a composite picture of a pastoral world. In tone and image each singer's pictures are consistent. Corydon portrays a humble rustic who dedicates his trophies of the hunt to Diana and promises if all goes well (*si proprium fuerit*) to honor the goddess with a marble statue (28–32). Thyrsis takes the part of a poor worshiper of Priapus reminding the god of their mutual poverty and of the golden image he may have if he will increase the herd (33–37). Corydon praises Galatea in images drawn from the choicest refinements of nature: she is sweeter than Hybla thyme, whiter than swan's down, lovelier than the pale ivy (37–40). But Thyrsis concentrates upon the disappointed lover who feels more bitter than crowfoot weed, sharper than thorns, cheaper than the cast-up seaweed as he waits out the long day wherein love fails to answer his call (41–44). Corydon sings of the shade that protects the flock from summer heat (45–48) and Thyrsis of the smoky hearth fires that keep the herdsmen safe from the north wind (49–52). Corydon sings of the fullness of autumn when Alexis is in the country — he fears

[63] For extensive analysis of the diction and prosody of the contrasting strophes see esp. Pöschl and Putnam.

the drought of absence (53–56)—but Thyrsis sees the hills dry and the vines barren, hoping for Phyllis to come and bring greenness and cause Jupiter to pour down showers of rain (57–60). The final stanzas present the most subtle contrast.[64] Corydon peoples the grove with trees beloved by the gods:

Populus Alcidae gratissima, vitis Iaccho,
formosae myrtus Veneri, sua laurea Phoebo;
Phyllis amat corylos: illas dum Phyllis amabit,
nec myrtus vincet corylos, nec laurea Phoebi.   [7. 61–64]

(The poplar is most pleasing to Hercules, the vine to Bacchus, the myrtle to beautiful Venus, and his own laurels to Phoebus. Phyllis loves the hazels; so long as Phyllis loves them neither the myrtles, nor the laurels of Phoebus will surpass the hazels.'

The trees are emblems of the gods in nature; Corydon's woodland gains dignity from its associations with deities. Phyllis, a human figure who lacks the nobility of the gods, has chosen one of the humblest trees for her emblem; consequently the poet's task is to elevate Phyllis' hazels to a place in the symbolic unity of the grove. Corydon finds his poetic challenge in creating ideal meanings for the objects of the natural world.

Thyrsis, in his turn, mentions the trees whose beauty dominates the places where each is best suited to grow:

Fraxinus in silvis pulcherrima, pinus in hortis,
populus in fluviis, abies in montibus altis:
saepius at si me, Lycida formose, revisas,
fraxinus in silvis cedat tibi, pinus in hortis.   [7. 65–68]

---

[64] H. Fuchs, "Zum Wettgesang der Hirten in Vergils siebenter Ekloge," *MH* 23(1966):218–222, argues that the two strophes 53–56 and 57–60 should be reversed, giving both Phyllis songs to Corydon. The first of these, in his opinion, lacks the smoothness that characterizes Corydon's more exemplary pastoral singing, while the optimistic hope of rain suits his perspectives. The more negative anticipation of drought is fitting to the cynical Thyrsis. Pöschl, pp. 148–149, suggests that Thyrsis' last two strophes show the influence of Corydon's more elegant artistry, changing from dissonance to harmony, incorporating a unity of nature and love. Klingner, pp. 123–124, finds such a change only in the penultimate strophe, while Putnam believes that Thyrsis' songs are consistently inferior: "Although Thyrsis' contrasting comparison at first seems apt, the result is only that Lycidas is equated with a tree and the speaker is allied to the woods, gardens and streams amid which the tree is placed" (*Virgil's Pastoral Art*, p. 250).

(The ash tree is the loveliest in the forests, the pine tree in gardens, the poplar in streams and the fir tree in the high mountains. But if you return to see me often, beautiful Lycidas, the ash in the forests will give place to you, the pine in the gardens.)

In contrast to Corydon's unified, emblematic picture, Thyrsis' is merely a catalogue. He has divided the natural world into four separate locations and chosen, rather arbitrarily, one outstanding object in each. For Thyrsis the trees have no ideal associations, and his more practical aesthetic is ready to give a human figure precedence over nature. Thus the final stanzas bring the songs back to their beginnings with Corydon establishing a divine presence in nature while Thyrsis insists upon a more limited and human point of view. His version of Arcadian song may be linked with the wilderness landscapes of *Eclogues* 8 and 10, where the lovers see only a world that mirrors their disappointments and uncertainties.

In a burst of enthusiasm that seems to recreate his immediate response to the contest, Meliboeus assigns the victory to Corydon:

> Haec memini, et victum frustra contendere Thyrsin,
> ex illo Corydon Corydon est tempore nobis.   [7. 69–70]

> (These things I remember, and that defeated Thyrsis competed in vain; from this time Corydon, Corydon is for me.)

Thyrsis' failure might be predicated from the third poem, where the failure of both singers indicates that pastoral song does not succeed by defamation of the natural world. Critics have pointed out that Thyrsis' songs are not only unlovely, but also contain violations of decorum and taste.[65] The golden Priapus, the cast-up seaweed, the smoky hearth-fire, and the somewhat sexual rainfall are grotesque images, out of keeping with the moderation of the rural ideal. Pöschl has added a degree of dramatization to the contest by suggesting that Thyrsis' songs are parodies of Corydon's; that the bolder, less refined singer seeks victory by humorous, ironic deprecation of his rival's quiet idealism. But all agree that Thyrsis' negative per-

---

[65] E.g., Putnam, *Virgil's Pastoral Art*, pp. 236, 238, 248.

spectives are somehow necessary to the poem, even if they do no more than give impetus to Corydon's creative idealizing.[66] If the poem is to be related to the *Eclogue* book as a whole, its songs must be weighed in this context. Michael Putnam has spoken of Corydon's landscapes as a fulfillment of the pastoral dream of the earlier Corydon, but this is perhaps to give too much credit to that misguided swain.[67] The Arcadian Corydon is cheerfully aware of the limitations of man and nature. His small Micon is self-effacing; his summer sun is hot; his beloved may leave the pastoral world. Unlike the monologue singers, this Corydon does not see the pastoral world as a self-centered paradise, but rather, like Meliboeus in the first poem, finds an ideal in making the best of little. Such idealism does not court disillusionment. At the same time, Thyrsis, although skeptical in his view of nature, does not resort to the invidious back-biting of the rustic Menalcas, but merely represents the other side of Corydon's idealizing, the awareness that nature can mirror man's grievances as well as his hopes. His subjects are not foreign to the *Eclogues:* the dry summer heat and the rejected lover belong to the world of nature; the protective hearth fire appears in the first poem and again in the cycle of seasonal festivals in the fifth. The relationship of Thyrsis' stanzas to Corydon's is like that of disappointment to expectation, or of Tityrus' farm to the hard world outside its borders. The two sets of stanzas are complementary, and Thyrsis' is a necessary perspective, a creative counter to Corydon's persistent idealizing; for it is when the uncontrolled ideal obliterates reality that we find the disillusionment of an unhappy lover or a Corydon. The songs of this contest are not songs of pastoral withdrawal but explorations of the interrelationship of nature and man. Taken together, they present the pastoral world as a microcosm of human emotions.[68]

[66] Pöschl, pp. 118–119 is, I think, accurate in his description of Thyrsis' tone as one of detached, perceptive irony, a shrug of the shoulders: " 'ridendo dicere verum.' " See Putnam, *Virgil's Pastoral Art,* pp. 251–252.

[67] *Virgil's Pastoral Art,* p. 247.

[68] Pöschl, p. 150: "The stanzas of Corydon and Thyrsis together make a still greater whole. For that which is narrow, aggressive, unpoetic, and spiteful is, after all, an element of life and forces itself, as Vergil well knows, into poetry. Corydon and Thyrsis embody the two possible sides of the bucolic." Klinger,

Even so, this limited microcosm does differ from the more expansive ideal vision of *Eclogue* 5 with its hopes of world order, of personal tranquillity within a cosmic frame. It is, in fact, a retrenchment rather than a renewal of that ideal. As the contest offers Meliboeus only a temporary respite from his labors, so also it represents no more than a temporary interpretation of the pastoral world. There is something puzzling and incomplete in Corydon's victory, a note of ambiguity that remains suspended until the ninth poem, when pastoral idealizing is once more tested against the historical world.

In the third through the seventh poems, versions of pastoral song are composed by separate speakers as if they represented congenitally opposite points of view that the reader must reconcile or distinguish for himself. In the ninth poem, this situation is inverted and the songs of one poet are judged by two speakers. The dialogue is studded with song fragments attributed to the fictional poet Menalcas.[69] Their function is to elicit comment and interpretation and thus a final evaluation of the tensions in pastoral poetry and the pastoral singer's achievement.

The songs are sung in the course of a journey toward the city, but they look backward toward the pastoral world. Unlike other songs, they do not pretend to spontaneity but are recalled from memories of former times. The singers do not enjoy the

---

Virgil: Bucolica, Georgica, Aeneis (Zurich, 1967), pp. 124–125, sees the same kind of complementary pairing in the two worlds of Meliboeus and Daphnis; both perspectives are necessary for the larger "Vergilian world picture."

[69] That these several fragments represent portions of earlier Vergilian poems is a view expressed by F. Leo, "Virgils 1 und 9 Eklogue," *Hermes* 38(1903):14–17, but refuted by Rohde, p. 24, who argues that Vergil composed the fragments for this poem alone with the intention of creating a historical perspective, a vision extending beyond the limitations of the pastoral world. Likewise a traditional identification of Menalcas and Vergil has been challenged by modern critics. H. Oppermann, "Virgil und Octavian," *Hermes* 67(1932):197–219, suggests that all three poets are masks for the author; the alternating optimism and despair in their songs is a symbolic contrasting of past and present powers. C. Segal, *"Tamen cantabitis Arcades,"* p. 255, puts the case in a new way. Vergil has made extensive use of phrases and themes from Theocritus' seventh *Idyll,* a poem that combines autobiographical suggestions with an examination of poets and poetry. The use of song fragments in *Eclogue* 9 points up the similarity of the two poems. See also Klingner, p. 154, on Vergil's reversal of motifs from the *Thalysia.*

otium of Tityrus and other herdsmen. This, too, is in the past. Both are admittedly less skillful than Menalcas and are ready to appreciate his pre-eminence as they rehearse his works. For them Menalcas is the spokesman and symbol of the pastoral life; yet their judgments are affected by the fact that the pastoral life has fallen on hard times.[70]

The ninth poem resembles the first in its apparent questioning of the bucolic mode, but the questions are deeper and more serious. Whereas in *Eclogue* 1 the disappearance of a Theocritean paradise made way for an orderly agricultural landscape within the threatening framework of nature, now this landscape is fading away. Many echoes of the earlier poem show that the pastoral life has grown more precarious.[71] No Tityrus has come home to freedom, but another farm has been lost. The soldier, who before came only to possess the farmland, has now almost murdered the poet. The animals once sold for the farmers or driven into exile are now sold for the soldier's profit. Once more prophetic birds have warned of disaster.

The dialogue is conducted under the shadow of a journey that seems symbolic of a need to abandon the pastoral world. The opening words present the theme of departure: "Quo te, Moeri, pedes? an, quo via ducit, in urbem?" (Where are you walking to, Moeris? Is it where the way leads, to the city?) The road itself points to the city, which now dominates the rural world. In this context, Moeris, an old man depressed and discouraged, has lost faith in the pastoral life.

As if he could not bear to admit to his destination, Moeris does not answer directly, but instead pours out the bitter thoughts induced by his journey:

[70] For Oppermann, p. 211, this means a loss of faith in the efficacy of pastoral. Similar opinions are expressed by Otis, p. 132, Galinsky, pp. 185–186; and Putnam, *Virgil's Pastoral Art*, pp. 293–341. But Büchner, p. 221; Segal, "*Tamen cantabitis Arcades*," pp. 244ff.; Klingner, pp. 154–158; and Van Sickle, pp. 499–500, find an affirmative explanation of pastoral song.

[71] The point of these retrospective motifs is often obscured by those who think that the ninth poem was composed first, and represents an initial failure to save the farm, while the first poem represents a final success. E.g., Oppermann, pp. 212–213; Otis, pp. 131–133, 134–136. For criticisms of this view see Carl Becker, "Virgils Eklogenbuch," *Hermes* 90(1955):316–318, who argues that the loss of the farm is not Vergil's major theme.

O Lycida, vivi pervenimus, advena nostri
(quod numquam veriti sumus) ut possessor agelli
diceret: 'haec mea sunt; veteres migrate coloni.'
nunc victi, tristes, quoniam fors omnia versat,
hos illi (quod nec vertat bene) mittimus haedos.   [9. 2–6]

(O Lycidas, I have lived to see what I never even thought to fear: that the foreign possessor of my little farm should say: "These things are mine, go away, you old tenants." Now, beaten and sorrowful, since chance overturns all, I am sending off these kids for him — and I hope they don't sell.)

The phrase *vivi pervenimus* intimates Moeris' preoccupation with time, old age and loss. The parenthetical *quod numquam veriti sumus* recalls feelings of security associated with better times — feelings now proven illusory. As a result of his new knowledge, Moeris has come to look on human life as uncertain and unpredictable: "quoniam fors omnia versat." *Fors* represents his understanding of the link between man and history; it is his idea of a universal power. The pastoral world that had once seemed exempt from such powers has proven vulnerable, and Moeris has become a homespun philosopher late in life. Yet his gloomy philosophy implies a one-time false protection from reality: an illusion of innocence. Such a philosophy suits old age; yet it is strange for an old man to be learning of misfortune for the first time.

When Lycidas asks if the poet Menalcas had not saved the farm by his songs (7–10), Moeris extends his pessimistic reflections to include the failure of poetry in a hostile world:

Audieras, et fama fuit; sed carmina tantum
nostra valent, Lycida, tela inter Martia quantum
Chaonias dicunt aquila veniente columbas.   [9. 11–13]

(You had heard it; there was a rumor, but among the weapons of Mars, Lycidas, our songs have just so much force as people say of the doves of Chaonia when an eagle comes among them.)

The eagle and the prophetic doves are birds of Zeus, yet the stronger turns against the timid and weak.[72] To Moeris, poems

---

[72] Servius, III, 110–111 *ad* v. 13, suggests that the lesser augury, that of the doves, yields to the greater authority of the eagle.

seem fragile, in need of special protection and appreciation in the great world.

He goes on to explain not only the vulnerability of song, but also that of the poet, telling how he and Menalcas, engaged in a quarrel with the soldier, had a narrow escape from death (14–16). Moeris, the practical and superstitious, had heeded an omen and saved the poet's life. Although the precise nature of the event is vague, it seems to shatter all idealistic beliefs concerning the special nature of the poet. Menalcas participating *in litibus* has slipped out of his proper role and undertaken something beyond his strength. The very occurrence of such a quarrel shows the vulnerability of poetic nature in the face of actual affairs.

Moeris believes that Menalcas' career has been clouded by failure. His quotation of an uncompleted song praising Varus is ironic:

> Immo haec, quae Varo necdum perfecta canebat:
> 'Vare, tuum nomen, superet modo Mantua nobis,
> Mantua vae miserae nimium vicina Cremonae,
> cantantes sublime ferent ad sidera cycni.' [9. 26–29]

> (Sing rather those verses, not yet finished, which he was making for Varus: "Varus, your name, if only our Mantua remains ours — Mantua, alas, all too near the unhappy district of Cremona — the singing swans shall bear aloft to the stars.")

The song was a promise of gratitude, but only a conditional promise. Now it remains incomplete, for the appeal to Varus is lost even before the poet could polish his verses. In retrospect the lofty phrasing seems absurd.[73] Once again the poet had embarked on a venture beyond his powers, but this one was even within his own proper field.

The pessimism of Moeris' thinking is reflected in his choice of songs. He is reluctant when Lycidas begs him to sing something (32), but he remembers an old song about Galatea:

> 'huc ades, o Galatea; quis est nam ludus in undis?
> hic ver purpureum, varios hic flumina circum

---

[73] The swan, as bird of Apollo, is suited to heroic contexts: e.g., *Homeric Hymns* 21. 1; Hor. *C.* 4. 2. 25; Lucretius 3. 6–7.

fundit humus flores, hic candida populus antro
imminet et lentae texunt umbracula vites.
huc ades; insani feriant sine litora fluctus.'   [9. 39–43]

(Come here, O Galatea, for what sport is there among the
waves? Here shines the rosy springtime; here the turf around
the rivers pours forth flowers of mixed kinds; here the silver-
bright poplar leans over the cave and the slender vines weave a
diminutive shade. Come here; leave the raging waves to beat
on the shore.)

As an adaptation of the Cyclops' invitation to Galatea (*Idyll*
11. 42–49) this pretty song expresses a dream destined to
remain unfulfilled, and in this new context its futility is magni-
fied. As he sings of the eternal springtime of the *locus amoenus*
— a refuge from the real and restless ocean — Moeris gives voice
to his own longing to turn back from present reality. His choice
of a song shows regret for a fantasy world that has vanished,
and despair arising from a sentimental fixation upon the past.[74]

In direct contrast is the song of Caesar's star that Lycidas
remembers. It is an injunction to turn away from the past and
think of the present in terms of the future:

'Daphni, quid antiquos signorum suspicis ortus?
ecce, Dionaei processit Caesaris astrum,
astrum quo segetes gauderent frugibus et quo
duceret apricis in collibus uva colorem.
insere, Daphni, piros: carpent tua poma nepotes.'   [9. 46–50]

(Daphnis, why do you watch for ancient star signs to rise. Behold, the star of Venus' Caesar has marched forth; the star by
whose influence the seeded fields should rejoice in fruits; by
whose power the grape should lead forth its color over the sunny
hillsides. Graft now your pear trees, Daphnis; your grandsons
will gather the fruit.)

The farmer may claim a special, privileged relationship to the
future, for he inaugurates enterprises for posterity. In the *Cato
Maior*, Cato quotes a verse from Caecilius to express similar

---

[74] Putnam, *Virgil's Pastoral Art*, pp. 314–316, finds a somewhat pathetic futility
in the choice of a song so unsuited to present circumstances.

feelings concerning the work of the farm: "serit arbores, quae alteri saeclo prosint" (He sows trees so that they may be of use to another generation [7. 24]). Like Cato, Lycidas remembers that the harvest is not only for the farmer who plants, but also for posterity. The gratification of exercising foresight may be substituted for the self-indulgent pleasure of more immediate rewards. By foresight the farmer participates in the order of nature. Lycidas' perspective is dynamic, looking toward the future, waiting for things to come.[75]

His song recalls *Eclogues* 1 and 5. In 1, the words *insere piros* were ironic, spoken by Meliboeus in the bitterness of his loss. But the star of Caesar celebrates the apotheosis that Menalcas, the singer of *Eclogue* 5, has interpreted as the beginning of a new harmony between nature and man. Both the lost farm and the apotheosis are consequences of the death of Caesar: loss and promise mingled together. History is neither entirely benevolent nor entirely destructive. Although the immediate moment seems dismal, a balance of forces can be anticipated with time. Unlike Moeris, Lycidas maintains faith in things not yet accomplished, and sings of an order not yet known.

The contrast between the songs illuminates that between the speakers, for in choosing their favorite pieces from the works of Menalcas they have made his poems expressive of themselves. For Moeris, absorbed in his memories, the pastoral ideal is a reminder of degeneration. His attitude embodies the discontentment of man, mourning and seeking the golden age, amidst an imperfect nature. He remembers youth as an idyllic time when he could while away long days with singing:

Omnia fert aetas, animum quoque. saepe ego longos
cantando puerum memini me condere soles.

[75] If the song is not taken as an indication of Lycidas' personality, it can, of course, have other meanings. H. Wagenvoort, "Vergil's *Eclogues* 1 and 9," in *Studies in Roman Literature, Culture and Religion* (Leiden, 1956), p. 261, sees it as an urgent address to Caesar, containing a bitter echo of the optimistic 5. 50. Holtorf, pp. 228–229, calls it a tactful address to Octavian and a reminder of the importance of poetry in the great world. Otis p. 132, emphasizes the connection with Meliboeus' remarks in *Eclogue* 1: "This is what the promised blessings of Caesar have come to." Klingner, p. 156, sees an expression of hope in a new age under Octavian, the *divi filius*.

nunc oblita mihi tot carmina, vox quoque Moerim
iam fugit ipsa: lupi Moerim videre priores.
sed tamen ista satis referet tibi saepe Menalcas.   [9. 51–55]

(Age carries off everything, and also the spirit; I remember how
often in my boyhood I buried the long days with my singing.
Now all my songs are forgotten, and even Moeris' voice has now
run away: the wolves saw Moeris first—but Menalcas can tell
you the same tale often enough.)

Nature has robbed the singer of his voice, even as time has
weakened his memory. To Moeris, Menalcas seems also a poet
of bitter experience and failure. Thus he will often repeat the
old man's gloomy tale.

For Lycidas, the present moment is everything. Song is
always effective as a creative power. Lycidas is not concerned
with the poet's fate in the historical world, but only with nature's need for his art:

quis caneret Nymphas? quis humum florentibus herbis
spargeret aut viridi fontis induceret umbra?   [9. 19–20]

(Who would sing of the Nymphs? Who would scatter the ground
with flowering grasses or darken the fountains with green
shade?)

This fragment recalls the idealism of the Arcadian Corydon,
an idealism that sharpens man's awareness of the beauty of
nature. So Lycidas reveres Menalcas, the master singer, but the
central passage of the *Eclogue* comprises his definition of a
lesser poet: himself.

et me fecere poetam
Pierides, sunt et mihi carmina, me quoque dicunt
vatem pastores; sed non ego credulus illis.
nam neque adhuc Vario videor nec dicere Cinna
digna, sed argutos inter strepere anser olores.   [9. 32–36]

(The Pierian Muses have also made me a poet. I have songs of
my own and the shepherds even call me a bard, but I am not
ready to trust them; for I consider myself not worthy to speak
with Varius and Cinna, to honk like a goose among melodious
swans.)

Unlike such singers as Damoetas and Thyrsis, Lycidas claims neither pastoral superiority nor the attention of the great world. He cares more for his *carmina* than for the name of *vates*, a title he feels unworthy to claim. But although he accepts his rustic limitations, he is not oblivious to the great world. His preference for the song of Caesar's star indicates a desire to bind together the orders of nature and history.

Lycidas adds to his definition of poetry by tempering Moeris' dismal picture of the futility of song. Song always gratifies the singer; it can lessen hardship and make a long road less painful. Unlike Meliboeus, who drove his goats silently toward exile, Lycidas goes toward the city singing:

> cantantes licet usque (minus via laedet) eamus;
> cantantes ut eamus, ego hoc te fasce levabo.   [9. 64–65]

> (Let us go singing as far as we may—the way is less painful. To make our singing easier, I will relieve you of that burden.)

These verses complete a dramatic reversal in the roles of the two singers. At the beginning of the poem, the gloomy Moeris with his awareness of change and uncertainty had seemed the more realistic. Now Lycidas is more practical as he carries his ideal of order onward into an ambiguous world. He does not need to turn back from reality or seek refuge in sentimental memories. Twice he urges that Meliboeus forget his troubles in an exchange of songs (32, 56). But he does not forget to offer assistance in bearing the older shepherd's load.

Amidst oppressive circumstances, the younger singer merely acts for the best.[76] As we begin to see how Moeris' despair is fixed in emotional bondage to the past, how his love for pastoral singing is dependent upon the stability of the pastoral world, we also see the superiority of Lycidas' commitment to the future and his ability to act without question or complaint. His desire for song is whetted by the discussion of Menalcas' poetry. Even as he talks, he stops to notice the world around him:

[76] Perret, pp. 97–98: "It is Lycidas who is at the center of the poem, the most attractive, perhaps of all the characters that Vergil has depicted in the *Bucolics:* spontaneous, refined, confident of his talent, happy to receive something of his just deserts, capable of having lived through catastrophes without being tarnished by them, the very figure of youth."

et nunc omne tibi stratum silet aequor, et omnes,
aspice, ventosi ceciderunt murmuris aurae.
hinc adeo media est nobis via; namque sepulcrum
incipit apparere Bianoris. hic ubi densas
agricolae stringunt frondes, hic, Moeri, canamus;
hic haedos depone, tamen veniemus in urbem.   [9. 57–62]

(And now the whole level surface of the plain lies quiet before
you, and see, all the gusty murmurs of the breeze have ceased.
This place is midway in our road, for the tomb of Bianor begins
to be visible. Here where the farmers cut the thick leaves, here,
Moeris, let us sing. Here put down your kids. We will still arrive
in the city.)

In this prospect there are elements of melancholy. A distant
tomb is the travelers' landmark; the bundled leaves foretell the
approach of winter; the tranquillity of the evening portends
rain. The singers are midway in their journey, approaching the
terminus of the pastoral world. Yet Lycidas sees peace and unity
in this portentous calm, a setting not inappropriate for song.
Even if they rest and sing, they will finish their journey.[77]

By contrast, Moeris' insistence on completing the necessary
task with no relaxation seems single-minded and restrictive:

Desine plura, puer, et quod nunc instat agamus;
carmina tum melius, cum venerit ipse, canemus.   [9. 66–67]

(Say nothing more, boy, and let us do what is urgent. We will
sing our songs better when he himself has come back.)

Rejecting the suggestion that the immediate moment may be
made less burdensome, or even enjoyable, Moeris waits for the
absent Menalcas to return and inspire better singing. His hopes
are not truly placed in the future, but rather in a recovery of
the past.

The singers are opposite in mood and philosophy, and thus
in their evaluations of pastoral song. They are not, however,
opposed in sympathies. Each hopes for a better world; each,
in his way, is a seeker after a pastoral ideal.

[77] Putnam, *Virgil's Pastoral Art*, p. 329, suggests an opposite meaning: that
Lycidas fails to understand that the conclusion of the journey will mean the end
of pastoral song.

Moeris, like Corydon and the unhappy lover, cherishes the myth of natural innocence: a passive tranquillity that is shattered by the coming of experience as song has been injured by confrontation with the historical world. To one who thinks in this manner, the awareness of change is bound to be tragic, leaving no more than a fading vision of a once-happy world.

Lycidas, on the other hand, sees that pastoral order is created by poets who interpret an indifferent world by their art. The pastoral ideal is recurrent, reborn in all times and circumstances. The poet need never be silent in his quest for ideal order; he can satisfy desires by giving them articulation, even as Lycidas pleases himself by the discussion and exchange of songs. Beyond this, the singer sees a nature that is not unrealistically perfect, but capable of accommodating disorder and surviving temporary disturbances. Unlike the lost paradise, this nature may always furnish new material for the poetic imagination. For the poet who takes an active rather than a passive role, there is the hope of relegating disorder to a subordinate place in a universal scheme. Thus in the face of civil war and the lost farm, Lycidas sings of the promise given to the future by Caesar's star.

Neither triumphs completely. Although the optimism of Lycidas is engaging and makes a strong bid for the reader's sympathy, Moeris has the last word. Their debate is incapable of full resolution for human nature follows the way of Moeris as readily as that of Lycidas. The pastoral songs of Menalcas are equally productive of optimism and despair.

In the last of the dialogue poems, when the pastoral landscape is fading into memory, the symbolic tensions surrounding the lost garden must inevitably reveal their significance for the great world. Menalcas, the master poet, may never return to the pastoral. But in Vergil's later works, the pastoral dream does recur in all its original freshness to provoke once more a meeting of innocence and experience. In the greater world of the *Aeneid* this conflict is no longer restricted to the theoretical exploration of modes of poetic imagination, but takes on new urgency in the crises of the active historical life. Now Italy itself is the pastoral sphere, where golden-age longings conflict with reality as individuals oppose their wills to a changing historical

world. The opposition of withdrawal and commitment is mag-
nified in the persons of the two Italian kings, Evander and
Latinus.

Both are pastoral rulers and, like the herdsmen of the *Eclogues*,
have much in common. Each is united through ancestry with
the Trojans. Each knows of a prophecy linking the destiny of
his kingdom with that of Aeneas. Each has a single child whose
fate will be intertwined with that of Aeneas. At the moment
of Aeneas' arrival in Italy, each rules his wilderness domain in
peace. Each is aware of the legend of Saturn and the tradition
of the Italian golden age. But here the two differ, for each has
his own understanding of the meaning of this golden age.
Latinus, who traces his lineage from Saturn, sees himself as the
recreation of his divine ancestor, the preserver of an unaltered
tradition of peace:[78]

> ne fugite hospitium, neve ignorate Latinos
> Saturni gentem haud vinclo nec legibus aequam
> sponte sua veterisque dei se more tenentem.   [7. 202–204]

> (Do not flee from our welcome; and do not be ignorant of the
> Latins, a race of Saturn, just without bond or laws, holding itself
> by its own free will to the precedent of the ancient god.)

Latinus' ideals are those of innocence. His faith in spontaneous
virtue implies superiority to law, which is to him no more than a
chain (*vinclum*), a base means of compulsion. But Evander
gives a different account of the Saturnian ideal:

> haec nemora indigenae Fauni Nymphaeque tenebant
> gensque virum truncis et duro robore nata,
> quis neque mos neque cultus erat, nec iungere tauros
> aut componere opes norant aut parcere parto,
> sed rami atque asper victu venatus alebat.
> primus ab aetherio venit Saturnus Olympo
> arma Iovis fugiens et regnis exsul ademptis.
> is genus indocile ac dispersum montibus altis
> composuit legesque dedit.   [8. 314–321]

[78] For Latinus' relationship to the Saturnian kingdom and the weakness of his
vision see W. S. Anderson, "Juno and Saturn in the *Aeneid*," *Studies in Philology*
50(1958):519–532; Kenneth Reckford, "Latent Tragedy in *Aeneid* VII. 1–285,"
AJPhil. 82(1961):252–269.

(The native Fauns and Nymphs possessed these groves, and a race of men born from tree trunks and hard oak who had neither customs or culture, not knowing how to yoke the bulls or gather together their resources or spare their substance. But the hard food of the bough and the hunter nourished them. Then first came Saturn from lofty Olympus, fleeing the arms of Jove, an exile whose domains had been snatched away. He brought together this intractable race scattered over the high mountains and gave them laws.)

Looking backward to the inhumanity of a life that is no more than a spontaneous existence in nature, Evander understands the need for law, to him neither constraint nor bondage but a guide to a harmonious life in human communities, the true foundation of the golden age:

aurea quae perhibent illo sub rege fuere
saecula: sic placida populos in pace regebat.   [8. 324–325]

(Men say that the ages under that king were golden; thus did he rule his people in tranquil peace.)

Unlike Latinus, Evander places the lost world behind him. Knowing that greed and discord have undone the ideals of Saturn, he thinks of himself as no more than a ruler in a lesser age, an exile who has founded his city amid the ruins of a glorious past.

To each of these monarchs Aeneas comes as the bringer of inevitable change, and each, in his response to the stranger, shows the effects of his individual temperament and philosophy. Latinus is unimpressed by Aeneas' heritage from a heroic past, by gifts snatched from the ruins of Troy and mementoes of the defeated Priam (7. 249–258). With his thoughts fixed on future glory, he welcomes Aeneas, accepting the alliance that promises to carry the name of his race to the stars (7. 96–107). Still, he is unprepared for the future. Already he overlooks the dangerous restlessness of Amata his queen and young Turnus, whose more chauvinistic adherence to the Saturnian tradition opposes the acceptance of a foreign prince in Italy.[79] From them

[79] Anderson, p. 528, suggests that Juno, as daughter of Saturn, regards the Saturnian Age as the status quo of Italy. As her followers, Amata and Turnus become forces resistant to change.

and from his people, Latinus appears to expect the spontaneous obedience that is his own ideal. His very surroundings reveal his blindness to the real nature of Italy. In his ancestral temple, surrounded by images of his warlike forbears, kings descended from Mars,[80] he sits on his high throne proclaiming peace (7. 182–191). But the green and golden surface of Latium masks the violence of human anger. For Latinus, torn between his desire for the fulfillment of the prophecy and his wish to preserve his illusion of innocence, there is no course save futile retreat. Closing himself within the recesses of his citadel (7. 599–600), he refuses emotional commitment to the war that determines the fate of his kingdom.

Evander places a higher value upon the heroic past. He sees in the arrival of Aeneas the re-enactment of a cherished memory: the visit of the noble Anchises to his boyhood home in Arcadia (8. 155–168). Now his reverence for Anchises is repeated in Pallas' attraction to Anchises' son, and without question of the future the father dedicates his son to the cause of justice in Italy. A veteran of old wars at Praeneste, Evander knows that Italy is no land of peace, and his shrewd advice sends Aeneas to seek his needed allies among the Etruscans (4. 470–503). With the defeat of the brutal Mezentius, he hopes to see the beginning of a better age. Unlike Latinus, whose happiness rests upon false security, he is conscious of human limitations and ready to accept the conflicts of an imperfect world. Yet before Aeneas leaves Pallanteum, Evander also speaks of the ideals of moderation that govern his humble life (8. 364–365). Clearly he is the king who truly embodies the traditions of ancient Saturn, the more because he does not presume to recognize the parallel himself.[81] Thus Vergil has extended his contrasting of the pastoral dreamer and the realist as a paradigm of human responses to the forces of historical change. The awareness that man cannot successfully

---

[80] This point is especially clear if we consider the similarity between Latinus' temple and the Forum of Augustus with its military images and temple of Mars Ultor that Henry Rowell discusses in "Vergil and the Forum of Augustus," *AJPhil.* 62(1948):261–276.

[81] Michael Putnam discusses Evander's golden age in *The Poetry of the "Aeneid"* (Cambridge, Mass., 1965), pp. 130ff.

shape his immediate environment or his vision of the future upon the pattern of a static mythological ideal is, as a scholar has recently suggested, a lesson that the author of the *Aeneid* may be proposing to Augustus, the creator of the Roman golden age.[82]

[82] Robert Rowland, "Foreshadowing in Vergil, *Aeneid* VIII. 714–28," *Latomus* 27(1968):832–842.

CHAPTER 6

❦ Prophecy and
❦ Retrospect

In reading the rustic poems we have seen how an increasing sense of the futility of pastoral innocence is tempered by a compensatory awareness of new possibilities for pastoral poetry as a microcosm of the world of experience. In more literary and philosophical terms these possibilities reach their fullest development in *Eclogues* 4 and 6, the songs of the Eclogue Poet whose common theme is history, both national and universal, presented with colorings of prophecy and retrospect.[1]

Eclogues 4 and 6

The link between the two poems has been described by Brooks Otis as a contrast of moral perspectives, to which the fourth poem contributes an optimistic history raising man from an iron age to a golden and the sixth, a history that follows pessimistically from creation and the golden age to the decline of man.[2]

---

[1] According to Servius, *Servii Grammatici qui feruntur in Vergilii Carmina Commentarii*, ed. G. Thilo and H. Hagen, vol. III: *Servii Grammatici qui feruntur in Vergilii Bucolica et Georgica*, ed. G. Thilo (Leipzig, 1887: repr., Hildesheim, 1961), p. 3, the two poems (along with *Eclogue* 10) stand apart because they are *non merae rusticae*. The fourth poem he considers a *genethlicon* (birth celebration) and the sixth a *theologia*, suggesting that Vergil had composed these apastoral pieces either from a desire to include *res altiores* in his collection or for the sake of variety.

[2] "The Silenus Song falls into a quite recognizable pattern: Creation, Golden Age, Fall and Flood (Prometheus, Pyrrha), Age of Heroes and first expedition on the sea (Hylas); then a series of *amores* (Pasiphaë, Atalanta) and *amores-metamorphoses* (Phaethontides, Scylla, Tereus, Philomela) all illustrations of *amor indignus*, love gone wrong, love *after* the golden age or *Saturnia regna*" (Brooks Otis, *Virgil: A Study in Civilized Poetry* [Oxford, 1963], pp. 136–137, 138).

216

But the moral distinction may also be seen as a function of differing kinds of myth; the one presenting mankind as he wishes to be, the other an attempt to grapple with man and nature as they are. This contrast provides a focal point for the essential myth of pastoral: man's troubled quest for a renewal of identity. Together the two poems present the essential conflicts of the *Eclogues*.

In speaking of the visionary England in Spenser's *Faerie Queene*, Angus Fletcher makes a point important to the understanding of the prophetic poem: "The major prophetic writings of the west belong to a tradition that is only partially predictive, a tradition that balances anticipation of the future with a concern for the past, and even more important, for the present . . . History is useful and necessary to the prophet because it presents him with a theoretical wholeness of past, present and future."[3] Such is the disposition of the fourth *Eclogue*. Although the poet speaks with prophetic confidence, his intention is to create a model for the future in terms of the deficiencies and strengths of the past and the needs of the present. Uniting the perspectives of myth and philosophy, he discovers an ideal pattern for mankind: a literary revelation to give dignity to the pastoral and a political vision to perfect the course of Roman history. Thus it is unnecessary to question the alliance of politics and pastoral in the *Eclogue*, or even to insist that the work is primarily a pastoral poem. Its golden age is appropriate both to history and to pastoral, for it is by this image that man has conventionally shaped his historical legends as an articulation of his social desires. But in their double association, the images of the golden age are removed from their familiar, retrospective context to become metaphors within a structure of philosophical allegory. By exploiting its figurative capacity the pastoral can most surely fulfill its ambitions of creating a microcosmic view of the world. A need for metaphor is implied in the opening lines, where the poet speaks of creating forests

[3] "The modern era, beginning with the sixteenth century, sees the term 'prophecy' gradually pick up a connotation which the critic of Spenser will have to reject: the notion that a prophetic utterance gives a sharp, unequivocal vision of the future" (Angus Fletcher, *The Prophetic Moment: An Essay on Spenser* [Chicago, 1971], pp. 3–5).

of consular dignity ("si canimus silvas, silvae sint consule dignae," [4.3]). In the course of the poem, the forests turn to farmlands, a Roman symbol of order and unity.

The first words of the prophecy proclaim a new and startling coalescence of time:

> Ultima Cumaei venit iam carminis aetas;
> magnus ab integro saeclorum nascitur ordo.
> iam redit et virgo, redeunt Saturnia regna,
> iam nova progenies caelo demittitur alto.
> tu modo nascenti puero, quo ferrea primum
> desinet ac toto surget gens aurea mundo,
> caste fave Lucina: tuus iam regnat Apollo.   [4.4–10]

(The furthest age of Cumean song now has come; the great order of time's divisions is born anew. Already the virgin has returned; the kingdoms of Saturn have returned; already a new offspring is sent down from the lofty sky. Grant favor, chaste Lucina, to the child now being born, with whom the iron race will cease and a golden race spring up over the entire world. Already your Apollo reigns.)

Ultima is an ambiguous word that can mean both earliest and last. Past and future unite in this term and both are at hand in the reappearance of the virgin Astrea, symbol of justice, and of the Saturnian Age. Return has become birth and a beginning. Present and future come together with the advent of the child for whom the iron age will give way to a golden. The *gens aurea* is a race whose nature embodies its goal. Quite possibly Vergil is thinking of a passage in the *Republic* where Plato distinguishes the qualities of real men by these designations, regarding the traditional gold, silver, and bronze as the metals or tempers of the soul. As an offspring of the gods the child seems to stand for the organizing spirit of the new age. His life will be synonymous with the perfection of human society. By this token, we may identify the child as a manifestation of the Jungian archetype of the divine child: a figure that represents man's longing for, and confidence in, an idealized better self.[4]

---

[4] On time and especially the insistence of the future in the language of the poem's first verses see John Van Sickle, "The Fourth Pastoral Poems of Virgil and Theocritus," *Atti e Memorie dell'Arcadia*, series 3a, 5 (1969):2–7. *The Republic*,

In the central passages of the poem, the future takes form in pastoral terms as the poet looks ahead to a world that will grow with the child, pairing each stage in his development with a new stage of alteration in nature. Thus he creates a hypothetical landscape that is specific in detail yet whose lack of topographical organization and visual perspective links it with the *locus amoenus* of the monologue poems. The unreal quality of the landscape is a constant reminder that it is, at best, a fragile poetic vision. But unlike other, more static visions, this embodies dynamic principles of growth, moving toward the transformation of a wilderness into a spontaneous agricultural paradise. This clear symbolic progress keeps the vision from becoming either private or hedonistic and maintains its ties with the historical world.

The first stage of the description provides for a moderate amelioration of nature:

> At tibi prima, puer, nullo munuscula cultu
> errantis hederas passim cum baccare tellus
> mixtaque ridenti colocasia fundet acantho.
> ipsae lacte domum referent distenta capellae
> ubera, nec magnos metuent armenta leones;
> ipsa tibi blandos fundent cunabula flores.
> occidet et serpens, et fallax herba veneni
> occidet; Assyrio vulgo nascetur amomum.   [4. 18–25]

(But for you, child, earth with no cultivation will pour forth her first small tributes; the wandering ivy everywhere, with wild nard and colocasia mixed with smiling acanthus. The goats themselves will bring home udders swollen with milk and the flocks will not fear great lions. Your very cradle will pour

---

3. 415a: "God in fashioning those of you who are fitted to hold rule mingled gold in their generation, for which reason they are the most precious—but in the helpers silver, and iron and brass in the farmers and other craftsmen." C. G. Jung, *The Archetypes and the Collective Unconscious*, trans. R. F. C. Hull (New York, 1949), pp. 160–166. For discussion, see Eleanor Winsor Leach, "*Eclogue* 4: Symbolism and Sources," *Arethusa* 4(1971):167–169. An equivalent symbolism, with more specific religious associations, is posited by Eduard Nörden, *Die Geburt des Kindes: Geschischte einer religiosen Idee* (Leipzig, 1924), who identifies the child with the Alexandrian god Aion, a figure representing the cyclical renewal of time.

forth harmless flowers, and the serpent will die away, and the
herb that deceives with its poison will die. Everywhere Assyrian
incense will be born.)

The verbs *fundet* and *fundent* supply an exuberant motion that
answers to the *surget* of verse 9; and *nascetur*, echoing *nascenti*,
reiterates the theme of birth, drawing together the natural and
human worlds. The phrase *nullo cultu* prefigures golden-age
spontaneity. In tribute to the child, the world is becoming a
liberally furnished *locus amoenus*, the garden of a fruitful,
maternal *tellus*. It is an exotic garden that draws together *flora*
from Italy and the far corners of the earth, combining natural
luxuriance with hints of symbolic stylization. The acanthus that
grows wild among rocks but lends itself to graceful artistic
designs, the ivy that wreathes the cups of Menalcas and is an
emblem of inspired poetry, and the *baccar* that wards off the
evil eye mingle with Egyptian *colocasia* and Assyrian incense.[5]
This is a *locus amoenus* universalized, a garden containing the
abundance of the whole world. It is also an ideal pasture where
the goats, the most wayward of the herdsman's charges, come
home with full udders as, in Callimachus' *Hymn* (1. 47–48),
Amaltheia comes to nourish the infant Zeus in his Cretan cave.
It is a harmonious pasture where the lions, newcomers from the
great world, live peacefully with the bucolic herd. Yet some old
perils are absent. The disappearance of the *fallax herba* signifies
that nature has no more deceptive snares for man. The death
of the serpent suggests a triumph of civilized order such as that
implied in legends of Hercules or Apollo, but here no struggle
is necessary; nature herself has taken the serpent away. In its
eclecticism and random juxtaposition of images, this garden
maintains the outlines and freedom of a wilderness, but it is
a wilderness purged of danger where nature has become a
sponsor and friendly companion of man.

The transformation that marks the child's adolescence combines two motifs. New changes in nature contrast with the
repetition of old historical patterns:

[5] *Acanthus:* Vitruvius *De Arch.* 4. 9. *Baccar:* see *Ecl.* 7. 27–28; Servius, III, 48
ad 4. 19; and the discussion in Michael Putnam, *Virgil's Pastoral Art* (Princeton,
1970), p. 147.

at simul heroum laudes et facta parentis
iam legere et quae sit poteris cognoscere virtus,
molli paulatim flavescet campus arista
incultisque rubens pendebit sentibus uva
et durae quercus sudabunt roscida mella.
pauca tamen suberunt priscae vestigia fraudis,
quae temptare Thetim ratibus, quae cingere muris
oppida, quae iubeant telluri infindere sulcos.
alter erit tum Tiphys et altera quae vehat Argo
delectos heroas; erunt etiam altera bella
atque iterum ad Troiam magnus mittetur Achilles.   [4. 26–36]

(But as soon as you can read the praises of the heroes and the
deeds of your fathers and can recognize what the nature of
virtue may be, little by little the wild fields will turn golden with
soft grain, and the grape will hang reddening from unattended
thorn bushes, and the hard oaks will sweat dewy honey; however
a few traces of ancient error will survive in order to spur [men]
on to try the sea with ships, to gird their towns with walls, and
to cut furrows into the earth. There will be another Tiphys and
another Argo which will carry chosen heroes, and again a great
Achilles will be sent to Troy.)

The child's education prepares him to take his part in the
actions of the political and historical worlds. Learning of heroic
glory and of the ancestral deeds that are his own tradition, and
of the philosophy that should frame his standards, he prepares,
in a Roman manner, to meet the demands of the civilized world.
Accordingly, wild nature organizes herself toward fruitfulness.
Slowly the *campi* take on the garb of the farmland while the
thorn trees turn to a vineyard and the sap of the oaks becomes
honey. The wilderness garden yields to a broader agricultural
prospect, better adapted to the needs of man. Yet civilization
and nature remain at cross purposes. Traces of the first human
evil recur as man with his ships, his fortifications, and his plow
imposes his willful, greedy domination upon the earth. As in
the past, these activities preface war. The conflicts of the heroic
age repeat themselves; the historical and the agricultural
worlds remain separate. Nature's alterations reflect the growing
hope of the child but have not yet changed human life.

Finally, when the child has reached maturity, man's labors

cease, and the whole world assumes the pattern of the self-cultivating farm (37–45):

> hinc, ubi iam firmata virum te fecerit aetas,
> cedet et ipse mari vector, nec nautica pinus
> mutabit merces; omnis feret omnia tellus.
> non rastros patietur humus, non vinea falcem;
> robustus quoque iam tauris iuga solvet arator.
> nec varios discet mentiri lana colores,
> ipse sed in pratis aries iam suave rubenti
> murice, iam croceo mutabit vellera luto;
> sponte sua sandyx pascentis vestiet agnos.   [4. 37–45]

(At the time when age confirmed in strength will have made you a man, the trader will give up the sea; the seafaring pine will exchange no cargoes; every land will bear all things. The ground will not endure rakes nor the vine the pruning hook. The sturdy plowman will loosen the yoke from his bulls. Nor will the fleece learn to lie by means of its varied colors. In the meadows, the ram himself will color his fleece, now with a sweetly blushing purple, now with a yellowed saffron. A vermilion hue will spontaneously clothe the feeding lambs.)

The limitations of natural law are lifted. Constraint and violation cease. No longer is man compelled to live by struggling against nature with his agricultural weapons. There is freedom for man and animal as the plowman releases his bulls from the yoke. Such freedom is typical of the golden-age dream. But one new miracle sets this Roman era apart from other legendary ages. No longer will man employ his artifice in teaching nature to deceive for human pleasure, for the browsing sheep have put on the brilliant colors of the civilized world.[6] The new age brings forth a unique sign of accord between nature and man.

Despite the vivid accretion of specific details, an air of mysterious elusiveness hangs over this prophecy. A reader would be

---

[6] Macrobius *Sat.* 3. 7. 1–2, proposed that these remarkable colors might be inspired by an Etruscan legend and quotes a passage translated from an Etruscan book: "If a sheep or ram is sprinkled with purple or gold color, this will increase the prosperity of the leader of a social class or a people; his people will bring forth offspring of distinction." This notion should support the poet's use of golden-age abundance as a metaphor for the abundance attending upon civic virtue.

very naïve to take it for literal prediction.[7] Superficially, it is a return to man's mythic origins, for the climax of the golden age clearly recalls the Hesiodic image of that ideal past before the decline of man commenced and evil crept into the world. The world-farm stands for a reversal of this process, for the disappearance of ancient evil from the organization of human society.

Yet throughout the vision, emphasis is not on man's return to nature, but rather on nature's approach to the human world. In place of regression is a movement away from an old, imperfect reality toward a definite new goal. This movement is fostered by the double vision of the prophecy, the pairing of stages wherein nature, like the child, passes through infancy, adolescence, and maturity. With its emphasis on *facta* and the continued conflicts that accompany nature's gradual transformation, the prophecy speaks also to heroic aspiration. The spirit of the Roman pastoral impulse, the moral bond between the countryside and the state, is solemnized in Vergil's intermingling of civic and rural motifs. A Roman desire for fame and achievement—a desire that has no ·place within the Hesiodic golden age—is brought into accord with man's perpetual wish to live in harmony with his natural environment. A Roman, we may be sure, would no sooner live in a primitive golden age than John Milton in his own Garden of Eden.

Specifically, I suggest that Vergil does not propose to revisit the lost dream world of the past. His literary allusions ask the reader to recall passages where the golden age is more than a mythical memory, existing outside its legendary chronology as a model for the contemporary world. In Chapter 2 I mentioned the way in which Hesiod and Plato rationalized the archetype, removing it from the irretrievable past to take on new meaning

---

[7] Conventionally, the prophecy has been taken for a free adaptation of the Hesiodic world myth, a reversal of the pattern of decline. See F. Klingner, *Römische Geisteswelt*, 2d ed. (Munich, 1961), p. 301; H. J. Rose, *The Eclogues of Vergil* (Berkeley, 1942), p. 184. The problems posed by this interpretation are sharply outlined by G. Jachmann, "Die vierte Ekloge Vergils," *Arbeitsgemeinschaft für Forschung des Landes Nordrhein Westfalen* (Cologne, 1953), pp. 46–47; Jachmann investigates the paradoxical existence of two golden ages: that announced for the year 40 which has already begun, and that projected into future time.

as a counsel of civic perfection. Hesiod speaks of a people who might recapture the spirit of the early life by the practice of justice and righteousness, and, in consequence, might realize the favor of the gods with abundant returns from nature and a peaceful life:

> But when men issue straight decisions
>   to their own people
> and to strangers, and do not step at all
>   off the road of rightness,
> their city flourishes, and the people
>   blossom inside it.
> Peace, who brings boys to manhood, is in their land,
>   nor does Zeus
> of the wide brows ever ordain that hard war
>   shall be with them.
> Neither famine nor inward disaster comes the way
>   of those people
> who are straight and just; they do their work
>   as if work were a holiday;
> the earth gives them great livelihood,
>   on their mountains the oaks
> bear acorns for them in their crowns,
>   and bees in their middles.
> Their wool-bearing sheep are weighted down
>   with fleecy burdens.
> Their women bear them children
>   who resemble their parents.
> They prosper in good things throughout.
>   They need have no traffic
> with ships, for their own grain-giving land
>   yields them its harvest.   [*Works and Days* 225–237][8]

The ideals here are simplistic as befits the practical moral philosophy of the *Works and Days*. Unlike the legendary innocents, these people labor, yet their tasks are not such a burden as those of ordinary men. Above all, they are self-sufficient, free from the foreign commerce that leads man into war. In the *Laws*, Plato has removed the myth from its agricultural setting and added more sophisticated rationalization and an

[8] Richard Lattimore, *Hesiod* (Ann Arbor, 1959).

allegorical meaning. Within the structure of contemporary societies and governments, a nation that pursues virtue under the leadership of a just ruler may re-establish the harmony and abundance of the legendary era. Thus the tradition of the golden age is to be interpreted as a moral allegory whose lesson is "that we ought by every means to imitate the life of the age of Chronos, as tradition paints it, and order both our homes and States in obedience to that mortal element within us, giving to reason's ordering the name of 'law' " (*Laws* 713e).[9]

Both in Hesiod and in Plato the new golden age is produced, not by a passive or naïve goodness, but by the active virtues of a people striving for justice. Vergil also implies such a purposeful unity in his new Roman future. He has built his prophetic vision by combining Plato's political philosophy with Hesiod's agricultural atmosphere, but like Plato he regards the details of the legend, the images of material prosperity, as a metaphorical equivalent of the undefined goods and abundance belonging to a state where man has learned to live in harmony with man.

Still, the garden is too familiar an image of innocence to serve as an adequate symbol for the transformation of the future without the figure that relates it to history: the child born to be the leader of a new race of man. This child, whose presence gives unity to the entire poem, is a real infant who needs the favor of Lucina at birth, who must at last be encouraged to smile at his mother; yet by concealing his name and identity, Vergil has also made him an abstraction, a link to bind together the visionary world and the real. The child's birth gives concrete occasion for the beginning of change, and his human maturing provides a definite goal. The virtues of the child are opposed to the *scelus* and *fraus* of the past, and, although neither is fully defined, we sense the opposition of forces necessary to creative change.

Vergil's child enters history as a part of the gods' design for the recreation of the world. Plato's contemporary golden age

---

[9] The translations of *The Laws* are by R. G. Bury, *Plato: The Laws*, 2 vols. (Cambridge, Loeb, 1926). Additional discussion and citations may be found in Leach, pp. 176–181.

also requires the guidance of such a figure, a ruler or lawmaker who recalls the beneficent governors of the Saturnian kingdom, given to man by the gods. Plato explains the circumstances under which such figures may influence the state: "God controls all that is, and . . . chance and occasion cooperate with God in the control of all human affairs. It is, however, less harsh to admit that these two must be accompanied by a third factor, which is Art. For that the pilot's art should cooperate with Occasion — verily I, for one, should esteem that a great advantage" (709b).

"Opportunity" is manifested in the practical and material circumstances of a state; "chance" in the appearance of a ruler divinely endowed with the art that is necessary for his task: "When all the other conditions are present which a country needs to possess in the way of fortune if it is ever to be happily settled, then every such state needs to meet with a lawgiver who holds fast to the truth" (709c). Such conditions are approximated by the divinely reconstituted world order that inaugurates Vergil's poem. "Occasion," or the moment when the new course of history is destined to begin, is the year of Pollio's consulship. Accordingly, Pollio himself must be a leader under whose government traces of Rome's old wrongs will disappear:

> teque adeo decus hoc aevi, te consule, inibit,
> Pollio, et incipient magni procedere menses;
> te duce, si qua manent sceleris vestigia nostri,
> inrita perpetua solvent formidine terras.   [4. 11–14]

(With you, Pollio, as our consul, this great glory of the age will begin, and the great months begin to move forward. With you as leader, whatever imprints of our wrongdoing remain will dissolve, and release the earth from perpetual dread.)

Here Vergil echoes another of Plato's requirements for the betterment of the state: "a heaven-sent desire for temperate and just institutions . . . in those who hold high positions" (711d–e). In seeking to obliterate the crimes of the past, Pollio's government will anticipate that of the child's maturity.

The Platonic lawgiver is a being in whose nature virtue is instinctive. From communication with gods, daimons, and heroes he receives his inspired knowledge of the good (716c–717d). So Vergil's child participates in the society of the gods:

> ille deum vitam accipiet divisque videbit
> permixtos heroas et ipse videbitur illis.   [4. 15–16]

> (He will take on a life like that of the gods, and will look upon gods intermingled with heroes, and he himself will be noticed by them.)

Although the ideal ruler is, in a sense, a pastoral ruler, governing a world of ordered tranquillity, yet Plato specifies that he must be loyal to the traditions of his native land, honoring its best laws and preserving its institutions, giving reverence to ancestors and parents (717c–d). Thus Vergil's child re-establishes the best in ancestral tradition: "pacatumque reget patriis virtutibus orbem" (And he will rule a world made peaceful by such virtues as his ancestors knew [4. 17]). This is not to say that Vergil's creation of such a figure turns the *Eclogue* into a political document, much less that he is advancing a theory of monarchy for Rome. Not even the background of the *Laws* has this implication, for Plato keeps his own doctrine flexible, allowing that the best government may be carried out in accordance with a mixed constitution (712c–712e). Both here and in Plato, the ruler is ultimately no more than a theoretical figure, a figure longed for as a projection of man's desire to achieve the ideal.[10] But even if such rulers never exist in fact, they provide a conceptual model for governors and statesmen whose actions may rise above the common intrigues of politics. Vergil's only political doctrine is the moral injunction for present and future implied by his formulation of the ideal. In translating his Roman child into the divine leader of the golden race, he has recreated Plato's allegory of human perfection in poetic form.

The poem is not, therefore, a straightforward prediction, but the embodiment and elaboration of an idea. This idea is in-

---

[10] See F. Solmsen, "Hesiodic Motifs in Plato," in *Hésiode et son influence*, Entretiens sur l'antiquité classique, 7(Geneva: Fondation Hardt, 1960) pp. 193, 194. Plato argues that a "human being" cannot rule with justice, but only the divine and immortal element in man.

trinsically sufficient for the poet's literary elevation of the pastoral, capable of transforming the ancient and static dream of innocence into a new and dynamic myth. But the form of the poem also provides for a new dignity in pastoral, for Vergil has explored his subject within a clear traditional frame, modeling the rhetorical structure of his prophecy upon that of the *Homeric Hymns*.[11] The topical divisions of the hymnic pattern are obvious in the *Eclogue:* a celebration of the god's lineage; a tale of his birth; a record of his deeds and powers; a closing invocation. In itself the hymn combines archaic dignity with Alexandrian poetic sophistication, since the ancient form had been revived by Callimachus and adapted by Theocritus, who brought it to the fringes of pastoral in two poems: *Idyll* 24, the deeds of Heracles, and *Idyll* 17, the praises of Ptolemy. As Gordon Williams has suggested, *Idyll* 17 is closest in form to the *Eclogue*, showing many of the same structural features: a commentary on the ruler's parentage; a celebration of his birth; a lengthy, somewhat pastoral description of the fertility of Egypt; a promise of future divinity.[12] But although this poem attributes great virtues to Ptolemy and declares his worthiness to be celebrated in terms belonging to the gods, it remains a flattering encomium of a ruler. Vergil, whose unwillingness to flatter is clear from his abstract and symbolic treatment of the child, has chosen a slighter subject and made it nobler, restoring the secularized hymn to its archaic spirit. He has made the literary form function as a metaphor that transforms its human subject into a divine.

But Vergil's most original variation upon the hymnic form is in the two sections of seven verses each that follow upon the golden-age prophecy: his invocation of the ruler and his prayer for his own poetry.[13] In the hymns, both topics occur frequently, but they are formulaic and little related to the structure of the

---

[11] For specific discussion, see Leach, pp. 171–172.

[12] Regarding *Idyll* 24 see M. Bollack, "Le Retour de Saturne (une étude de la quatrième églogue)," *Rev. Et. Lat.* 45(1967):304–324. Gordon Williams, *Tradition and Originality in Roman Poetry* (Oxford, 1968), pp. 274–283.

[13] For the structural divisions of the poem see Van Sickle, p. 2. The divisions indicated by his grouping (3–7–7–28–7–7–4) correspond roughly with the topical divisions of the hymnic form.

poems. By calling upon the god for personal favor and promising, at some uncertain date, a new song, the singer gives a solemn and reverent conclusion to his work.[14] In the *Eclogue*, Vergil has expanded the personal element in these conventions, reshaping them as a self-conscious commentary upon his own prophetic gesture.

With his image of bright-fleeced sheep in the meadow the poet carries his golden-age vision to the limits of fantasy. He has, as it were, warned the reader that he is not composing a literal prediction, that he himself is not so naïve as to expect the future of Rome to spring up in the Saturnian pasture. A poet speaking in the darkness of the present cannot hope to give final shape and substance to the ambiguous and unlimited future. The illumination of a future in terms of the past, the revision of conventional images and fantasies, is as far as his vision can proceed. Thus, resigning to the Parcae, the traditional guardians of heroic destiny, the authority by which his better world may be confirmed, the poet turns back from his visionary farmland and speaks in the present moment, invoking the divine figure whom he himself has created:

> 'Talia saecla,' suis dixerunt 'currite' fusis
> concordes stabili fatorum numine Parcae.
> adgredere o magnos (aderit iam tempus) honores,
> cara deum suboles, magnum Iovis incrementum!
> aspice convexo nutantem pondere mundum,
> terrasque tractusque maris caelumque profundum;
> aspice, venturo laetentur ut omnia saeclo!   [4. 46–52]

("Run onward, twining the thread of such ages," the Parcae have commanded their spindles, speaking in concord with the stable, divine will of ordained fate. Move on toward great honors [the time will straightway be at hand] beloved offspring of the gods, great increase of Jove. See how the curved weight of the world beckons; see how the lands and the reaches of the sea and the endless sky all together rejoice in the new time coming near.)

---

[14] All the *Homeric Hymns* and Callimachus' *Hymns* 1, 3, 4, 5, and 6 conclude with invocations of two to ten verses. The following topics appear: success for the singer, 15. 9, 24. 5, 25. 6; victory in a song contest, 6. 19–21; peace and good fortune. 8. 115–117, 9. 5, 20. 8, 31. 16, Callimachus 6. 135–136; another song for the god, 2. 490–495, 3. 545–546, 4. 579–580, and elsewhere.

Man's present longing for a new age is far more certain than the details of its coming. This longing can be articulated in impressive, wide-ranging terms that are themselves suggestive of heroic aspiration. With these the poet must be contented until the passage of time has substituted a new reality for that which man knows.

Thus, as he resigns himself to the present, the poet pauses long enough to suggest that Rome's ultimate transformation will also bring a transformation of himself and an opportunity to realize his poetic ambitions in a new form:

> o mihi tum longae maneat pars ultima vitae,
> spiritus et quantum sat erit tua dicere facta!
> non me carminibus vincet nec Thracius Orpheus
> nec Linus, huic mater quamvis atque huic pater adsit,
> Orphei Calliopea, Lino formosus Apollo.
> Pan etiam, Arcadia mecum si iudice certet,
> Pan etiam Arcadia dicat se iudice victum.   [4. 53–59]

(O let the last part of my life be long, and let me have voice great enough to sing of your deeds. And neither Thracian Orpheus nor Linus may surpass me in songs, even if the mother of one should be near him, and the father of the other: Calliope aiding Orpheus; fair-formed Apollo giving aid to Linus. Even Pan, should he vie with me and Arcadia judge us, even Pan shall confess himself beaten with Arcadia as judge.)

Facta, the poet's desired subject, betrays ambitions tending toward heroic poetry. An age nobler than any in the past will ennoble his works. Beyond this he cannot penetrate but can only speak of his future in terms compliant with the pastoral: victory in an Arcadian song contest. This vague promise is itself an acknowledgment that the poet has not yet gone beyond pastoral, that the higher vision of his initial lines cannot be fully realized in the present. The present remains the moment of pastoral, of limited knowledge within a limited milieu. Only when the new age has become a reality can the poet be free from his bondage to traditional images and able to seek a new language for greater things.

Thus the final image of the poem is neither heroic nor pastoral. The divine child, seen for the first time as a real human infant, is encouraged to smile at its mother:

> Incipe, parve puer, risu cognoscere matrem
> (matri longa decem tulerunt fastidia menses)
> incipe, parve puer: qui non risere parenti,
> non deus hunc mensa, dea non dignata cubili est.   [4. 60–63]

(Begin, little boy, to acknowledge your mother by smiling. [Ten months have brought long weariness to your mother.] Begin, little boy; the child who does not smile at his parent will have no god's invitation to his table nor goddess's invitation to her couch.)

Ultimately, the child may follow a career such as Hercules', achieving deification or even a marriage with the gods.[15] Yet, again, he may not, should he fall short of human and divine standards. The future remains uncertain, for the achievement of a leader rests ultimately with his own capacities and energies and not in a poet's optimistic predictions. With its juxtaposition of lofty aims and slender beginnings, this final image confirms the tentative nature of the poem. Both the child and his poet are incomplete, full of a promise whose meanings and specific applications are unknown. The prophecy is no more than a poetic experiment: an attempt to portray the world of experience in images belonging to the world of innocence.

In the sixth poem the world of innocence disappears, its usefulness ended. Here, again, magic is present. The forces and desires that compel man's life are manifested in images of transformation: on the one hand the changing of human beings into trees, birds, and monsters; on the other the creative animation of nature through art. The worst and best in human potential exist side by side.[16] As a loss of human identity, metamorpho-

---

[15] The passage is clearly inspired by *Idyll* 17. 121–134, where Theocritus mentions the tributes that Ptolemy has paid to his parents and compares his marriage with that of Zeus and Hera. The poem closes with an image of the couch of the gods: "And single is the couch that Iris, virgin still, her hands made pure with perfumes, strews for the sleep of Zeus and Hera."

[16] For a new and comprehensive interpretation of the poem as a dialectic of good and evil, of creative and destructive *amor*, see Charles Segal, "Vergil's Sixth *Eclogue* and the Problem of Evil," *TAPA*. 100(1969):407–435. For bibliography see Segal's p. 407, n. 1, and Eleanor Winsor Leach, "The Unity of *Eclogue* 6," *Latomus* 27(1968):13, n. 1.

sis is man's ultimate withdrawal into nature. In recognizing such danger in a total capitulation to the pastoral impulse, the poet discovers the need to create visions of order amid the chaos of the natural world, thus assuming a firmer control over himself and his environment than that given by the hypothetical vision of *Eclogue* 4.

Dispensing with the formal and deliberately structured plan of the fourth poem, the sixth pretends to follow an accidental pattern. The poet's confidence in his powers of heroic vision seems weakened as he confesses how his lofty ambitions have been turned aside:

> cum canerem reges et proelia, Cynthius aurem
> vellit et admonuit: 'pastorem Tityre, pinguis
> pascere oportet ovis, deductum dicere carmen.'   [6. 3–5]

> (When I was singing of kings and battles, Cynthius plucked my ear and chided: "A shepherd, Tityrus, is supposed to feed his sheep fat and keep his songs thin.")

These lines may be understood as a reflection of the fourth poem, where heroic prophecy has led ultimately to a retraction, a falling back upon pastoral limitations.[17] Now the poet accepts Apollo's strictures with apparent resignation, agreeing to content himself with the humbler mode, abandoning his chosen historical subject — *tristia bella* and the *laudes Vari* — in favor of an energetic pastoral tribute: "te nostrae Vare, myricae/te nemus omne canet" (For you Varus our tamarisks, for you every grove will sing, 10–11). Momentarily the poet appears to have withdrawn into a world of his own creation.

A second gesture of withdrawal appears when he turns abruptly from personal reflection to fiction, portraying a mythological scene. Two shepherd boys — or young satyrs — have

---

[17] Jean Hubaux, *Les thèmes bucoliques dans la poésie latine* (Brussels, 1930), pp. 13–14, proposes that the *reges et proelia* do not, as Servius had suggested (III, 65 *ad* v. 3), refer to Vergil's plans for the *Aeneid* or to some other epic subject, but rather to the fourth poem. See my comments on the *recusatio* in "The Unity of *Eclogue* 6," pp. 25–27, and Karl Galinsky's in "Vergil's Second *Eclogue*: Its Theme and Relation to the *Eclogue* Book," *Classica et Mediaevalia* 26(1968):127; Galinsky interprets the *reges* as the heroes of *Eclogues* 4 and 5, and *proelia* as the wars of 4. 31–36.

come upon Silenus asleep in a cave.[18] Their success concludes a long-standing quest for a song, wherein the god has often playfully eluded his pursuers (18–19). Now they signal their triumph by binding him in flower chains, but he laughs at their wiles:

> ille dolum ridens 'quo vincula nectitis?' inquit,
> 'solvite me, pueri; satis est potuisse videri.
> carmina quae vultis cognoscite.'   [6. 23–25]

(He, laughing at their strategy, said "Why do you tie these chains; release me, boys, it is enough to seem to have exercised power; recognize the song you desire.")

Understanding the search for poetry, Silenus grants the boys their unspoken wish, yet reminds them that they have approached a power that can never be truly controlled by external force.[19]

The binding and capture of a nature god is a motif that occurs frequently in classical literature and is always associated with a quest for knowledge.[20] Homer's Telemachus seeks news of his father from Proteus; Theopompus and Cicero tell the tale of Midas' capture of Silenus. Etruscan mythology includes the apprehension of Cacus the seer by the Vibennae, and Valerius Antius gives a similar account of Numa's binding of Picus and Faunus on the Aventine. The capture of Silenus recalls this background, yet it is also — perhaps even more deliberately —

[18] Segal, pp. 415–419, explores the symbolic implications of the manifold nature of Silenus — "a poet whose song moves all nature in rhythmic harmony . . . and a mythical figure who brings into focus the problematical quality of human nature." The "pueri" are called "satyri" by Servius, III, 67, ad vv. 13 and 14, and then "homines" in III, 68, ad v. 24, and Segal presents evidence for accepting the first interpretation in "Two Fauns and a Naiad? (Virgil, Eclogue 6. 15–26)," AJPhil. 92(1971):56–61.

[19] The suggestion is Segal's, "Vergil's Sixth Eclogue," p. 416. Putnam, pp. 200–202, proposes that the garlands are symbolic of the creation of poetry.

[20] The legend of the binding of Silenus attributed to Theopompus is in Aelian, VH 3. 18; Cicero, Tusc. 1. 48. The Etruscan version of the Cacus legend is given by J. Heurgon in La vie quotidienne chez les Etrusques (Paris, 1961), p. 283. The Roman variant involving Numa is in Valerius Antias 2. 6 (Arnobius 5. 1). See H. Peter, Historicum Romanorum Reliquiae, 2d ed., I (1914, repr. Stuttgart, 1967), 238–239; Ovid Fast 3. 285ff.; Plutarch Numa 15. In this account, Faunus and Martius Picus are on their way to drink the sacred waters of Egeria's spring, but Numa tricks them with cups of wine to put them to sleep.

patterned upon another literary adaptation of the myth, that in the *Symposium*. Having wreathed Socrates' head with garlands, Alcibiades begs him for a speech.[21] Like the boys in pursuit of Silenus, he confesses that he has long found Socrates mocking and elusive (216 c–e). He compares the wisdom of Socrates' speeches to those golden idols of the gods hidden in ugly images of Silenus whose true beauty is only to be found by those who know how to seek beneath a rough and deceptively ironic exterior:

If you chose to listen to Socrates' discourses you would feel them at first to be quite ridiculous; on the outside they are clothed with such absurd words and phrases—all, of course, the hide of a mocking satyr. . . . But when these are opened, and you obtain a fresh view of them by getting inside, first of all you will discover that they are the only speeches which have any sense in them; and secondly, that none are so divine, so rich in images of virtue, so largely—nay, so completely—intent on all things proper for the study of such as would obtain both grace and worth.   [221e–222a]

Alcibiades attributes to Socrates the mysterious power of a nature god. He is a magical musician who can enchant men and bring them to transform themselves, if only they are capable of understanding and interpreting his wisdom (215b–d). Vergil's imitation of this scene serves as a guide to the reading of his poem. In contrast to the deliberative, Platonic scheme of the fourth poem, this relies upon a more cryptic Socratic revelation.[22] The Silenus song has a function similar to that of Soc-

---

[21] Compare Silenus' words to Aegle, the naiad: "huic aliud mercedis erit," and Alcibiades' jocular threat to Socrates (*Symposium* 213d): "ἀλλὰ τούτων μὲν εἰσαυθίς σε τιμωρήσομαι." The translation is by W. R. M. Lamb, *Plato: Lysias, Symposium, Gorgias* (Cambridge, Loeb, 1925).

[22] Philosophical interpretation of the song goes back to Servius, III, *ad* v. 13, who takes Silenus as a disguise for Vergil's Epicurean teacher Siro, and thus attributes an Epicurean coloring to the song. He refers not only to the description of the creation of the world, but also to the fables, which he explains as an Epicurean technique of moral instruction, a tempering of serious matters with pleasurable attractions to soften the hearts of young boys with admiration or catch hold of empty minds (p. 71 *ad* v. 41). The philosophical explanation of the song has had a consistent series of defenders, enumerated in E. de Saint-Denis, "Le chant de Silène à la lumière d'une découverte récente," *Rev. Phil.* 37(1963): 27–29. To these should be added Galinsky, who thinks that the song's purpose is philosophical, its content antiphilosophical: "the desire for *beatitudo* clashes

rates' speech on love in the *Symposium:* it provides new insight for problems whose solution has thus far seemed elusive.

Like the visionary child who represents man's unrealized potential, the figure of Silenus is archetypal. As an old man, both god and poet, he is a synthesizer of knowledge accumulated from the world's past, a knowledge pertinent to the poet's quest. Jung outlines the pattern of circumstances that commonly brings such a personage to the aid of a protagonist needing knowledge:

The old man always appears when the hero is in a hopeless or desper-ate situation from which only profound reflection or a lucky idea — in other words a spiritual function or an endopsychic automism of some kind — can extricate him. But since, for internal and external reasons, the hero cannot accomplish this himself, the knowledge needed to compensate the deficiency comes in the shape of a personified thought, i.e., in the shape of this sagacious and helpful old man.[23]

Such is the situation in the poem. Caught between his own ambitions and Apollo's canon of pastoral simplicity, the Eclogue Poet has momentarily lost his artistic bearings. Literary tradition offers neither precedent nor justification for the blending of pastoral and heroic experience. In accepting Apollo's injunction, the poet appears to have forsaken his desired identity, yielding to the limitations of his poetic form. The baffling search for Silenus is an emblem of his own artistic quest. In the Silenus song, Vergil supplies what his protagonist, the Eclogue Poet, is seeking: a new interpretation of pastoral and a new role for the poet in nature. In the nature god's wilderness cavern, away from the visionary garden and all that is traditionally encom-passed by pastoral, the world of experience opens out through myth. As critics have often suggested, the familiar legends recounted by Silenus are associated with many literary forms, especially with epic and tragedy.[24] Silenus reshapes them in a

---

strongly with the actual subjects of Apollo's and Silenus' songs, i.e. the *infelices* and *indigni amores* which are described in gruesome detail" (p. 178).

[23] Jung, pp. 217–218; see also p. 220.

[24] For the idea of the *Eclogue* as a "catalogue" poem, see Otto Skutsch, "Zu Vergils Eklogen," *Rh.Mus.* 99(1956):193–195; Zeph Stewart, "The Song of Silenus," *Harv. Stud.* 64(1959):183–199. Although this interpretation cannot

historical outline, reducing each tale to an essential moment of confrontation between man and nature. This revision of old literary experience opens new possibilities for the bucolic, deepening its involvement in human affairs. The wilderness becomes a landscape that reflects man's actions and mind.

The myths are drawn together not only by their common natural setting, but also by notable similarities of motif and theme.[25] The longest and most elaborate, the tale of Pasiphaë, forms the center of Silenus' catalogue and is interrupted by a brief account of the daughters of Proetus (48–51). The two are opposite variations on a single motif. Pasiphaë, taken by love for the bull (45–47), seeks after him in hill and grove (52–60), planning strategies to capture the object of her desire. The daughters of Proetus, under the illusion that they have been changed into cows (50–51), attempt to flee from themselves, fearing that their debased forms will lower them to the animal world (48–49). The desire of one is the other's aversion. Together the two myths form a thematic focus for the catalogue, presenting an image of man torn between the human and animal worlds. Recognizing within himself a force that drives him toward nature, he may either seek vainly to fulfill this impulse, or draw back, clinging tenaciously to his dignity as a human being.

Both passages stand out for their comic dramatization of futile and extravagant actions. The Proetids adopt animal gestures, suffering to the fullest a shame that is only imaginary:

> Proetides implerunt falsis mugitibus agros,
> at non tam turpis pecudum tamen ulla secuta
> concubitus, quamvis collo timuisset aratrum
> et saepe in levi quaesisset cornua fronte.　[6. 48–51]

(The daughters of Proetus filled the fields with their unreal bellowing, but not one of them sought out shameful copulation with the herd, however much she feared dragging the plow

---

provide a complete explanation of the poem, the idea of an implicit comparison of literary genres should not be discarded.

[25] For the order and interrelationship of the myths see Leach, "The Unity of *Eclogue* 6," pp. 19–25; Segal, "Vergil's Sixth *Eclogue*," pp. 409–431.

with her neck and however often she sought the horns on her delicate brow.)

Pasiphaë, despite her lustfulness, cannot escape from the limitations of her human form. She would willingly undergo the metamorphosis feared by the Proetids; she has already undergone a metamorphosis of spirit as she seeks for a freedom and a new identity that will never be found:

> a! virgo infelix, tu nunc in montibus erras:
> ille latus niveum molli fultus hyacintho
> ilice sub nigra pallentis ruminat herbas
> aut aliquam in magno sequitur grege.   [6. 52–55]

> (Alas, unfortunate lady, you now wander in the mountains, while he, with his snow-white side crushing upon the soft hyacinths, slowly chews over pale herbs beneath the dark ilex, or follows some heifer among the large herd.)

Pasiphaë's quest is a parody of the bucolic dream.[26] The bull, who negligently reclines among the hyacinths or pursues the heifer of his fancy, enjoys the casual *otium* of a carefree pastoral swain. The objects that surround him — dark ilex and pale grasses — preserve the charming and conventional aesthetic balance of dark and light. Instead of composing meditative songs, he slowly chews his cud. But Pasiphaë, like the frustrated dreamers of the love poems, remains alone in the wilderness, cut off from her bucolic ideal. In equally comic fashion, the Proetids present the return from the pastoral. Struggling to maintain their human identity, they fear the yoke, the emblem of man's subjection of nature, and will not mingle with the herd. Silenus makes the Proetids a moral example for Pasiphaë. Man should not turn to nature to find escape from his human self.

This pair of myths marks a thematic turning point in Silenus' history. The first myths of the series — those of Pyrrha (41), Prometheus (42), the Saturnian kingdoms (41), and Hylas (43–44) — embody man's struggles against nature: the longing for human companionship amid the desolation of the flood, the struggle for the betterment of man, the dream of an ideal

---

[26] Segal has a slightly different view: "The bull's quiescence in the pale grass is nature's reproach to Pasiphae's wild search" ("Vergil's Sixth *Eclogue*," p. 427).

society, the adventurous quest for the golden fleece. They are recapitulated in the Proetids' struggle to save themselves from natural degradation. The myths that follow are allied with that of Pasiphaë. In the stories of Atalanta (61), the sisters of Phaeton (62–63), Scylla (74–77), and Philomela (79–81), bodily transformations follow in consequence of man's yielding to natural impulse. But the comic touches that give perspective to the humorous situations of the two central myths are absent from these other stories that deal with dire and unhappy events, not merely with desire and illusion.

The myths of Silenus present man alone against a background of nature, in a world that offers dangerous freedom to his emotions and impulses yet makes no sympathetic compromise with his desires. The mythical kinship between nature and man that was so important to the poetic fictions of *Eclogues* 4 and 5 has totally vanished. The autonomy of nature is established by the first part of the song, where Silenus gives a purely scientific account of the world's creation: one that neither includes man nor makes provision for his point of view.[27] Natural forms arise through a coalescence of the elements, and each part of the world spontaneously assumes its place within a general order. There is emphasis on the interrelationship of natural phenomena. Verbs that personify natural forces create a sense of action and response within nature:

> iamque novum terrae stupeant lucescere solem,
> altius atque cadant summotis nubibus imbres,
> incipiant silvae cum primum surgere . . .   [6. 37–39]

> (And now the earth is amazed by the new, glowing sun; and the rains fall far down from the clouds moved on high; as soon as the forests begin to spring up . . .)

With the alternation of sun and rain and the respondent growth of natural life, the great cycles of the world begin. Nature displays a coherence of her own, obeying the orderly laws that go on without concern for human life. The climax of creation leaves man conspicuously absent: "rara per ignaros errent ani-

---

[27] On this topic see Antonio La Penna, "Esiodo nella cultura e nella poesia di Virgilio," in *Hésiod et son influence*, p. 221; Stewart, pp. 184–185.

malia montis" (Scattered animals wander over unfamiliar mountains [40]). Nature is now the opposite of civilization, and there is no protective barrier between man and the wilderness. At its peril, the pastoral may forget this impersonal world, the reality that lurks behind bucolic illusion. It is not a nature that fosters dreams of innocence, but it is the same world that the unknown scientist of Menalcas' cup had described, the world that Orpheus must tame by his art. It is the inexorable, ceaselessly active nature that closes the first, second, and tenth poems as well as the sixth.

In such a world man's isolation and solitude are inevitable. Little sense of human fellowship or society enters into the landscapes. Loneliness surrounds the first human figures: Pyrrha casts her stones, and Prometheus endures his torture among the wild, Caucasian cliffs. The loss of a human companion is the theme of the myth of Hylas:

> his adiungit, Hylan nautae quo fonte relictum
> clamassent, ut litus 'Hyla, Hyla' omne sonaret.   [6. 43–44]

> (He added to these tales how the sailors cried out for Hylas left at the spring, until the whole shore resounded with their "Hylas, Hylas.")

His comrades do not understand his disappearance. Baffled, they seek him amid a nature that gives no answer save the echoes of their own voices. The daughters of Proetus are isolated in their madness. Pasiphaë's lonely search contrasts with the felicity of the bull who enjoys the companionship of the herd. The sisters of Phaeton grieve alone for their brother until their sorrow overcomes their human identity; their forms are cut off from humanity, encased in bitter bark (62–63). In the two myths that conclude the catalogue, an even greater isolation falls upon the perpetrators of crime. Metamorphosis confirms their alienation from the human world. Not only does the once lovely Scylla turn monstrous, but she also attacks the ships of Ulysses and becomes one of the terrors of nature, an enemy of mankind:

> Quid loquar aut Scyllam Nisi, quam fama secuta est
> candida succinctam latrantibus inguina monstris

Dulichias vexasse rates et gurgite in alto,
a! timidos nautas canibus lacerasse marinis.　[6. 74–77]

(Or what shall I say of Nisus' daughter, Scylla, who, as the
story goes, after her white thighs had been girded with barking
monsters, tormented the ships of Ulysses in the deep whirl-
pool? Alas, with her sea dogs she tore the timid sailors limb by
limb.)

The transformed Philomela is a melancholy figure. She turns
toward lonely places (80) and flies sadly above her former
home: "quibus ante/ infelix sua tecta super volitaverit alis"
(80–81).

Although Philomela's crime is the most extreme example
of subhuman conduct, the final words of her story suggest a
theme prevalent in several of the myths: that of seeking or
wandering. Philomela seeks out deserted places (*deserta peti-
verit*). The comrades of Hylas search the shore. The sisters of
Phaeton have sought their brother. Ulysses, attacked by Scylla,
is himself a wanderer. In the myth of Pasiphaë, the theme of
wandering is most explicit and forms of *errare* occur twice.
Pasiphaë wanders in the mountains ("tu nunc in montibus
erras" [52]) and traces the wandering footsteps of the bull
("si qua forte ferant oculis sese obvia nostris/errabunda bovis
vestigia"—If, by any chance, the footsteps of the bull so likely
to wander should cross before my eyes, 57–58). Wandering is
a condition natural to animals, and the phrase *in montibus erras*
recalls the earlier *rara per ignaros errent animalia montis* (40), the
description of the animals in the newly formed world. Tracking
her hopes for the fulfillment of animal desire, Pasiphaë follows
the bull into the condition of wandering, a condition unsuited
to human beings yet symbolic of man's uncertainty and frustration amid the natural world.

A second pattern of recurrent thematic suggestions centers
on the idea of bondage or capture. Prometheus is punished by
bondage to nature. The sisters of Phaeton are surrounded by
bitter bark, and Scylla is girt about with monsters. The Proetids
fear the yoke. Pasiphaë is captured by madness ("quae te
dementia cepit" [47]) and in turn seeks to capture the bull
(56–59). The young boys are unable to hold Silenus in bonds.

Man's longings cause him to struggle for control over nature, yet he must either recognize his weakness before this greater force, or become nature's prisoner himself.

The isolation of man in nature, his confused wanderings, and his liability to put himself in bondage direct us to understand nature as an expression of man's deep, discordant emotions, the desires and impulses that cut him off from society. The myths of Silenus show exaggerations of the pastoral impulse, yet, by their literal enactment of the return to nature, they dramatize the futility and self-destructiveness of man's hopes from the natural world. As we read the myths, we may understand that the search for innocence is only an optimistic interpretation of the impulse toward nature; a realistic version must also include folly, passion, and crime. The Silenus song is an entertainment that reveals the whole tragicomedy of man's desire for a natural life. Man, by nature, is always restless, always in search of what he cannot have. The historical pattern that organizes the myths shows that humanity has always been caught up in its futile search.

Before he ends his poetic catalogue, Silenus includes one contemporary scene: a tale of the poetic initiation of Gallus. When first we see him, Gallus is also a solitary figure, wandering by the River Permessus. An analogous passage in Propertius (2. 10. 25–26) suggests that the Permessus is an allusion to elegiac poetry. Gallus too wanders in a world of discordant natural emotions, but he does not long remain alone. The Muses greet him, leading him to the seat of Apollo where he receives new subjects for his verse:

> tum canit, errantem Permessi ad flumina Gallum
> Aonas in montis ut duxerit una sororum.   [6. 64–65]

> (Then he sang of Gallus, wandering toward the streams of Permessus, and how one of the sisters led him toward the Aonian mount.)

In these verses, *errantem* and *duxerit* present a thematic contrast. If *errare* suggests a lack of direction in nature, *ducere* is associated with an order to be gained through art. *Deductum* is the word by which Apollo described the kind of verse suited to the shepherd poet. *Deducere* appears here as Linus speaks to Gallus, describing the control over nature effected by Hesiod in his verse:

> ut Linus haec illi divino carmine pastor
> floribus atque apio crinis ornatus amaro
> dixerit: 'hos tibi dant calamos (en accipe) Musae,
> Ascraeo quos ante seni, quibus ille solebat
> cantando rigidas deducere montibus ornos.
> his tibi Grynei nemoris dicatur origo,
> ne quis sit lucus quo se plus iactet Apollo.'   [6. 67–73]

(As Linus, a shepherd of godlike song, his head crowned with flowers and bitter parsley, spoke these things to him: "To you the Muses give these reeds—behold, accept them—that belonged to the old man of Ascra long ago. With these he used to lead the unbending ash trees down the mountainsides in response to his song. With these you will tell of the origins of the Grove of Gryneus, so that no grove may there be wherein Apollo has more pride.")

Linus' words fill out the incomplete picture begun by Apollo's command to the Eclogue Poet, but the order he designates is no longer a restrictive one. The trees yielded to the power of Hesiod. The word *rigidas* implies an unbending quality in nature that art can overcome. The poet achieves what emotional man fails to realize, a control over the world that reflects human desires; he alone can influence intractable nature, drawing man's alien environment into harmony with the civilized world.[28]

Now Gallus must exercise this art in his own poem on the origins of the Grynean Grove. Apollo himself will recognize the work, which will place the grove first among his haunts. From Servius' description, we may gather that the grove is a subject conducive to poetry, a *locus amoenus* endowed with pleasant trees, fountains, and flowers. Yet its history is darkened by an act of human violence. According to Servius, Euphorion's

---

[28] Segal, "Vergil's Sixth *Eclogue*," pp. 418–421, accurately regards this expression as a metaphor for the creative powers of poetry but distinguishes between the Hesiodic power, which implies an "element of direction and constraint," and the Dionysian power of Silenus that "seems able to allow nature a greater measure of its inherent spontaneity, a greater freedom on its own terms."

poem on that subject recounted the story of a mocking quarrel between two soothsayers, ending in murder.[29] Other details of the initiation have similar backgrounds. Linus, the son of Apollo, was Hercules' tutor in song, murdered by his pupil but now become a shepherd of godlike art. The parsley crown that he wears is a symbol of mourning for another untimely death, translated into an emblem of triumph: a wreath to crown victors and poets.[30] In the juxtaposition of these symbols we see indications of man's determined subordination of violence and futility to the powers of creation and order. Even Hesiod fits this pattern, for he is the shepherd whom the Muses roused up in the hard pasture to sing divine truth for men bound in poverty and ignorance. As a human poet, Hesiod teaches both civilization and theology, making the world endurable and comprehensible for man. Within the *Eclogue* itself, literary reminders of his poetry are present in the form and mythical content of the Silenus song.[31]

In composing his song on the Grynean grove, Gallus will follow in the steps of Hesiod, a human model well suited to a poet of Alexandrian leanings, but the greater model for both singers is Silenus, who is now creating an order-giving song out of a history of chaotic and baffled emotions. Despite the violence of its subject, the song has a rhythm that moves the treetops and sets the wild beasts and fauns dancing, bringing gaiety and animation to nature. The savage energy of the wilderness yields

[29] Servius, III, 78 *ad* v. 72. There are two versions of the quarrel, the first concerning a ritual prohibition on wine drinking, the second, given by Servius *auctus*, a quarrel between Chalchas and Mopsus over their skills as augurs. The latter is attributed to Euphorion, whose poem was Gallus' source.

[30] Theocritus *Idyll* 24. 103 makes Linus an old man who tutored Hercules. Apollodorus 2. 4. 9 recounts the murder: Hercules' enraged response to Linus' striking him with the lyre. Servius, III, 77 ad *v.* 68: "Certain writers say that this kind of crown was chosen as a symbol of death either because its lowly herb signifies the untimely mourning for Archemorus or because the boy was killed by a serpent while creeping over this very herb.

[31] *Theogony* 22–34. On the importance of Hesiod see Marie Desport, *L'incantation virgilienne: Essai sur les mythes du poète enchanteur et leur influence dans l'oeuvre de Virgile* (Bordeaux, 1952), pp. 190–196, and La Penna, pp. 217–218. Desport, p. 198, gives the Hesiodic references for the myths which I reproduce here: Deucalion, frg. 21–24R$_2$; *Saturnia regna, W & D* 109; Prometheus, *Theog.* 510; Hylas, frgs. 77, 178; *Proetides*, frg. 52; Atalanta, frg. 220; Scylla, frg. 172; Phaethontides, frg. 220; Ulysses, frg. 89; Tereus and Philomela, frg. 125.

to artistic design, taking on characteristics of the human world. Thus we may understand that the poet bridges the gap between nature and civilization. What is chaos in reality becomes order under the influence of the poet. His role is to satisfy man's unfulfilled desires for nature by allowing for their fictional realization in verse. The poet is an interpreter of man in nature and nature in man. By means of the Silenus song, man's longings for innocence and his inevitable bondage to experience are put into perspective. His emotions are absorbed into the great context of nature, where they appear for what they are: a part of the whole panorama of the workings of the natural world.

Thus, where the idealistic fourth *Eclogue* must ultimately defer to a future reality, the sixth urges an awareness of the world here and now; its historical retrospect becomes a vehicle for the exploration of universal characteristics of mankind. In this poem, Vergil goes beyond his Roman commitment to the harmony of nature and civilization, which must hereafter appear as only one aspect of a more vital and psychological interdependency. In his reluctant withdrawal into nature, the Eclogue Poet discovers the pattern by which the naïve aspects of the pastoral impulse are displaced—the process by which man's experience in nature must be intellectualized, ordered, and interpreted as a source of knowledge and self-discovery. The identity that awaits the poet in nature is no magical transformation of self but a new definition of his artistic role. In this sense it offers a genuine and palpable rebirth.

CHAPTER 7

The Role of
the Eclogue Poet

Three different types of poet figure in the *Eclogues:* the rustic singer, the urban poet, and the mythological bard. As the poems, in various ways, bring these three different poetic types together, we are invited to compare their successes in poetry and their interpretations of the art of song. The aggressive rustic, Damoetas is the possessor of an Orpheus cup that symbolizes sublime song. Damoetas brags of the favor of Pollio, while the more attractive Lycidas is too modest to compete with Varius and Cinna. The mythological song of Silenus brings Gallus before Linus to receive the pipes of Hesiod. Gallus the love poet begs to be celebrated by Arcadian singers and dreams of becoming a pastoral swain. In all their encounters, there remains a distance between the rustic, the urban, and the mythological poets. One cannot enter into the role of another, and those who try to do so fail.

Still there is one poet who stands outside the three categories, although at times he participates in each. This is the Eclogue Poet himself.[1] In the fourth poem, he awaits the time when he

---

[1] Little attention has been given to the Eclogue Poet as a fictional speaker. He is traditionally considered a nonfictional character, a thin disguise for Vergil. See F. R. Hamblin, *The Development of Allegory in the Classical Pastoral* (New York, 1928), p. 66. In keeping with this belief, Wilhelm Kroll, *Studien zum Verstandnis der römischen Literatur* (Stuttgart, 1924), pp. 228ff., finds unity in the poet's use of historical allusions and the names of contemporary figures, while Georg Rohde, *De Eclogarum Vergilii Forma et Indole* (Berlin, 1925), pp. 65–68, finds the introductory passages chiefly responsible for Vergil's creation of a uniform pastoral coloring. E. A. Hahn, "The Characters in Vergil's *Eclogues*," *TAPA* 75 (1944): 196–241, discusses evidence of Vergil's changing attitude toward the pastoral and the development of his self-confidence as he pursues his work,

245

will conquer Pan in an Arcadian song contest, thus claiming mythological status. When Apollo, in the sixth, addresses him as "Tityrus," he seems to have cast himself in a rustic role. In the tenth, he is a Roman poet singing for Gallus although he has placed himself in an imaginary pastoral setting. Because of his multiple roles, the Eclogue Poet does not precisely fit any of his own definitions of the poet and keeps his personality more elusive than any character in the *Eclogue* book.

If we compare the Eclogue Poet as a first-person speaker with those in other Republican or Augustan poems, we find this impression of his elusiveness confirmed. He reveals no such intense personal convictions as Lucretius in the *De Rerum Natura*, nor does he relate his subject to man's daily life. He indulges in none of the exploitation of personal tastes and humors that characterizes Horace's *Satires* and his *Odes*. Unlike Catullus and the elegists, the Eclogue Poet does not pose as a man formulating deep-seated emotions—or what passes for them—into objective, articulate verse. Rather, his sole concern is with composing a new kind of Roman poetry and seeking out subjects appropriate to his chosen form. The Eclogue Poet gives himself almost no identity at all save what he acquires as the maker of his book.

In this role, however, he makes certain ideas and topics distinctly his own. He speaks in five poems—2, 4, 6, 8, and 10— with a voice and manner quite apart from those of any other character. By his pride in his own innovations and in the novelty

---

but her comments are based upon the supposed order of the poems' composition rather than their order in the *Eclogue* book.

A few more recent studies allow for fictional elements in the characterization. Marie Desport, *L'incantation virgilienne: Essai sur les mythes du poète enchanteur et leur influence dans l'oeuvre de Virgile* (Bordeaux, 1952), p. 93, believes that he means to portray himself as an imitator of Pan. Carl Becker, "Vergils Eklogenbuch," *Hermes* 88(1955):314–349, comments on the speaker's uniform point of view and his function in relating single poems to the design of the whole book. He is a poetic rather than an autobiographical speaker, to be compared with speakers in Horace's *Epodes*. Karl Galinsky, "Vergil's Second *Eclogue:* Its Theme and Relation to the *Eclogue* Book," *Classica et Mediaevalia* 26(1968):177–188, believes that the poet holds Epicurean ideas on the healing power of music; and John Van Sickle, "The Unity of the *Eclogues:* Arcadian Forest/Theocritean Trees," *TAPA* 98(1967):501–508, attempts to identify him with other persons whose names are mentioned in the poems.

of his form, he sharpens our awareness of pastoral as a literary mode. By revealing his association with notable Roman contemporaries, he establishes himself as an intermediary between the bucolic world and that of Rome. His intermittent comments on his literary progress and ambitions call attention to the unity of the collection of poems. The self-imposed limitations of pastoral are in conflict with the Eclogue Poet's aspiration. On the one hand he reveals an inclination to break out of his narrow genre and produce something more imposing in subject and style. On the other, he shows a poet's compulsion to go on composing verses whatever the generic restrictions his work must obey. This humorous tension between detachment and commitment serves to temper his involvement in the emotions of his fictional characters and to establish a qualified skepticism toward pastoral idealism and freedom. The poet surveys his own role-playing with an amusedly critical eye.

In his self-dictated task, the Eclogue Poet adopts a sophisticated perspective that at times makes him superior to his characters and even to the pastoral mode. In the second poem he has gentle criticism for the unsuccessful efforts of Corydon. His subtle introduction and evaluation of the singer imply that he is already well versed in pastoral while his protagonist is a bumbling amateur. The Eclogue Poet is the sole speaker in the fourth poem, where his formal role is that of a Roman poet striving to outdo his Greek model, Theocritus. Sophistication, the keynote of the opening verses, stems partly from his dissatisfaction with traditional Sicilian pastoral, partly from claims of insight into Rome's political future.

In *Eclogue* 6, the poet's sophistication receives a check as Apollo calls him a *pastor,* insisting on the creation of thin-spun verse (*deductum carmen*). He himself had been wrapped up in loftier subjects (*reges et proelia*) and this reminder of conventional limitations is no small slight to his inventiveness. In *Eclogue* 8, he is once more introducing pastoral singers, but now he reveals more strongly his growing impatience with pastoral and his desire to be about more spectacular tasks. His ideal has changed from heroic to tragic: "Sophocleo . . . carmina digna cothurno" (songs worthy of the buskin of Sophocles [8. 10]). The beginning of the tenth poem shows him once more con-

tented with the pastoral as he asks the fountain Arethusa to let
him sing his own final song. His sense of superiority now
emerges in an implicit contrast between himself and Gallus,
who has fallen into the role of unsuccessful pastoral dreamer.
Thus the role of the Eclogue Poet develops progressively
throughout the book and must be understood as a facet of its
order and design.

The Eclogue Poet distinguishes himself from other singers by
his higher degree of literary self-consciousness. Although both
the poet and his characters discuss the impulse to compose
pastoral verses, only the former regards these verses as a formal
work of art. In the first poem, both Tityrus and Meliboeus associate singing with the order of a happy life. Spontaneous song
has its origins in freedom: the shepherd's license to play whatever songs he desires: "et ipsum/ ludere quae vellem calamo
permisit agresti" (1. 9–10). Such song is a vehicle for personal
expression, undisturbed by thoughts of literary ambition.

Other rustic singers display higher aspirations than Tityrus,
often desiring victory in a song contest or the title of master
singer. But their standards of literary judgment are in keeping
with the bucolic milieu. Mopsus and Menalcas in the fifth poem
have the most sensitive emotional response to song, which for
them shares its sublimity with the dynamic forces of nature; yet
their praises of each other's songs are impromptu appreciations,
not deliberative literary evaluations. The optimistic Lycidas
likes cheerful songs and sings to lighten a long journey. The
elegiac poet Gallus thinks of pastoral song as a kind of magic
that can simplify his emotions and mode of life. Only the
Eclogue Poet places literary issues foremost, comparing the
bucolic poem with other kinds of verse.

The poet first declares plans for literary experimentation
with the opening words of *Eclogue* 4:

> Sicelides Musae, paulo maiora canamus!
> non omnis arbusta iuvant humilesque myricae;
> si canimus silvas, silvae sint consule dignae.   [4. 1–3]

> (Muses of Sicily, of a somewhat nobler subject let us sing!
> Neither orchard groves nor humble tamarisks give pleasure to
> all; if we sing of forests, let them be forests worthy of a consul.)

The *Sicelides Musae* refer to the previous *Eclogues*, especially to the more Theocritean poems 2 and 3, where Corydon's wooing of Alexis and Damoetas' flattery of Pollio provide comical treatments of a poet's desire to win recognition for his songs. In his plans to elevate the subject of pastoral, the Eclogue Poet differs from these singers who take their pastoral art for granted and pride themselves on simple rusticity. Although the self-satisfied Damoetas angles for Pollio's approval, he has not thought to alter his mode of expression to become more worthy of the great world. Both *Eclogues* 2 and 3 have failed to answer that need for the reconciliation of city and country suggested by *Eclogue* 1. To this subject the Eclogue Poet here addresses himself.

The *arbusta* and *humiles myricae* that cannot please a consul are likewise allusions to types of pastoral verse. *Myricae* (tamarisks) are common in the Theocritean landscape. Although they are mentioned in later *Eclogues*, they always seem exotic and out of place. In Damon's posthumous golden age they bear apples, and they weep for the metaphorical death of Gallus in Arcadia. Never do they appear in the agricultural landscape; their absence might be explained by the fact that Pliny calls the *myrica* a useless tree, not worth the planting.[2] But *arbusta* are different; they belong to the cultivated farm world of *Eclogues* 1 and 2. By linking the two, the Eclogue Poet suggests that his new and loftier pastoral mode demands a rejection, not only of the Sicilian pastoral, but also of his own rustic style.

Although the fourth *Eclogue* brings the golden age into pastoral and binds together the bucolic and heroic worlds, the poet's ambitions favor the heroic. His request to the young deity ("spiritus et quantum sat erit tua dicere facta" [4. 54]) declares his aims. As a singer he anticipates magnificent subjects for the future, subjects that will allow him precedence over the mythological bards. Gods will judge his singing and confess their own offspring defeated. Pan will no longer be supreme in his Arcadian homeland.[3]

---

[2] Pliny *HN* 24. 41. 1.
[3] Becker, pp. 339–340, sees a connection between the Arcadian song contest and the promise to surpass the bucolic mode.

The poet has chosen his loftier subject in preparation for the heroic age to come. He suggests that the prophetic *Eclogue* is no ultimate achievement, but only a declaration of what he wishes to achieve. When the prophecy is fulfilled, its usefulness will end. As he composes the prophecy the poet betrays his readiness to be dissatisfied with a world that is merely pastoral and offers only subjects for rustic song. In this respect his visionary idealism differs from Corydon's. Its end is not withdrawal or innocence, but rather a reorganization of experience.

The sixth poem is linked with the fourth by another discussion of subject and style:

> Prima Syracosio dignata est ludere versu
> nostra neque erubuit silvas habitare Thalea.
> cum canerem reges et proelia, Cynthius aurem
> vellit et admonuit: 'pastorem, Tityre, pinguis
> pascere oportet ovis, deductum dicere carmen.'   [6. 1–5]

(My Thalia was the first who deigned to toy with the verse of Syracuse, nor did she blush to live in the woodlands. When I was singing of kings and battles, Cynthius twitched my ear and chided: "A shepherd, Tityrus, is supposed to feed his sheep fat and keep his songs thin.")

Because this statement follows the convention of the *recusatio*, many have taken it to indicate that Vergil, at this time, had serious objections to composing heroic verse and needed to defend his preference for a lesser mode.[4] But such apologies are not the only function of the *recusatio*. By this formula the poet may also alert his reader to the possibility that his present subject might well have been treated, however differently, in some other literary genre. *Reges et proelia* recall the fourth poem where the pastoral encompasses heroic themes. The Eclogue

---

[4] Otto Skutsch, "Zu Vergils Eklogen," *Rh. Mus.* 99(1956):193–195, finds an allusion to the Alexandrian prohibition of epic, but J. P. Elder, *"non inussa cano,"* *Harv. Stud.* 65(1961):110, thinks Vergil wants us to know he composes pastoral by choice, not for want of something better. Wendell Clausen, "Callimachus and Latin Poetry," *GRBS* 5(1964):193, believes Vergil's personal distaste for war makes contemporary epic uninviting, but Galinsky, p. 177, takes the rebuke as a reflection on *Eclogues* 4 and 5 and sees a weakening of the poet's confidence in the power of poetry.

Poet has been interrupted in his meditations upon another heroic pastoral.

By the word *prima*, he claims to be the first Roman to write Theocritean verse, but *prima* also suggests that this manner was only a first stage in his work. Referring to the activity of his muse as playful (*ludere*), he implies that these first poems were simply exercises in preparation for the nobler works he has just been composing and for which he has just received Apollo's reprimand. The god undertakes the role of literary critic, insisting upon a conventional decorum for pastoral and a traditional *persona* for the pastoral poet. His function is to depict a prosperous countryside ("pinguis pascere oportet ovis") with finely crafted verse. The god calls the poet Tityrus. The name suits a feeder of fat sheep, but not a composer of heroic pastoral.

Touches of comedy in this passage convey indignation on the part of the poet whose efforts have been directed toward originality and new interpretations of tradition. Although the form of the *recusatio* is modeled on Callimachus' introduction to the *Aetia*, it is no profession of discipleship but, in fact, a burlesque. The fat sheep and thin muse are a humorous version of the Greek poet's fat victim and slender muse. Apollo is a comical champion of Alexandrianism. He does not touch the poet's shoulder, but tweaks his ear, a gesture intended to awaken memory but one to which no amount of sober commentary can succeed in giving dignity. It is the gesture by which a schoolmaster prompts a laggard pupil.[5] Unlike Callimachus, who is always aware of the demands of his proper medium, the Eclogue

---

[5] Thus Servius, *Servii Grammatici qui feruntur in Vergilii Carmina Commentarii*, ed. G. Thilo and H. Hagen, vol. III: *Servii Grammatici qui feruntur in Vergilii Bucolica et Georgica Commentarii*, ed. G. Thilo (Leipzig, 1887: repr., Hildesheim, 1961), p. 65 *ad* v. 3: The ear is sacred to Memory as the forehead to Genius, the fingers to Minerva, and the knees to Pity. Conington, *The Works of Vergil*, with a commentary by John Conington and Henry Nettleship, vol. I: *Eclogues and Georgics*, rev. by F. Haverfield 5th ed. (London, 1898: repr., Hildesheim, 1963), p. 75 *ad* v. 3, speaks of the gesture used to summon a witness as in Hor. *Sat.* 1. 9. 77 ("oppono aurem"). The context here suggests low comedy as also related uses of "pervellere aurem" in Val. Max. 1. 5. 8; Sen. *Ben.* 4. 36. 1; 5. 7. 6; *Ep.* 94. 55. Seneca talks about reminding oneself with a comical suggestion of bumbling absent-mindedness. In Plut. *Cat. Mai.* 20. 4: Cato does not want his son's ear pulled by a slave when he is slow to learn. Here the verb *ludere* ("practice") suggests the schoolboy.

Poet has forgotten the rules of pastoral. Finally, Silenus, to whom the poet transfers his difficult task of composition, is no true Callimachean, for he is intoxicated. Although his mythological song has traces of Alexandrian erudition, it does not stem from pure Castalian water, but from wine.[6]

Apollo's interruption is not pointless, nor is the humor of the passage gratuitous. The Eclogue Poet's bold *reges et proelia* points to a real danger: that the quest for poetic innovation might so radically transform the pastoral that it would cease to be pastoral at all. Yet the Callimachean parody demonstrates the futility of binding new poems to themes or artistic standards that belong to a literary milieu of the past. The extremes of poetic style suggested by the Eclogue Poet indicate the need for a productive compromise between new and old. Although the poet dutifully takes up the formulas of traditional pastoral, calling upon the Pierian Muses for his song, the poem is as unconventional as *Eclogue* 4. The catalogue of myths, with its roughly chronological arrangement, makes cosmic history a pastoral theme. Although the myths are traditionally associated with poems of other genres, Silenus transforms them into a unified series of pastoral vignettes, reducing the actions that belong to epic or tragedy to the simplest terms. The heroes of the Argo become confused sailors wandering on the shore; the dreadful queen of Crete is no more than a *virgo infelix*. The common theme of these legends becomes a pastoral theme: man's search for identity and self-fulfillment in the natural world.

The song of Silenus slips around Apollo's injunction by defending the inclusive capacities of the pastoral mode. Still the inspired mythological bard reveals a wisdom that the ambitious Eclogue Poet has not discovered for himself. His song contains no overt heroics, no far-flung prophecies for the Roman future, but deals with the familiar, unchanging nature of man, a theme better suited to the poetry of nature than actual historical deeds.

As the discussion of a proper subject for the pastoral links

---

[6] See Gilbert Lawall, *Theocritus' Coan Pastorals: A Poetry Book* (Cambridge, ass., 1967), pp. 102–108. Poetry written under the intoxication of wine will not be an artificial, learned poetry, but poetry in touch with emotional reality.

Eclogues 4 and 6, so the expression of a desire to break away from this genre links 6 and 8.

> tu mihi, seu magni superas iam saxa Timavi
> sive oram Illyrici legis aequoris, — en erit umquam
> ille dies, mihi cum liceat tua dicere facta?
> en erit ut liceat totum mihi ferre per orbem
> sola Sophocleo tua carmina digna coturno?   [8. 6–10]

> ([Tell] me, whether you are now riding above the rocks of great Timavus or hugging the shore of the Illyrian sea — will that day ever come when you permit me to speak of your deeds? When will it be time for me to proclaim through all the world your songs that alone are worthy of the Sophoclean buskin?)

The Eclogue Poet has taken Apollo's lesson to heart. Once more, as in 4, he addresses Pollio, but now he neither sets himself to interpret the great world in pastoral images nor strives to elevate the pastoral mode. Instead he confesses his longing to relinquish the pastoral. Already his thoughts follow the deeds of the proconsul in the historical world, and Pollio's tragic poems stir his imagination. But despite these loftier ambitions, he is still bound to his genre, still singing of the muse of Damon and Alphesiboeus. Such activity is little more than a manner of biding time, of idling away last moments before his departure from the bucolic world.

As if to emphasize the poet's growing impatience with his limited form, Vergil has made the dramatic arrangement of *Eclogue* 8 the most formal in the book. It is neither an overheard lament, such as 2, or a spontaneous contest, such as 3 and 7, but the report of a staged performance. The poet introduces his speakers with a grand gesture, describing their prowess in hyperbolic terms:

> Pastorum Musam Damonis et Alphesiboei,
> immemor herbarum quos est mirata iuvenca
> certantis, quorum stupefactae carmine lynces,
> et mutata suos requierunt flumina cursus,
> Damonis Musam dicemus et Alphesiboei.   [8. 1–5]

> (I sing the muse of the shepherds, Damon and Alphesiboeus, whose contest left the wondering heifer forgetful of her grazing;

by whose song the lynxes were struck silent, while the rivers,
transformed, stood still in their channels. I sing the muse of
Damon and Alphesiboeus.)

Such elevated formality, such an abundance of polysyllabic
words applied to a slight subject, creates not heroic, but mock-
heroic verse. In introducing the second song, the poet once
more calls on the Muse:

> Haec Damon; vos, quae responderit Alphesiboeus,
> dicite, Pierides: non omnia possumus omnes.   [8. 62–63]

> (This was Damon's song. As for what Alphesiboeus sang in
> response, you tell it, Pierian Muses; not all of us can do every-
> thing.)

The final phrase, with its perversion of the golden age formula
omnis feret omnia tellus, turns the mock-heroic into travesty. The
poet can hardly seem to take Alphesiboeus seriously when he is
not even able to recite his song.

Mock-heroic exaggeration also colors the pastoral singing.
With comical self-importance, Damon's unhappy lover looks
for his own death to restore the golden age. In Alphesiboeus'
song, *carmina*—the sordid love-spells of a country girl—lay
claim to a power like that of Circe's incantations:

> carmina vel caelo possunt deducere lunam,
> carminibus Circe socios mutavit Ulixi,
> frigidus in pratis cantando rumpitur anguis.   [8. 69–71]

> (Magic songs have power to lead the moon down from the sky.
> By magic songs Circe enchanted the comrades of Ulysses. The
> cold serpent in the meadows is shattered by magic singing.

The characters in the songs are fictional *personae* whose
identities should not be confused with those of their creators,
Damon and Alphesiboeus. Damon, whose song halts rivers in
their courses, is certainly not a lover ready for death. His composition imitates Theocritus' third *Idyll*, the love song of the
sentimental goatherd, but its extravagant despair makes it a
heavy-handed imitation of its witty, light-hearted model. Alphesiboeus is even more openly fictionalizing as he sings the

incantatory song based on *Idyll* 2, and he also is an awkward imitator. His rough country maiden, who has procured her love-charms from a ghoulish enchanter (95–99) lacks the grace and pathos of Theocritus' abandoned Simaetha. Her Daphnis has strayed to the city and the repetition of this word in her refrain ("ducite ab urbe domum, mea carmina, ducite Daphnin") makes the song reflect the rivalry of the pastoral and the great world. The use of magical *carmina* (spells) hints that pastoral songs alone would be insufficient to recapture the wanderer whose attention has been distracted from the bucolic world. When a barking dog seems to herald the lover's return, the enchantress is not sure if her magic has succeeded or if her triumph is only a lover's illusion (106–108). The two songs balance each other by contrasting the loss and restoration of pastoral love, yet both are exaggerated, overingenious treatments of the theme.

The Eclogue Poet expresses no genuine involvement in this far-fetched contest. He hardly belongs to the stupefied audience of animals and streams. Rather, his fantastic setting and inflated diction place the singers far from himself. His detachment contrasts with the active excitement of Meliboeus in *Eclogue* 7 who gives a song contest precedence over all his duties. More than ever he exhibits tolerant superiority toward the pastoral. Having abandoned the problem of relating bucolic poetry to historical reality, the Eclogue Poet no longer attempts to control the credibility of pastoral fictions, but allows his two singers to imitate traditional poems at will and lose themselves in images of pure fantasy. Nor does he contribute a final evaluation of the singers as he has done in *Eclogue* 2. Having handed over the task of repeating Alphesiboeus' song to the Muses, he abandons all obvious concern for the poem.

The poet's gesture is no less self-important than those of his characters. In fact their own aspirations toward tragic emotion and heroic magic reflect, in lesser form, the poet's high literary ambitions. In his new indifference to the bucolic, he is, like Damon's lover, the destroyer of a world his own imagination has created. He looks for this destruction to give birth to a better world with greater opportunity for his talents. Thus the comedy of the eighth poem is not confined to its rustic characters but includes the restless, aspiring Eclogue Poet. In the pastoral world, heroic ambitions can easily make the aspirer ludicrous. Unlike his characters, the Eclogue Poet finally takes account of this possibility. His search for heroic pastoral subjects culminates in mock-heroic, and at this point it disappears. In the tenth poem it is Gallus, not the Eclogue Poet, who is dreaming of heroic status in the pastoral world.

More positive aspects of the poet's ambition appear in the tenth *Eclogue*, whose opening verses declare a return to the pastoral world. The intellectual indifference of the Eclogue Poet in the eighth had been echoed by the physical absence of Menalcas, the master poet, in the ninth. There Moeris lamented the incoherence of the pastoral world without the presence of its organizing mind, and Lycidas had attempted to fill the role of organizer but failed to convince Moeris of the usefulness or feasibility of his attempt. In the ninth poem, the Eclogue Poet's earlier hints of withdrawal from the pastoral reach their climax in an insistent theme of departure, a sign of the impending close of the *Eclogue* book. But in the tenth, all the lost elements have come back: pastoral *otium*, the pastoral landscape, and the Eclogue Poet himself.

The poet's new, carefree posture resembles that of Tityrus at the beginning of *Eclogue* 1:

> incipe: sollicitos Galli dicamus amores,
> dum tenera attondent simae virgulta capellae.
> non canimus surdis, respondent omnia silvae.   [10. 6–8]

> (Begin. I will tell of the troubled love of Gallus, while the monkey-faced goats are shaving off the tender leaves from the shrubs. I will not sing to deaf ears; the forests will echo all my words.)

But unlike the singing of Tityrus, this composition of the Eclogue Poet's has a topic and purpose external to the pastoral world. As a setting for the song of Gallus, the pastoral will become a vehicle for literary discussion, but first the poet celebrates his own mastery of the form:

> Extremum hunc, Arethusa, mihi concede laborem:
> pauca meo Gallo, sed quae legat ipsa Lycoris,

carmina sunt dicenda, negat quis carmina Gallo?
sic tibi, cum fluctus subterlabere Sicanos,
Doris amara suam non intermisceat undam.   [10. 1–5]

(Grant, Arethusa, this final labor to me: a few songs must be
sung for my Gallus, but such songs as Lycoris herself may read.
Who will refuse songs to Gallus? Thus, for you, when you glide
down under the Sicilian seawaves, let bitter Doris not inter-
mingle her current with your own.)

The words *sic tibi* link the elegiac poet and the fountain; each
receives a tribute from the poet's verse.

The address to Arethusa echoes a passage in Moschus:

When Alpheus leaves Pisa behind him and travels to the sea, he
brings Arethusa the water that makes the wild olives grow; and with a
bride gift coming, of pretty leaves and pretty flowers and sacred dust,
he goeth deep into the waves and runneth his course beneath the sea
and so runneth that the two waters mingle not, and the sea never knows
of the rivers running through. So it is that the spell of that impish
setter of nets, that sly and crafty teacher of troubles, Love, hath taught
even a river how to dive.[7]

In this passage the wedding of the rivers is a part of the endless,
productive cycle of nature. But Vergil has emphasized only
Arethusa's secret course under the sea. He promises the fountain that she will preserve her identity, even as she inevitably
leaves her homeland to become a part of the greater world. His
words will keep the waters of Arethusa from obliteration in the
great salt sea. Thus the note of finality that sounds in the poem
is tempered by the claim that the poet makes for his own art.

The running of a stream to the sea is as inevitable as the
pastoral poet's final turning away from his landscape. The word
amara may suggest qualities of the larger world into which he
must go. This is the world that will receive his poems once he
himself has ceased to make them. Once he has turned firmly
toward the world of experience, the poet, too, faces a danger of
obscurity: a loss of the identity he has discovered through song.
The world his *Eclogues* must encounter is not only the perilous

[7] Moschus 6. The edition used is *The Greek Bucolic Poets*, trans. J. M. Edmonds
(Cambridge: Loeb, 1912), p. 461.

world of critcs and readers, but also the great world of poetic
tradition where the individual poem may scarcely stand out
among others of its kind. It is in order to establish his own
identity beyond question that the poet demands to speak for
himself in the last poem, and he does so by comparing himself
with Gallus as an interpreter of pastoral song.

The poetic careers of the two have much in common. Both
are young poets, still experimenting with their subjects, still
defining their places in the literary world. But Gallus comes
inexperienced to the pastoral, seeking a new identity within his
imaginary Aracadia. When he discovers the impossibility of
changing, he goes as he came, uniquely himself. Although
bucolic dreaming cannot answer his needs, he has reality to fall
back on and engages with greater conviction in the warfare of
love.

For Gallus, the pastoral experience is one of self-discovery,
although it does not give him the new self he had desired. In
a different manner, the Eclogue Poet has also completed a
discovery; he speaks as one whom trial and error have made
experienced in the pastoral until at least he knows its limitations
and its strengths. Through his amused sympathy for Gallus,
he clarifies his definition of himself. As the tenth poem closes,
the two poets stand in strong contrast, each in his own proper
world and yet interrelated, as nature unites the pastoral and the
historical worlds.

At the same time that Gallus abandons his fantasies of nature,
the Eclogue Poet reasserts the power of nature and of pastoral
song. In the final scene of the *Eclogue* book he is at home in his
pastoral environment as never before. At ease, but not idle, he
plaits a rustic basket as he sings. Servius identifies this basket
as a symbol for the creation of artful bucolic verse (*tenuissimo
stilo*),[8] but it has, I think, a much larger significance than this.
The weaving of baskets is the useful task that the poet recommends to Corydon when he criticizes the futile courtship song.
It is an occupation proper to the Roman agricultural scene.
Notably, this basket has the rustic name *fiscella* rather than the

---

[8] III, 127 *ad* v. 71. He sees an association between the work and the singing:
"ac si diceret: nisi hac re occupatus, minime canarem."

more elegant *calatha* (the baskets that Corydon's nymphs were to heap with flowers). The weaving of the basket symbolizes Vergil's analogy between the country man's physical ordering of nature and the poet's recreation of its order in verse. The Eclogue Poet has become an industrious rural singer, combining work in nature with song.

In this poem there is no more striving to exceed the limits of pastoral, no more impatience with the form. The Eclogue Poet's relaxation contrasts with the restlessness of Gallus; yet it allows him to pay one final tribute to Gallus, a tribute that only he can offer. Through the sponsorship of the poet who has affectionately ridiculed his disorderly love and his fantastic visions, Gallus at last receives a place in the pastoral world. The *amor* that impels the lover is felt by the poet in a different form:

> Gallo, cuius amor tantum mihi crescit in horas
> quantum vere novo viridis se subicit alnus.   [10. 73–74]

> (Gallus, for whom my affection grows greater hour by hour, just as the green alder pushes itself up in early spring.)

This love, expressed in an image of tranquil vitality, is in keeping with the ways of nature.

The shepherd singer is now alone, singing at the close of day and urging his goats home. Even for him the natural world is not entirely benevolent:

> surgamus: solet esse gravis cantantibus umbra,
> iuniperi gravis umbra; nocent et frugibus umbrae.
> ite domum saturae, venit Hesperus, ite capellae.   [10. 75–77]

> (Let us rise: the shadow is usually ominous to singers; the juniper shadow is ominous, and the shades do harm to the fruits. Go home well fed; Hesperus comes; go home, goats.)

To remain too long in the pastoral world is dangerous; the shadows can also suggest that obscurity feared by poets.[9] Re-

---

[9] The point is made somewhat differently by Steele Commager in his introduction to *Vergil: A Collection of Critical Essays* (Englewood Cliffs, 1966), p. 2: "But perhaps Vergil also implies that the time has come to move on to a larger genre: *surgamus.* Shade, characteristic element of the pastoral landscape that the poet creates, has at last proven too private, too isolating."

calling the loss of identity that threatened the waters of the fountain, we may see that both the entry into the larger world and isolation within the small world are perilous.

But the Eclogue Poet is not truly isolated. His love for Gallus is an assurance of his identity in the world of Rome. With the words *meo Gallo*, he has placed himself within its sophisticated literary milieu. The poet writes to command the attention of Lycoris: "quae legat ipsa Lycoris" (10. 2). Although this phrase may simply echo words from Gallus' own love poems, it may also refer to the actress's reading of contemporary poets in the Roman theatre. (According to Servius, Lycoris did recite Vergil's sixth *Eclogue*.)[10] In writing poems for Lycoris to read, the poet indeed professes to move within a fashionable literary world.

Thus another of the unique functions of the Eclogue Poet is to link bucolic poetry with the literary world of Rome. Other singers are aware, and even envious, of this world, but only the Eclogue Poet sets himself to meet its artistic challenge. Although he boasts of being the first poet to attempt the Sicilian pastoral, he regards this achievement as minor without success in adopting his material to his own world. His introductory addresses and apologies to Pollio, Varus, and Gallus show us a poet seeking — with just a degree of comical eagerness — recognition among the literary figures of his time.

To these distinguished contemporaries the poet attributes the motivation of his historical themes. Their literary influence takes precedence over that of the Muses. While several rustic singers keep the convention of reverent homage to the Muses, the Eclogue Poet treats them casually, as familiar associates of whom he feels little awe. In the fourth poem he informs them that their previous work will not do for Pollio. In the sixth, where he names Varus as the moving power of his song, a resigned *pergite Pierides* instructs the Muses to produce the rustic poem that Apollo has commanded. Damon and Alphesiboeus have their pastoral Muse, but the poet is interested only in the deeds and songs of Pollio. In the tenth poem, he addresses the fountain Arethusa as a Muse, but only to demand

[10] III, 66 *ad* v. 11.

the right to compose his song himself. He invites the Muses to commend the finished song to Gallus.

Thus, in a manner very independent and modern, the Eclogue Poet assigns a secondary role to the Muses.[11] Their place is taken by the Roman statesmen whose deeds are potential sources of inspiration even when they cannot be directly incorporated into the poems. Pollio, especially, is more than a patron. He is the model of a Roman career in politics and letters. Through such men, the modern world gives promise of becoming heroic. By his insistence on his intellectual energy and literary ambition, the Eclogue Poet shows himself ready for the challenge of a transformed world.

The restlessness that characterizes the poet's experimentation with the pastoral shows that he thinks of himself primarily as a Roman poet, for whom the writing of bucolic is the assumption of a temporary role. As a maker of pastoral verses, he is impersonal and analytic; he cannot afford the spontaneous simplicity that is traditional for rustic singers. Such self-expression as that of Tityrus is unknown to him. He is interested in the differences between his own work and that of others and is not afraid to weigh the pastoral against epic and tragic verse. As he waits out his time in a bucolic milieu, preparing himself for an undefined future greatness, we may see in him traces of the old Roman ideal of growing up in the country—the legend perpetuated by Cato the Censor. Like Romulus he is ready to cast off his shepherd's disguise and take his place in the greater world.

By restricting the personal comments of the Eclogue Poet to matters of literary theory and stylistic endeavor, Vergil allows him to give no attention to the serious contemporary issues that play a part in the poems. He has nothing to say of the crises of Italian agriculture, displaced farmers, lost farms, and civil war that distress the rustic characters. By contrast, the Eclogue Poet is almost artificially optimistic in his enthusiasm for coming ages and new deeds.

Because of this apportionment of themes, we must under-

---

[11] On the Republican poets' use of the Muse as a metaphor for poetic inspiration see Steele Commager, *The Odes of Horace* (New Haven, 1962), pp. 2–15.

stand that neither the Eclogue Poet nor any other character in the *Eclogues* is to be taken as a definitive spokesman for Vergil, or as a representative of his personality or ideas.[12] The Eclogue Poet is a composer of introductions and an inventor of pastoral fictions. Vergil is the author of the *Eclogue* book. The book itself is not merely a series of Vergilian opinions on pastoral, history, or agriculture, but rather an exploration of the artistic and symbolic possibilities of a given literary form. The design that guides the reader through this exploration unfolds by a subtle interweaving of repeated patterns of character, setting, and theme.

Despite his sophisticated literary perspective and high aspirations, the Eclogue Poet is only one figure in this design, more persistent in his appearances than other characters, yet lacking their deep involvement in the natural world. The pastoral singers represent poetry as an image of human action, while the poet makes it a species of intellectual endeavor.

At the same time, the poet's search for a style and a subject is a theme contingent upon many others in the book. His impatience with fantasy and unmitigated rustic simplicity reveals his awareness of the loss of the garden and embodies the Roman's skeptical attitude toward inexperience or withdrawal from the historical world. In his wish to unite bucolic and heroic, he approximates the Roman desire to unite country and city: a version of man's archetypal longing for a reconciliation of innocence and experience.

The poet takes pride in mastering his literary form as the farmer or political leader prides himself on giving order to his segment of the world. His aspirations toward literary recognition are his own version of man's search for identity and security in whatever part of the world must be his home. In discovering the limitations and possibilities of the bucolic, the Eclogue Poet does, in his own way, make peace with nature, but his search for a place in the great world is unending and has only begun with the poems' close.

The thematic and structural unity that the Eclogue Poet

---

[12] For typical identifications see H. Holtorf, *P. Vergilius Maro: Die grösseren Gedichte*, vol. I: *Einleitung, Bucolica* (Freiberg and Munich, 1959), pp. 224–227.

creates by his comments has support from a more formal principle of design in the arrangement of the poems. The five poems introduced by this speaker alternate with five dramatic dialogues wherein the rustic characters speak for themselves.[13] Thus the pattern of the book develops through the juxtaposition of two distinctly different forms with different symbolic possibilities. When the Eclogue Poet speaks, pastoral nature is set within a framework of literary self-consciousness. The rustic speakers present nature directly, through the medium of spontaneous song.

Both direct and indirect presentations of the pastoral landscape have their precedent in Theocritus, but the earlier poet's use of the two principles is random.[14] By creating a regular alternation of the two types of composition, Vergil allows the wide-ranging natural variety of the *Eclogues* to be controlled within an orderly pattern. The alternation is analogous with man's double view of nature, which is sometimes wild and spontaneous, sometimes carefully ordered and cultivated.

Here, as in the case of Vergil's wild and civilized landscapes, we may find a coincidence with forms of contemporary experimentation in Roman art. Closely analogous to these framed and unframed poems are the framed and unframed landscape paintings of the second style. Within a short period of time, two schemes of wall decoration were almost equally popular: the prospect enclosed by an *aedicula* and the landscape that seemed to open the entire wall.[15] The first type makes use of an elabo-

[13] P. Maury, "Le secret de Virgile et l'architecture des *Bucoliques*," Lettres d'humanite 3(1944):71–72, dismissed the idea of a dialogue-narrative alternation as a principle too simple to be the structural basis of so complicated a work as the *Eclogues*. The principle has never been popular with critics, but it is defended by E. de Saint-Denis, "Douze années d'études virgiliennes: L'architecture des 'Bucoliques'," IL 6(1954):139–147; by Skutsch, pp. 195–197; and by Galinsky, pp. 161ff., who sees an alternating pattern of the successes and failures of song in alleviating passion. Thomas Rosenmeyer, *The Green Cabinet: Theocritus and the European Pastoral Lyric* (Berkeley, 1969), pp. 13–14, considers the alternation symptomatic of pastoral's arbitrary use of dramatic forms.

[14] Lawall identifies Theocritus' use of the frame and inset pattern with his highlighting of pastoral visions or ideals (e.g., the Daphnis song in *Idyll* 1, the songs of Lycidas and Simichidas in *Idyll* 7). But Theocritus does not consistently assign his framing passages to a first-person speaker.

[15] For a chronology of developments within the second style see H. Beyen, *Die pompeianische Wanddekoration von zweiten bis zum vierten Stil, I* (The Hague,

rate *trompe l'oeil* setting that creates the impression of a recessed window open on a natural scene. From its contrast with beams, pilasters, and cornices, the landscape stands out with startling simplicity, no matter how formal or stylized its composition may be.[16] The open-wall landscapes have been variously described as a breaking down of spatial boundaries, as an extension of the room into nature, and as a bringing of the outside world into a confined space.[17] In fact, the effect of the composition depends upon the viewer's interpretation. In the first category belong several of the paintings I have mentioned earlier: the green monochrome landscape from Herculaneum (Figure 2), the Boscotrecase panels (Figures 8–10), and especially two pairs of religious landscapes from the Palatine houses known as those of Livia (Figures 1 and 14) and Augustus (Figures 15 and 16) that I use for illustration here. In the second category are the well-known murals from the *cubiculum* of the Villa of P. Fannius Synistor at Boscoreale (Figure 17) and the garden room of the Villa of Livia at Prima Porta (Figure 18).[18]

The Palatine landscapes are sacral-idyllic compositions, without human figures, placed in the centers of elegant, sym-

---

1938), 32–33, and Christopher Dawson, *Romano-Campanian Mythological Landscape Painting, YClS* 9(1944):61–65. The development of the framed picture within an architectural setting is traditionally considered later than that of open-wall compositions, but it is obvious that no one form ever totally dominated the field at a given time.

[16] Dawson, p. 62, remarks that in certain cases it is difficult to tell whether a framed landscape should be interpreted as a natural prospect or as a picture. A valuable estimate of the Roman predilection for framed landscapes is in Frank Brown's description of views of nature seen from inside a villa: "Life in the country looked outward, as well, through the eyes of the villa. Its shell was pierced by view-finding apertures. Its outer rooms were turned upon formal prospects. From its height it directed the outlook of the owner as firmly as it did the notion of his daily life; sorting vistas out of the field of vision and cutting the spread of landscape into significant segments" (*Roman Architecture* [New York, 1961], p. 21).

[17] Phyllis Lehmann, *Roman Wall Paintings from Boscoreale in the Metropolitan Museum of Art* (Cambridge, Mass., 1953), p. 131, remarks on the blending of illusion and reality in the Boscoreale *cubiculum*.

[18] Guilio Emmanuele Rizzo, *Monumenti della pittura antica scoperti in Italia*, section 3, vol. III: *Le pitture della Casa di Livia* (Rome, 1936), pp. 52–59; Gianfillipo Carettoni, "Due Nuovi Ambienti dipinti sul Palatino," *Boll. d'Arte* 46(1961):189–199, Pl. IIb and figs. 5–8. Lehmann, pp. 82–131; Muriel Gabriel, *Livia's Garden Room at Prima Porta* (New York, 1955), pp. 6–23.

14. Landscape depicting a sacred grove in the Hall of Landscape Paintings in the House of
    via on the Palatine in Rome. Reconstruction drawing from G. E. Rizzo, *Monumenti della pittura
    tica scoperti in Italia*, sec. 3, vol. 3: *Le pitture della Casa di Livia* (Rome, 1936), fig. 35.

metrically designed walls. In the House of Livia (Figures 1 and
14) these walls are decorated with encrusted panels surmounted
by architraves and a narrow, figured frieze. In each, the projecting roof of the *aedicula* seems to overhang a recessed window
flanked by pilasters supporting its beam. The longer wall is
the more elaborate, including an arch within the *aedicula* and
slender decorative columns and candelabra. In the House of
Augustus (Figures 15 and 16), the architectural illusion is even
more highly developed, and a pattern of recession and projection covers the entire wall. The foregrounds stand out in brilliant colors, while the recessed landscape panels gain further
distance because of their subdued pastel tones. The addition of
theatrical masks and of double doors with porticoes on either
side of the *aediculae* has led Gianfillipo Carettoni to suggest
that the arrangement imitates the design of a stage setting in
which the central landscape panel is to be considered as the
painted scene.[19]

[19] Carettoni, p. 194.

15. Landscape depicting a sacred grove. Fresco from the Room of the Masks in the so-called House of Augustus on the Palatine in Rome. Photograph by courtesy of the Gabinetto Fotographico Nazionale E 47767.

The landscapes of the two houses are similar in their subjects and in the basic outlines of their designs. Two of the panels — one from each house — show a conical *betylus* shrine, crowned by a disc. In the backgrounds are *scholae* surrounding the sanctuaries. Offerings are placed at the foot of each shrine, and in the Livia landscape are also hung on the *betylus*. This landscape is the more complicated, with three statues of Hecate arranged on its *schola*, a flight of steps and a bridge leading to the raised sanctuary, and a small stream, populated by ducks, flowing toward the foreground.

The second pair of paintings are even more similar. The central figure of each is a Doric column, topped by a covered urn. Sacred trees wind about the columns, extending their branches symmetrically on both sides. Low walls define the

16. Landscape depicting a sacred grove. Fresco from the Room of the Masks in the so-called ...use of Augustus on the Palatine in Rome. Photograph by courtesy of the Gabinetto Foto-...phico Nazionale E 48632.

limits of the sanctuaries, while in the backgrounds a row of dimly seen trees suggests the world outside.

The effectiveness of these decorations depends upon their juxtaposition of elegance and simplicity.[20] Their perspective arrangements make the fabric of a highly refined interior into a

[20] Peter H. von Blanckenhagen and Christine Alexander, *The Paintings from Boscotrecase MDAI(R)*, Supplement 6 (Heidelberg, 1962), p. 27, sets these apart from other sacral-idyllic paintings: "In either case, the landscape is a highly formalized and, as it were, symbolic setting without people. The ducks, the birds, the sheep are almost ornaments. In all these aspects, the newly discovered panels in the 'House of Augustus' appear very similar. The stillness and authority of the paintings derive from their strangely austere composition and not from the evocation of the atmosphere of a landscape. There is neither the intimacy nor the charm of a bucolic spot; no air and no space, no action and no sentiment, but an almost forbidding strictness."

framework for glimpses of an ever-present nature. The world of these religious panels is tightly constructed; the lines and shapes of the natural objects are closely interrelated with those of the monuments. Sacred trees bend around the shrines as if by attraction; fountains spring up at their feet; wooded barriers cut off the outside world. Even the offerings piled by the shrines are scarcely sufficient to suggest a human intrusion upon the order of the divine sanctuaries. Man seems to have had no hand in their arrangement. Their quiet harmony appears to spring from a spontaneous interrelationship between nature and the controlling divinity of the shrine. Only by recalling the unruly spontaneity of real nature can the viewer break the spell of their organization. Nothing, in fact could be less natural and more pictorial, more heavily influenced by artistic planning and design.

The illusion created by the larger landscapes is entirely different. They encompass the spectator with their prospects. In the *cubiculum* of the villa at Boscoreale (Figure 17), he stands amid great ornamental gateways, storied towers, terraces, balconies, and colonnades. At the back of the room, this impressive architecture yields to a less formal scene: the grotto and trellis that seem to offer entry into a wilder, rustic world. In the garden room of the villa at Prima Porta (Figures 18 and 19), a foreground of low flowering plants and ornamental trees bearing fruit and blossoms stands against a background of massed shrubbery that seems to form the outer boundary of the cultivated enclosure. The trees and the air are filled with birds, and the plants bloom without regard to season.

The walls of these rooms dissolve into receding and advancing planes that increase the sense of space for the spectator, yet his attention is less firmly controlled and directed than in the panel rooms.[21] He is uncertain whether he stands in a garden, on a

[21] Lehmann, pp. 148–150, believes that the spectator's experiencing of these landscapes is very close to the process by which he would study a natural scene: "Frequently, after having surveyed the scene as a whole and perceived its fundamental interrelationships, he lingers over a succession of individual details that attract his attention. While he concentrates upon one such detail, he retains only the faintest visual awareness of its periphery, which tends to recede or disappear, causing him, for the moment, to virtually detach the object of special attention from its context, to temporarily cease to see it in relationship

17. Architectural prospects. Fresco from a bedroom in the Villa of Fannius Synistor at Bosco-ale, now in the Metropolitan Museum of Art in New York. Photograph, Alinari 44315.

terrace, or within a room. The arrangement of the pictures on all sides—and especially the symmetry of the Boscoreale room—is openly unrealistic; so also is the organization of so great a multitude of images within so limited a space.

The combination of detailed foreground and receding perspective constantly baffles the eye. Seen quickly, the landscapes are active and full of motion; the eye travels rapidly over images and planes. When studied for a longer time, they become static and designed. The details seem almost too carefully wrought to give the illusion of actual nature. In the garden room, the spectator begins to notice that the light falls inconsistently from several directions, that the shadows are sometimes too

---

to its surroundings. Precisely this shifting of attention from a larger to a smaller field, from the general to the particular, is assumed to be characteristic of the visual-psychological behaviour of the Roman spectator" (p. 150).

deep, that the birds hang suspended in the air.[22] But a change in the spectator's position renews the freshness of his impressions, and the pictures once more become real. He cannot long be certain whether he is participating in an actual scenic prospect or inspecting an image that has been immobilized in order to command admiration for its artfulness alone.

The confused beholder may wonder if the garden is random or ordered; if the order appears in the image or in his own mind. But unlike the framed panels, these all-encompassing scenes invite varying interpretations. The spectator can move freely in and out of the compositions, accept or reject their organizations, consider them as artificial or lifelike. Lacking the bare, controlled simplicity of the religious panels, they do not attempt to limit his concept of the natural world.

Similar patterns of organization appear in the *Eclogues*. At their outset, the framed poems establish a distance from nature. In their concern for formalities of theory and criticism, the Eclogue Poet's introductions are comparable to the architectural decoration of the paneled walls. These technical, self-conscious discussions of pastoral provide a framework for visions of innocence and natural simplicity. But the search for innocence is the traditional subject of pastoral, and Vergil has emphasized the traditional, literary quality of these songs with a heavy burden of Alexandrian allusion that belies their apparent simplicity.

The images of nature in these poems are either fantastic (as in Corydon's dream idyll and in the golden-age prophecy) or wild (as in Silenus' cavern, his mythological vignettes, and the Arcadian visions of Damon's lover and Gallus). The fantasy suggests man's search for a paradise garden; the wilderness evokes the unrestrained quality of human emotion. In these

[22] The perspective is regular, but as Gabriel, p. 19, observes: "The blue color of the background does not portray an actual sky. There is no shading near the horizon such as we see in a number of landscapes from this period. The appearance of solid form in the garden is created by the arrangement of masses of light and shade, but the light falls from different directions and the wind that turns the leaves is also inconsistent." For the flowers and seasons see p. 11, and for the general design, pp. 18–19: The flowers seem to be set out in regular receding planes, while the interrelationship of the forms is created by "a Sienese rhythm of dancing lines in the inter-laced stalks and branches."

18. Garden landscape. Fresco from the Villa of Livia at Prima Porta, now in the National Museum of the Baths of Diocletian in Rome. Photograph by courtesy of the Gabinetto Fotographico Nazionale, C 1080.

five poems a movement from the fantasy garden toward the wilderness associates man's search for natural innocence with his discordant passion and emotion.

In *Eclogues* 2, 8, and 10 the visions of innocence are personal visions, expressing their makers' disillusionment with reality,

19. Garden landscape. Fresco from the Villa of Livia at Prima Porta, now in the Natio᷉
Museum of the Baths of Diocletian in Rome. Photograph by courtesy of the Gabinetto Fo᷉
graphico Nazionale, C 1085.

their rejection of oppressive experience, and their withdrawal
from a world in which they no longer desire to live. In *Eclogues*
4 and 6, where the poet is the chief speaker, the golden age and
the wilderness are historical rather than personal visions, representing a desire to associate pastoral fictions with the real world.

In his impatience with the traditional pastoral, the Eclogue Poet adopts a critical attitude toward the seekers after innocence; yet, paradoxically, he shares in their discontentment, and he also is a fiction-maker. So long as he remains a pastoral poet, only his ambitions and his commitment to reality can set him apart from the lesser artists in his design.

The framed poems are countered by the rustic dialogues, where pastoral literature is never mentioned and no external voice informs us of the extent of limitations of the fiction. These poems remind us of the world of Italian agriculture. With their frequent juxtaposition of foreground and background scenery and their coherent topographical details, they invite us to enter rustic landscapes peopled with farmers and shepherds whose primary concern is to preserve the stability and order of nature.

Like the open-wall compositions in landscape painting, these rustic poems are more ambiguous than those of the more stylized, literary type. When the speakers seem to touch on historical issues, we are never entirely certain whether to credit these simple characters with complete understanding of the questions they raise. We are uncertain whether they, or Vergil, speak with a double meaning.

Tityrus seems unable to identify his *deus*. We do not know if he is deliberately cryptic or dazzled by rustic awe. Damoetas speaks of Pollio but gives no reason why the name of this distinguished person should be familiar to him. Although we can see that the Daphnis of Mopsus and Menalcas is greater than an ordinary shepherd swain, we do not know if the apotheosis song is a spontaneous tribute to a nature god or a calculated allusion to a historical figure. The Thyrsis of the seventh poem may be engaged in a petulant, naïve argument with Corydon, or he may be raising deliberate artistic objections to his rival's excessive idealism. In the ninth poem no one says clearly whether Menalcas is a pastoral singer or an urban pastoral poet; he is simply a figure who has captured the imagination of the farmers because his works seem relevant to their lives. By creating so rich and suggestive a texture of symbolism, yet leaving its ultimate meaning uncertain, Vergil invites his reader to see what he will in these poems. He does not declare any opinions or take any stand.

Still, there is, as I have suggested, a hint of a developing pattern in the contrasting of negative and optimistic perspectives in the dialogue poems. The speakers' attitudes are formed by their success or failure in attempting to order the world of nature to stave off the impending chaos of the historical world. As the poems continue, the more optimistic speakers gain ascendancy. Thus, in the first and third poems, the despairing Meliboeus and the wet-blanket Menalcas appear to give the more reliable interpretations of the world, while the naïve Tityrus and brash Damoetas strike a false note. But in the last three poems, the cheerful speakers find a better world within their natural environment and make some gesture toward the subordination of disorder. In the apotheosis song, Moeris resolves the shepherds' grief for Daphnis. The idealistic Corydon pleases Meliboeus, the scrupulous and dedicated farmer, while Lycidas urges acceptance of the historical world. Despite their rustic simplicity, these characters have not withdrawn from confrontation with the experienced world.

The two types of poems—framed and unframed—support each other. Each represents one aspect of the pastoral. Neither is sufficient to stand alone. The pastoral fantasies of the framed poems must be contrasted with more stable, objective images of nature. The rustic poems need the sophisticated context created by the Eclogue Poet to assure us that their ambiguous symbolism is genuinely pertinent to the historical Roman world.

Given, however, Vergil's wild and cultivated landscapes, his two types of character (the frustrated shepherds and the optimists), and the many interweavings of theme and idea that I have discussed in previous chapters, we may see that the alternating poems present a continuous dialogue of fiction and reality. The search for innocence and the urge to involve oneself in experience are opposing impulses, but they work together to create a comprehensive pattern of withdrawal and return.

In interpreting the *Eclogues* we cannot ask that either the actions or the characters should reveal the outlines of a clear and progressive plot.[23] There is no gradual step-by-step unfolding

---

[23] Attempts to discover a consistent progress of ideas and themes in the poems are largely influenced by the work of Maury, pp. 102ff., who sees in their development the pattern of a philosophical initiation, following a symbolic course

of an idea to a logical or predictable conclusion at the end. Especially, there is no triumphant arrival at a paradise garden, but only a continuous searching throughout the natural world. The design of the poems is contrived for exploration, not for argument. Yet when we reach the concluding poem, we notice that our own attitudes, and those of Vergil's characters, seem somewhat different from before. Certain aspects of pastoral experience have become clearer. The relationship between emotion and the search for innocence is more sharply defined when the unhappy lovers go to Arcadia, identifying that harshest of pastoral countries with their rejection and their grief. Likewise, the acceptance of experience seems more possible when Lycidas places faith in Caesar's comet, and when Gallus returns to the warfare of love.

Vergil's changes and modifications of the pastoral experience come home in *Eclogue* 10, where, rather surprisingly in such a highly literary context, he has created echoes of the rustic *Eclogue* 1. First of these is the resemblance between the Eclogue Poet and Tityrus, but many other situations of the opening poem now appear in reverse. There the impious *miles* was close at hand, symbolizing history's threat to pastoral order. Now Gallus, a very different, very human *miles*, expresses his longing for a pastoral identity and a pastoral home. The soldier, like a shepherd, is susceptible to emotion, deeply involved in a quest for a better world.

---

that leads from earth to sky, and then, with Gallus' disorderly passion, once more back to earth. *Eclogues* 4–6 constitute the climax of the initiation; the apotheosis of Daphnis in 5 is "the epiphany of a divine figure." Maury emphasizes the correspondences of form and subject between poems 1 and 9, 2 and 8, 3 and 7, 4 and 6, and on this point he is followed by Becker, pp. 315–319, and Brooks Otis, *Virgil: A Study in Civilized Poetry* (Oxford, 1963), pp. 128–143. The predominance of erotic themes in the final poems and their negative relationship to the philosophical or pastoral tone of the *Eclogues* is observed by Maury, Otis, and Galinsky (pp. 188ff.), while Van Sickle studies Vergil's progressive clarification of "Arcadia" as a poetic and pastoral ideal. Michael Putnam, *Virgil's Pastoral Art: Studies in the "Eclogues."* (Princeton, 1970), pp. 392–393 and elsewhere, sees a growing tone of pessimism in the poems and sees the poet at last forsaking an ideal world of poetry to return to the real world: "The battles of life cannot be fought from the ivory tower of disengagement but from hand to hand combat with the enemy, be it the weeds which choke the weary farmer's field or the civil wars in which brother destroys brother in needless slaughter" (p. 393). Thus the conclusion of the *Eclogues* points toward the *Georgics*.

At the same time, threats of war and historical chaos have moved far off. The barbarous *miles* has taken Lycoris to Gaul. Gallus is at the other end of the Roman world. He speaks of taking his pastoral visions with him, of feeding his sheep under the Aethiopian star, but he knows that what really goes with him is the chaotic warfare of love. Gallus has replaced Meliboeus as the wanderer, the symbol of man's search for elusive tranquillity and rest.

As the poem draws to its close, the falling shadows recall those of *Eclogue* 1, but now they have a positive rather than a negative meaning. Evening comes on, once more declaring the end of the shepherd's song, and the dangerous shade of the juniper warns the poet home. His response to this sign shows his understanding of nature, his acceptance of his place within the pastoral world. The goats, once hungry and headed toward exile, are now well fed and going home. Hesperus rises, but not to interrupt the singer, for he has already finished his song.

As the poet's last words recall the first *Eclogue*, we see in them a meaning both changed and renewed. There, in a momentary glimpse of agricultural order, the prospect of Tityrus' farmland stood out amid widespread chaos. Now the course of the poems has followed the image of disorder from its apparent source in a world outside pastoral to its permanent roots in the human mind. Man is no better ordered than the world he lives in; he has no magical better self to be discovered in escape from the actual world.

❧ Index

Vergil's *Ecologues*

Designed by R. E. Rosenbaum.
Composed by Kingsport Press, Inc.
in 10 point linofilm Baskerville, 2 points leaded,
with display lines in Baskerville.
Printed offset by Kingsport Press
on Warren's Olde Style India, 60 pound basis.
Bound by Kingsport Press
in Holliston book cloth
and stamped in All Purpose foil.